Praise for *The Third Chapter*

"*The Third Chapter* is a compassionate rendering of the challenges of entering uncharted post-career years, followed by an eloquent vision of the joys that lie ahead for those who put giving at the center of living."
— Rosabeth Moss Kanter, Harvard Business School professor and bestselling author of *Confidence* and *America the Principled*

"Sara Lawrence-Lightfoot follows her subjects on an extraordinary journey. Read this book and be inspired by the diverse ways these women and men redefine their lives, adding purpose, passion, and reflection as they grow older."
— Marian Wright Edelman, President, Children's Defense Fund

"In this singular book, Sara Lawrence-Lightfoot introduces a new stage of life, delineates its intriguing and unexpected contours, and draws lessons that are meaningful for every human being."
— Howard Gardner, author of *Good Work: When Excellence and Ethics Meet*

"Sara Lawrence-Lightfoot, one of our most graceful and gifted chroniclers of the changing psychological landscape, has produced a biography of the new life stage emerging between the end of the middle years and the arrival of old age. This remarkable tale is conveyed through the nuanced stories of individuals navigating their way through their fifties, sixties, and seventies, and is punctuated by Lightfoot's arresting observations. The result is not only the best book yet about the changing life course, but an inspiring roadmap for individual and social renewal in the emerging Third Chapter. As ten thousand baby boomers turn sixty each day, the timing of this book is as exquisite as its insights."

—Marc Freedman, author of *Encore: Finding Work That Matters in the Second Half of Life* and founder/CEO of Civic Ventures

SARA LAWRENCE-LIGHTFOOT

The Third Chapter

Sara Lawrence-Lightfoot is the Emily Hargroves Fisher Professor of Education at Harvard University and the former chair of the board of the MacArthur Foundation. As a sociologist, she examines the culture of schools, the patterns and structures of classroom life, socialization within families and communities, and the relationships between culture and learning styles.

ALSO BY SARA LAWRENCE-LIGHTFOOT

Worlds Apart:
Relationships Between Families and Schools

Beyond Bias: Perspectives on Classrooms
(with Jean Carew)

The Good High School:
Portraits of Character and Culture

Balm in Gilead: Journey of a Healer

I've Known Rivers:
Lives of Loss and Liberation

The Art and Science of Portraiture
(with Jessica Hoffmann Davis)

Respect: An Exploration

The Essential Conversation:
What Parents and Teachers Can Learn from Each Other

THE THIRD
CHAPTER

THE THIRD CHAPTER

Passion, Risk, and Adventure

in the 25 Years After 50

SARA LAWRENCE-LIGHTFOOT

SARAH CRICHTON BOOKS

Farrar, Straus and Giroux   New York

Sarah Crichton Books
Farrar, Straus and Giroux
18 West 18th Street, New York 10011

Printed in the United States of America
Published in 2009 by Sarah Crichton Books
First paperback edition, 2010

Grateful acknowledgment is made for permission to reprint excerpts from the following previously published material: "Age" (7 1. extract), "Adulthood II" (6 1.), and
"Patience" (5 1.) from *Cotton Candy on a Rainy Day* by Nikki Giovanni, copyright ©
1978 by Nikki Giovanni; reprinted by permission of HarperCollins Publishers /
William Morrow. Transcript of Bill Moyers's interview with the author, reprinted by
permission of *Bill Moyers Journal* and the Public Broadcasting Service.

The Library of Congress has cataloged the hardcover edition as follows:
Lawrence-Lightfoot, Sara, 1944–
    The third chapter : passion, risk, and adventure in the 25 years after 50 /
by Sara Lawrence-Lightfoot.— 1st ed.
        p.   cm.
    (Sarah Crichton books)
    Includes bibliographical references.
    ISBN: 978-0-374-27549-5 (hardcover : alk. paper)
    1. Older people—United States—Interviews.   2. Aging—Psychological
aspects.   3. Old age—Social aspects—United States.   I. Title.

HQ1064.U5L39 2009
305.260973—dc22

                                                                2008029147

Paperback ISBN: 978-0-374-53221-5

Designed by Jonathan D. Lippincott

www.fsgbooks.com

9 10

For Paloma Sara
the newest among us
a miracle

CONTENTS

PREFACE TO THE
PAPERBACK EDITION

The book you hold in your hands was first published in a hardcover edition in January 2009. It was a terrible time economically, the worst January on record. And as I set out on a cross-country book tour, I wondered what I would find. I steeled myself for stories of lament and discouragement, fear and despair. The message of my book was one of creative reinvention and personal renewal. Was it the right message for times like these?

Simply put: yes.

The Third Chapter explores the ways in which men and women between fifty and seventy-five—folks "neither young nor old"—have been finding new ways to adapt, explore, and channel their energies, skills, and passions. But in a still youth-obsessed society that continues to regard older adults as diminished and declining, how do you challenge those archaic assumptions and keep learning and growing? How do you find the courage to change direction, to become an innovator, a risk-taker?

On radio talk shows, through e-mails and blogs, in bookstores, libraries, and auditoriums, folks from all walks of life told me their stories. And instead of the anxiety I'd anticipated, what I heard were tales of resilience and adaptation, determination and creativity—yes, even in economically challenging days.

A fifty-seven-year-old laid-off factory worker in Detroit told of using his welding skills to create huge sculptures of dinosaurs. When he first started, he sold them for next to nothing at flea markets—then, as he mastered his craft, for handsome sums to art galleries.

In Vermont, a seventy-two-year-old Realtor whose business had "shrunk to nothing" said she'd signed up for a stint in the Peace Corps in Senegal; she feels for the first time that she is "making a difference on our planet."

A seventy-year-old gynecologist/obstetrician in Texas felt "burnt out" from the tedium of his practice and his "involuntary participation in a deteriorating and unjust health care system." So he returned to his childhood love of Broadway theater, plunged back into training, and is now performing the classic songs on cruise liners. Not only that: when he's ashore, he volunteers as an obstetrician in the central valley of California, delivering the babies of migrant farmers.

It was exhilarating to hear these stories. And as varied as they were, I was struck by how similar they were to one another—and to the stories of Third Chapter folks I recount in this book.

The men and women all seem to follow similar steps on their journeys. First, if they are facing a new reality in their lives—a job loss, a decline in their income and savings—after an initial sense of fear and loss, they then, with a fierce resolve, manage to turn crisis into opportunity. The new and unwelcome constraints force a kind of risk-taking and innovation.

Second, at this point in their lives they are willing to risk vulnerability and failure. They stand ready to challenge our culture's views of what is "age-appropriate" for older adults.

Third, after years of striving to climb the ladder of success and to make their individual mark, their impulse is now to "give forward" to the next generations, to leave a legacy, to be of service. Their forced sacrifices turn into altruism.

And fourth, in giving forward, they see the value of cross-generational projects; young and old working and learning together, not competing for access, opportunity, and resources. As they reinvent themselves, the Third Chapter folks often turn to young people for mentoring, for their expertise and energy, for the ways they can see into the future. In turn, the young recognize the Third Chapter folks' valuable contribution to these encounters; the wisdom and patience, the restraint, humility, and perspective that come with aging.

In those insecure early months of 2009, I also heard many of these themes of reinvention echoed in a larger public discourse. I was impressed, for example, by how, in his speeches, President Obama managed to navigate the borders between a message of crisis and one of optimism—between asking people to sacrifice and encouraging them to be innovative and resourceful. He called for us to bring our best selves—our most hopeful dreams and productive energies—to the task while managing to speak to the country's anxiety and fears without burying us in the blues. He worked hard to paint a realistic picture of the hardships we face without throwing us into a deepening anxiety. The speeches were high-wire performances, weighing the measures of substance and style, teetering on the edges of idealism and cynicism.

To my surprise, I have heard this same balance resonating in voices across the country as I've traveled. Like the tonal calibrations of darkness and light that we have heard in President Obama's speeches, reinvention and giving forward in the Third Chapter require a delicate balance of truth-telling and inspiration, loss and liberation, urgency and patience, sacrifice and generosity.

The Third Chapter—those years when we're neither old nor young—can be the most transformative time in our lives, just as long as we have the courage to challenge the ageist stereotypes, the creativity to resist the old cultural norms, the curiosity to be open to new learning, and the adventurousness to pursue new passions and experiences.

Sara Lawrence-Lightfoot
August 2009

THE THIRD
CHAPTER

Introduction: Facing the Mirror

Perhaps it is my age. I am sixty-two, and for the last several years my conversations with friends, colleagues, and even casual acquaintances have often been punctuated by what I have now come to call "confessional moments." Certainly there is the expected chatter and grumbling about minor and major infirmities or unwelcome signs of deterioration—lower-back pain, varicose veins, bald heads, and gray hair—and there is the usual whining about offspring, now finished with college, maybe even married with young children, who return home to live and still need to be provided with health care and spending money. When I refer to confessional moments, however, I do not mean the habitual grumbling about our inevitable decline as we grow older. (One of my friends refers to these gripe sessions as "organ recitals.") Nor am I referring to the odd and troubling sensation of gazing into the mirror and seeing not yourself, but someone decades older than you imagine yourself to be—someone who looks very much like your mother.

I am, instead, talking about moments when we manage to resist the signs of burnout, make peace with the old/new mirror image, and refuse to be preoccupied with our chronic laments about aging or our sadness about our vanishing youth. These are moments when our faces light up, when there is a palpable surge of energy and we begin to reveal stories about learning something new. These are stories told most often by people who are—like me—in the "Third Chapter" of our adult lives, the years between fifty and seventy-five, the generative space that follows young adulthood and middle age. And these stories are recited with intrigue, passion, and self-discovery—stories that reveal themselves like mysterious secrets; tales often striking in their contradictions and paradoxes.

My friend Jacob, an ardent intellectual and a distinguished journalist with a Ph.D. in political science, has a quick mind and a subtle wit. Born in Hoboken, New Jersey, the only son of Jewish immigrant parents, he is a man of expansive warmth, whose greatest pleasures are relational and social and whose currency of discourse has always been language: a rapid-fire delivery blending a New York Bronx dialect with a sprinkling of Yiddish, for emotional effect. Now sixty-two, he tells me of his first experience attending a seven-day silent retreat where—after much resistance, fear, and panic; then resolve and determination— he began to let down his barriers and inhibitions and learn to live in the stillness. This still-raw understanding and practice of meditation has opened a whole new discipline and perspective that seem to "challenge old inhibitions and raise questions" about who he is "becoming," and about his capacity to be alone with himself. He says dramatically, "Meditation is the most counterintuitive thing I could have possibly tried to learn to do."

Roma, a fifty-seven-year-old physicist I met at a dinner party, who has spent all of her professional career in the laboratory enjoying the quiet and order of the space, the exacting, familiar rituals of the scientific process, and the pursuit of the objective, quantitative evidence, recently began to feel—after thirty years—the limits and constraints of her existence. The solitude and discipline of her work, which used to feel safe and generative, started to feel claustrophobic. The rituals began to seem routine. The questions that used to inspire curiosity began to strike her as dull and formulaic. But mostly she sensed the need to "make a difference on our planet" in a more direct and immediate way; she yearned to teach, to serve, to give back. Cutting back on her hours in the lab, Roma signed up for a mentoring program where she teaches middle-school black, brown, and poor students in an after-school program the subject that always fascinated her the most when she was a young adolescent: astronomy. In her first year of teaching, Roma admits that this is the hardest, most challenging work that she has ever done: learning the science now long forgotten and finding a palatable and relevant way to present it; learning to relate to and discipline the children and capture their imaginations; learning to recover from the awkwardness and public failures that come with being a total novice. "I'm so completely uncool," she says with a smile. Like Jacob, she has chosen "the most difficult path," strewn with minefields and misunderstandings, and rare, unexpected successes along the way.

And there is Robert, the seventy-two-year-old retired mechanical engineer whom I meet at an ice-cream joint on the side of the road in rural New Hampshire. He and his wife of fifty years are out on their ritual Sunday drive, and they are looking to pick up an interesting conversation with a stranger. They sit down next to me at the picnic table and begin in a place where we all meet: with family stories. I listen to their proud tales about their grandchildren scattered all over the country and admire the photographs of their smiling faces. But soon, with a bit of gentle prodding from his wife, Abbie, the conversation turns to Robert's "new passion," and he goes to the car to fetch his drawings, postcard-size pen-and-ink sketches of birds. He has always loved birds: listening to their songs in the morning light, watching them visit the bird feeders outside his kitchen window, observing the "social interactions" among them. And he has always said, "I wish I had an artistic bone in my body, so I could draw the beauty I see in them." A week after his retirement party, as he faced the "surprising emptiness" in front of him, he took the leap of faith and signed up for three drawing courses—"a total immersion"—at the adult-education center. "This has become my life!" he says in confessional tones, as I remark on the steady improvement I see in his portfolio of work, and as he talks about the exhilaration and vulnerability of learning something new.

For women and men in the Third Chapter, the process of learning something new feels both familiar and strange, exciting and terrifying, mature and childlike, both in character and out of body, like returning home and setting out on an adventure to an unknown destination. This is true whether we are talking about learning a new skill, craft, or art form—like learning to speak a foreign language, play jazz piano, or become a playwright—or whether we are learning to feel and express a broader and deeper emotional repertoire—freeing us from the bondage of the rigid requirements of decorum forged in our childhood—or whether we are learning to grieve after the death of a loved one—learning to make ourselves vulnerable and not retreat from intimacy—or whether we are talking about shifting the focus of our energies and priorities, from solitary, individualistic, and competitive to community-based and collaborative; from making it up the ladder of success to making an imprint on the lives of others.

This book focuses on the creative and purposeful learning that goes on in the Third Chapter of life. I explore the ways in which men and women between the ages of fifty and seventy-five find ways of changing, adapting, exploring, mastering, and channeling their energies, skills, and passions into new domains of learning. I believe that successful aging requires that people continue—across their lifetime—to express a curiosity about their changing world, an ability to adapt to shifts in their developmental and physical capacities, and an eagerness to engage new perspectives, skills, and appetites. This requires the willingness to take risks, experience vulnerability and uncertainty, learn from experimentation and failure, seek guidance and counsel from younger generations, and develop new relationships of support and intimacy.

In writing this book, I wanted to understand what motivates people in this Third Chapter of life to want to learn something new. What are our sources of inspiration; what are our greatest fears and inhibitions; what are the major barriers to learning; and what allows us to pursue adventures? I also wanted to know how the processes of learning, adaptation, experimentation, and mastery are different during this period of life. Do maturity and life experiences support a greater sense of liberation and collaboration; a new level of patience, perspective, and confidence; and a sturdy sense of self that permits risk-taking? How do people break long-established patterns of behavior, old habits and inhibitions that no longer serve them well? How do people seek and make productive use of feedback and criticism when they are developing new skills and adapting to new realities? How do they hang on to their dignity, sense of authority, and self-respect when the awkwardness and imbalance of new learning make them feel infantilized? What needs to be unlearned if someone is to learn something new? How do people balance—and negotiate the tensions between—the losses and gains of new commitments? What are some of the things that people in their Third Chapters discover that they simply cannot learn; what are the physical, developmental, cognitive, and emotional limitations that prevent them from gaining mastery of new skills and taking the next developmental step? And, finally, what are the connections that can be drawn between individual learning, community building, and cultural creativity? What institutional innovations, shifts in cultural priorities, and educational reforms might support the translations from individual gain to public good?

I think that part of the reason we who are in our Third Chapters tend to speak of our new learning in "confessional tones"—in tentative, hushed voices that barely veil the excitement and the terror we feel inside—is that something in us feels we are being irresponsible, or inappropriate, maybe even unseemly, when we admit our lust for new learning. Somehow, we feel that people our age should be consolidating our experiences, integrating all that we've learned and accomplished, and resting on our laurels—not engaging in risk-taking projects, embarking on unmapped adventures, and enduring the awkwardness and vulnerabilities of new mastery. Maybe we even feel it is somehow undignified to be so childish in our enthusiasms and eagerness to explore new domains of knowledge, recover ancient passions, and try on new roles and costumes.

Our sense of inappropriateness is related, I believe, to deeply ambivalent, shifting societal expectations, institutional norms, and cultural presumptions about the "normal" developmental trajectories of aging. Some of these changing societal expectations are visible and quantifiable, reflecting demographic shifts, increases in educational attainment, and lifestyle changes for people in their Third Chapters. Each generation is living longer than the last one. Better health care, improved diet, more exercise, new medical innovations and interventions, and changes in the routines and rhythms of our work and play allow us to live much longer—stretching the time when we are fortunate enough to be energetic and productive.

U.S. Census statistics from 2000 tell the story of a recent and significant bulge in the population of older Americans who are healthier, better educated, and yearning for a productive and enjoyable alternative to retirement.[1] The arc of life and learning is continually being expanded and redefined. As a matter of fact, demographers who study the shifting patterns tell us that not only are people living longer and thus facing interesting questions related to how to compose their lives, but also that what I am calling the Third Chapter represents a significant and new developmental period in our culture, one that comes along only once a century. It seems that every hundred years or so a new developmental phenomenon emerges on our cultural horizon. It becomes noticed and named, and entered into the lexicon of our views and rhetoric about human experience.

Last century, we "discovered" and labeled "adolescence" as a distinct developmental period between childhood and adulthood. We began to see it as a time of enormous change, drama, and fluctuation, and as an explanation for new alignments in the strained relationships between parents and their teenagers. During adolescence, powerful peer relationships pull young people away from family expectations, rhythms, and rules and into a world in which parents have little control, access, or understanding. The "work" of adolescence—say developmentalists—is to differentiate, establish some measure of separation from family, and take the initial steps toward independence in the world. This is usually not a smooth or benign process; there is the predictable tumult, drama, awkwardness, and pain as the parent-child relationships are renegotiated and redefined. So, last century, the chronological period of adolescence emerged as a cultural construct that was stamped into our psyches and written into the social scripts of our families, schools, and communities.

In the twenty-first century, another phase of life seems to be emerging as significant and distinct, capturing our interest, engaging our curiosity, and expanding our understanding of human potential and development. Demographers talk about this new distinctive chapter in life as characterized by people—between fifty and seventy-five—who are considered "neither young nor old." In the Third Chapter we are beginning to redefine our views about the casualties and opportunities of aging; we are challenging cultural definitions of strength, maturity, power, and sexiness.

Signs of these shifts in our cultural regard and societal expectations have appeared in the media, in popular culture, and in everyday conversation. Helen Mirren stands on the stage, accepting the Oscar for her portrayal of Queen Elizabeth II—her white hair perfectly coiffed and gleaming, her shimmering, low-cut dress exposing a healthy cleavage, her sultry, seductive voice softening her British accent. As she walks up to receive her honor, she is called "hot" by her male presenter. She knows she's sexy; telling a reporter after the show that if she were offered a role that required a nude scene, she would be more than happy—at sixty—to bare it all. But it is not just movie stars; whole marketing campaigns are designed to court the humanly flawed and give a different face to aging. Dove commercials of older nude women in frontal poses challenge earlier standards of modesty and decorum, openly reveal their sagging bodies, gray hair, and lined faces to audiences still struggling to see and accept the new definitions of sexy. Documentaries offer inspiring narratives of Baby Boomers carving out new altruistic careers, and life-insurance commercials depict handsome, bronzed seventy-year-olds fly-fishing, snowboarding, and romping with their grandchildren—capturing the physical prowess and gentleness of confident, mature men.

This is a chapter in life, then, when the traditional norms, rules, and rituals of our careers seem less encompassing and restrictive; when many women and men seem to be embracing new challenges and searching for greater meaning in life. The Boomer generation—once defined by their youthful boldness, achievement, and opportunism—bring to the Third Chapter their wealth and resources and their social capital and sense of authority, as well as their appetite for new adventures and their yearning for inspiration and reinvention.

Even with these marked shifts in societal views and expectations, and in our identities and self-images, however, there is a palpable cultural undertow that continues to regard aging beyond fifty as defined by inevitable decline; by the slow deterioration of mind, body, and spirit. Our culture continues to be youth-obsessed. Beauty and strength, lust and passion, energy and optimism, daring and courage are still seen as embodied by people in their twenties and thirties; and women and men over fifty continue to mourn the ways in which their bodies no longer conform to those youthful ideals, lifting and Botoxing their faces, dyeing and thickening their hair, flattening their butts, reforming their breasts, and working their muscles. All of us—old and young and in between—to some extent still harbor a jaded and static view of life beyond fifty—a depressing image of people slowing down, losing interest, and fading away. It is a picture of disappointment and loss: loss of vitality, curiosity, sexiness, and drive. It is seen as a time for leisure and retreat, not challenge and engagement; a time for resting on our laurels, not meeting new challenges; a time for circling the wagons, not journeying forth. The "golden years" are perceived as anything but golden and lustrous. They do not shimmer with excitement and adventure; they grow rusty with routine. They mark the beginning of a slow decline toward death. In the twenty-first-century culture, then, there continues to be a preoccupation with all things youthful, and a prejudice—however veiled—against the symbols and signs of aging.

These contrasting, contrary images of aging express a profound cultural ambivalence, one that leads to oppositional attitudes, mixed metaphors, confusing imagery, and ambiguous societal signals about what is developmentally appropriate for us, about what is possible and achievable, and about what our dreams should be made of. And I believe that the confessional tones we use—our hushed disclosures of new adventures in learning that we would prefer to scream from the mountaintops—reflect our wary response to this cultural ambivalence.

This book offers a strong counterpoint to the murky ambivalence that shrouds our clear view of people in their Third Chapters. It challenges the still-prevailing and anachronistic images of aging by documenting and revealing the ways in which the years between fifty and seventy-five may, in fact, be the most transformative and generative time in our lives; it traces the ways in which wisdom, experience, and new learning inspire individual growth and cultural transformation. The women and men whose voices fill these pages tell passionate and poignant stories of risk and vulnerability, failure and resilience, challenge and mastery, experimentation and improvisation, and insight and new learning. Finally, this book explores the public benefits, the ways in which new learning in the Third Chapter—both individual and collective—might begin to reshape our culture's understanding of education, wisdom, productivity, and even work.

For two years, I traveled around the country interviewing forty men and women between the ages of fifty and seventy-five who saw themselves as "new learners," who were eager to reflect on their experiences, question their motives, celebrate their achievements, and tell their stories. I spoke to twenty-four women and sixteen men, from a variety of professions and careers, from diverse racial, ethnic, and religious backgrounds, and from a range of geographic regions around the country. Although many had grown up in poor and working-class families, the women and men whom I interviewed were all well educated (with college and advanced degrees), and relatively affluent (living middle, upper-middle, and upper class lives). "I have known a generous abundance in my adult life," said a former entrepreneur who had grown up in poverty and was now, at sixty, trying to master a pair of courses in quantum physics, "and that has allowed me the freedom to take the risks of creating a new reality for myself." Most of the people I interviewed, then, did not to have to worry about paying the mortgage, keeping their health insurance, educating their children and grandchildren, or funding their retirements. They enjoyed a "privileged place" that allowed them the resources and emotional space to explore new adventures, imagine different scenarios, and make unlikely choices they might never have anticipated in their first two chapters of life.

Using what sociologists call a "snowball" sample (asking each interviewee to recommend others who might be interested in joining the project), I searched out people who were embarking on new learning adventures; who were eager to examine their motives and the goals and processes of their learning; and who wanted to be intentional in shaping their journeys. I was interested in exploring what these men and women meant by "learning" and why it felt "new" to them. I asked them to trace in detail the initial impulses and motivations that led them to the learning experience, the barriers and breakthroughs they experienced, the path, pace, texture, and rhythms of their learning. I also wanted to know whether their learning was solitary and self-sustained, maybe even secretive (the stealth learner), or whether it was being supported by mentors, teachers, or coaches. What scaffolding was needed to support their efforts; whom did they go to for criticism, assessment, and feedback? Along the way, how did they stay motivated; how did they withstand the inevitable failures, setbacks, and criticism; and what did they mark as signs of progress and measures of achievement? Did the new learning become their life's central preoccupation, and in what ways did it impact their normal rhythms, routines, and relationships? Did the mastery of learning make them feel different about themselves—their capacities, strengths, and intelligence; their vulnerabilities, weaknesses, and challenges?

In addition to exploring the origins, processes, and trajectory of new learning, I also was interested in having people describe the context—historical, physical, relational, and cultural—in which the learning was embedded, and the ways in which the setting and timing shaped their engagement and mastery. How were they influenced by these external forces and events, those that were within and out of their control? Were there pivotal moments—of public achievement, personal crisis, serious illness, family realignments—that rocked their reality and inspired change in them?

I was also curious to see the imprint of the immediate context in the places where people were learning. I visited a sixty-three-year-old portrait painter in her studio, traced the history of her work chronicled in her large portfolio, and watched as she applied thin luminous layers of paint to a portrait in progress. I examined the Victorian cabinet of a seventy-year-old furniture maker and listened as his colleagues offered their tough critiques of his design. I toured the gorgeous studio of a seventy-year-old quilter, and watched her lure novices into working on a collaborative public exhibit, in the process turning the privacy and asylum of her studio into a space for public art. I sat for hours on the bench beside a sixty-two-year-old jazz pianist as he practiced his scales and played me some of his new compositions, and I observed Roma, the fifty-seven-year-old laboratory scientist in her first year of teaching adolescents in an after-school program.

I sat in the audience of a fifty-two-year-old woman who had worked with a voice coach for two years to become a more fluent and compelling public speaker, watched the dress rehearsal of a play written by a sixty-three-year-old new playwright, and enjoyed the debut performance of a fifty-eight-year-old former schoolteacher at the conclusion of his first year of studying acting. I stood on the beach and watched a fifty-five-year-old woman biologist take surfing lessons, bravely battling—rather than riding—the big waves, and stood at the finish line when a seventy-year-old man completed his first half-marathon, to raise money for cancer research. I followed in the footsteps of a seventy-year-old architect going on her first archaeological dig at the site of an African American meetinghouse that had been a stop on the route of the Underground Railroad, and watched a sixty-year-old former CEO working with activists and advocates from a nonprofit, to apply his business knowledge to their mission.

Each of these visits not only helped me visualize and document the settings in which learning was taking place, but also allowed me to observe those processes of mastery that people were not yet able to identify and articulate—the inchoate, often chaotic experience of newly emerging perspectives; the rawness of embryonic skills. My site visits allowed people to "show" me rather than "tell" me about what they were learning—for example, to witness the knowledge expressed through their bodies, rather than through thinking and language. And it helped me notice the almost imperceptible changes and tiny improvements in mastery of which people were often not aware. In the days and weeks following the interviews, people would often want to continue our conversation, fix a misstatement, embellish a point, or explain something further; they sent me e-mails and letters, published pieces and diary excerpts that they had written, photographs they had taken of new work, or drawings that mapped the progress of their learning since we last spoke.

As I observed and witnessed the learning of these men and women, I listened carefully for the ways in which the storytellers composed their central narrative. I was attentive to the talk and the silence; to those moments of expressivity and restraint; to those places where they feared to tread; to those revelations that surprised them; to those memories long buried. These were emotional encounters, filled with tears and laughter, breakthroughs and breakdowns, curiosity and discovery. Even narratives that might have begun as intellectual excavations often found their gravity and expression in the affairs of the heart, blending emotion and cognition, feelings and intellect. Talking about the present and the future almost always required journeys into the past. More than one person exclaimed, "This is like looking backward into the future." As I listened, I always pressed for details, for nuance, for complexity; for the subtext, the hidden underside of things palpable and tangible.

In her wonderful autobiographical account *One Writer's Beginnings*, my favorite storyteller, Eudora Welty, says about her craft, "What discoveries I've made in the course of writing stories all begin with the particular, never the general."[2] In the particular resides the general. Stories—well told, with detail and context—allow for texture, subtlety, and multiple interpretations, and they help us to discover the universals among us. As I traced the narratives and delved for the particulars of person and place, I listened for the patterns, the themes, the collective voice. I worked to discover the idiosyncratic even as I probed for the similarities and commonalities—the places where people's stories converged and overlapped, even when those people at first appeared to be so unalike.

Another important insight from Welty's exposition on craft focuses on the subtle but critical distinction between "listening to a story"[3] and "listening for a story."[4] The former, she says, is a more passive, receptive stance in which the interviewer waits to absorb the information and does little to give it shape or form. The latter is a much more engaged, discerning position in which the interviewer searches for the story, seeks it out, and is central in its creation. She does not compose or direct the unfolding drama; she does not impose her own story, drowning out the narrator's voice. But she is willing to enter into a dialogue that reveals part of her own journey, and she is aware of the part she plays as witness in shaping the story's coherence and aesthetic. In this work, I employed Welty's more activist, artistic approach of "listening for the story": for its shape, intensity, rhythm, and texture; for its substance and content; for its metaphors and symbolism; for the light and shadows.

As I listened to the voices of Third Chapter learners, I played many roles. I was the empathic and attentive witness, putting myself in their shoes, trying to decode the environment as they saw it, resonating with their anxieties and fears, reckoning with their inhibitions, challenges, and successes. I was the eager cheerleader, offering applause, appreciation, and acclaim for their creativity, their grit, and their courage. I was the discerning connoisseur, developing a taste for the shape of their sentences, the cadence of their language, the arc of their stories. I was the artist, painting the landscape, drawing their portraits, sketching in the light and the shadows. I was the spider woman, weaving together their life remnants, unsnarling the tangled

THE THIRD CHAPTER

threads of their stories, casting a net to catch them if they
should fall. I was the probing researcher, patiently gathering
data, asking the impertinent questions, examining their interpretations with skepticism and deliberation. And I was the
fellow traveler, walking beside them, watching their backs,
admiring the vistas, avoiding the minefields, and bringing my
own story to our dialogue. As a matter of fact, as I heard the narratives of these women and men, I felt myself deeply engaged in
new learning as well—echoing and reflecting the curiosity, vulnerability, risk-taking, and passion of their journeys in my own.
I looked into their eyes and saw my reflection, the refracted
images of my face in the mirror: a sixty-two-year-old woman
with "confessional moments" of my own.

ONE

Loss and Liberation

> All changes, even the most longed for, have their melancholy; for what we leave behind us is part of ourselves; we must die to one life before we can enter another.
>
> —Anatole France[1]

As people move from one developmental stage to the next, they are likely to experience the twin emotions of loss and liberation, despair and hope, pessimism and optimism. It is so difficult to "let go" of the familiar, the routine, the proven, the daily rituals; so hard to relinquish your solidity, your expertise, your status and station, and take the risk of embracing the new, the unproven, and the unfamiliar. The transition—sometimes abrupt and at other times protracted—is usually a time of fear, ambivalence, and chaos, during which it is hard to articulate where you are heading or how you will get there, and life feels out of balance and unfocused.

ENTR'ACTES

Emory Daniels is a developmental psychologist used to thinking about the journey of life as a series of stages that are not distinct and hierarchical, but overlapping and intersecting. Between the stages there are "transitions" that Emory calls "entr'actes" (her language is full of theatrical metaphors): times that often feel empty, threatening, confusing, and directionless, but that she believes we should see as opportunities for reflection, rest, recuperation, and self-interrogation. "These are brief intermissions that you could just slide through without noticing," she says. "It is much better to see these as precious moments for self-reflection . . . a time to make what you want to do a great curiosity . . . a time for thoughtful self-invention." Emory's embrace of these moments of transition reflects the fact that she has always seen her life as a "series of chapters filled with a series of precipitous events that rise and fall and lead to the next reinvention of the self." Emory's optimistic view of the movement of life, the preciousness of the moment, and the urge to live in the "existential present" point back to a terrible train accident that she barely survived at twenty, when she was badly injured and knocked unconscious. This early brush with death seems to have become a central touchstone for Emory. She counts every year since the accident as a gift—a gift, however, that could be taken away at any moment.

At sixty, Emory resigned from her job teaching at the university where she had founded and directed a graduate program. She admits that there are many ways in which she might tell the story of her leaving: a departure that she initiated, but one that was complicated and painful nevertheless. There are at least four versions of the story that she tells me, her voice still full of lament and regret. You could say that she left because the university administration was not giving her program the resources or support that it needed and deserved . . . or you could say that Emory left because she wanted more time to devote to her writing, a lifelong dream of hers . . . or you could say that she decided to leave because of the fragility of her husband's health ("There were signs of physical decline in him, but I left not to take care of him—I left so that I could be more available to him") . . . or you could say that she left because she was suffering from an increasingly difficult case of asthma, exacerbated by the environmental conditions of her office at the university, an illness that often made the physical requirements of her work incredibly hard. Story number four, referring to her own physical weakness and vulnerability, serves as a powerful metaphor for the ways in which her departure was life-saving and life-giving. "Leaving was like letting air into my chamber, into my body," she says, breathing deeply, her hand placed over her chest. "It turned out that my health was a big thing. By the time I left, I had a full-blown, hugely aggravated case of asthma, a collapsed lung, frequent pneumonia and bronchitis. I was coughing all the time, spitting up such thick guck. When I would stand up in front of my class to lecture, I'd cough into the microphone, and all my students would duck under their desks."

However she tells the story, Emory's decision to resign, pack up her office, and leave felt, at first, like a huge relief. "The first stage was definitely euphoria. This was my prominent emotion," she says, relishing the memory of her initial joy and pleasure at being released from the aspects of her work that felt imprisoning and exhausting. To Emory, it felt a lot like the way she felt when she and her husband moved from their suburban home, where they had raised their children, to a chic loft in center city perfect for two. She had loved their ritual of packing up and getting out. "I've always been directed toward new chapters in my life . . . so I thought, finally, we are moving. I loved the thought of changing the scenery and designing a new stage set." After the movers took all of the stuff out of her house, Emory walked through the empty rooms and saw the spaces filled with people.

She could see her middle son's crutches leftover from his snowboarding accident, the parties they had enjoyed in the living room, and the cup of coffee she had with a friend in her kitchen. Seeing the rooms filled with precious moments helped her feel good about leaving, and reminded her of the richness of her former life, not the losses or regrets.

Emory felt the same way after packing up her university office. "It was joyful. I felt ownership of my life that I hoped I deserved by this time. . . . I felt that my life was now under my control, that I was affecting some kind of change, and it felt very hopeful, very exciting. This was at the core of making my life comprehensible." Leaving with grace also seemed very important to Emory; she wanted to leave the university "setting an example" for her students. She wanted them to see her, at sixty, opening a new door, embracing the uncertainty, living in the moment. "I have always been very open with my students about where I am developmentally. I've always told them my age, shared my challenges—hoping to model for them a vital engagement in life."

Not surprisingly, the euphoria was short-lived; replaced relatively quickly by feelings of loss and assaults on her self-esteem. For so many years Emory's identity had been wrapped up in what she was doing, not who she was; now, suddenly, shockingly, it was hard to figure out what to call herself and how to structure her time. She had lived with a professional title, a business card, a handle that was easily described at dinner parties. "It is hard for me to say what I am now. What do I call myself? What do I put on my card? . . . I'm constantly trying to negotiate the balance between the prominence that exhausted me and the anonymity that makes me feel empty." The first summer after resigning, Emory purposely decided not to unpack her books from the office. She couldn't even stand to look at the boxes.

She was trying to stay very far away from any traces of her former life, not wanting to face the things that she was surely missing—her students, her schedule, being needed.

Instead, she began a project that turned out to be the beginning of her return to herself. Emory decided to paint a portrait of her best friend, a gift for her friend's sixtieth birthday. The painting, which she had expected to dash off in a couple of days, consumed five months of her time and went through many revisions. There are tears in her eyes as she recalls the tortuous revelatory process. "I was dedicating myself to this gift for my best friend. It was an opportunity, I thought, to explore my art. . . . Every day I would wake up, go to my easel, and work on the painting, and every day it changed. I tried painting from several photographs, choosing pieces from each—the mouth, the forehead, the eyes—trying to come up with an aesthetic whole on the canvas. I was painting in acrylic, so I was able to completely paint over everything and start all over. The first rendering that I did in just a couple of hours was probably my most successful. My son came in and said, 'That's it.' But I couldn't leave it alone; it became something of an obsession. After a while, I found myself putting a scarf on her head, which turned out to be my scarf that I bought at Neiman's . . . and then I put my red sunglasses over her eyes. If I hadn't forced myself to stop, pretty soon she would have had the same long, crooked nose that I have. . . . Just a little while longer and the portrait would have been me!" Now Emory is laughing at what she discovered in the emerging image: the surprising evolution from a painting of her best friend to a self-portrait. "I realized that this had become an imprint of my self-invention, an effort to make myself into an integrated whole."

Having completed the portrait—actually, she never thought it was finished, she finally just forced herself to quit—Emory still felt at loose ends. She missed the structure and purposefulness of her workweek. She did not like that Friday mornings seemed completely interchangeable with Thursday mornings, or that the weekends felt just like the weeks. Playing on her computer one day, she discovered the poker.com website, and she found herself joining six people in cyberspace around a poker table. Later on, she wrote about the odd collection of folks she met around the table. "There we all were: the portly man with the cigar in his mouth, the guy with the Afro and the ski sweater, the enormously well-endowed woman in the low-cut dress, the handsome man in the tuxedo, the tidy grandmother in the gray dress, and the square-shouldered thinker in the red running suit. The guy in the tuxedo was sometimes called "Dietcoke32" or "Lovemykids." Sometimes the man with the cigar was called "Gonefishin" or "Tigersfan." The woman in the revealing dress could be "Mindhead," "Snookcatcher," or "I've got the nuts."

Almost immediately Emory was hooked. "I didn't play for real money . . . but I loved the gambling, the betting. It was so much fun!" She could sit there, often perched on her bed, the covers pulled up around her, and play for several hours, enjoying the strategy, the competition, the motley company. "What was I doing?" she asks me in retrospect, her voice full of guilty pleasure. "I was enjoying the privilege of wasting time. This was the first time in my life that I had time to waste." She also claims that there was excitement in "learning something new" and in mastering "the rules of the game." Emory would often tell her friends—particularly those who were disbelieving or dismissive about how she was using her time—that she was playing because she wanted to write about it. She was merely being a participant observer, working in the best anthropological tradition. But she knew that this was a pretty weak cover for what she herself was finding interesting and pleasurable. "It was incredibly relaxing, mildly stimulating . . . I didn't mind at all entering the world of addiction."

From online poker, Emory "graduated" to online Scrabble, still enjoying the sensation of "wasting time," and relishing—in a life that seemed so lacking in structure—the sense of doing something that had a "beginning, a middle, and an end." Gradually, Emory began to wean herself away from the games; she could see the days disappearing, she could feel the boredom and angst brought on by repetition. In retrospect, however, and without apparent defensiveness or rationalization, she thinks about this period as a critical stage of "letting go," a stage that she labels "exhalation," and she reminds me that these stages are neither discrete nor hierarchical: they do not neatly follow one another up and down a ladder of complexity or self-knowledge. "Each stage persists and is felt and replayed from time to time," she says looking through her developmentalist's lens. So, even though it feels like a long time ago that her days were filled with poker and Scrabble, from time to time Emory still finds it pleasurable to revisit her cyberspace friends online, and waste her time.

Facing the task of making revisions on a book she had finished before her departure from the university finally allowed Emory to move ahead. She was able to use the reshaping of her academic text—her favorite part of the writing process—to remind herself of how much she enjoyed writing, and how much it was part of her "essential identity." It became the bridge to another writing project, which had been sitting on a back burner for at least twenty years, since her mother's death. Emory's mother had been the principal of a small progressive school, an unusual place that often admitted children who did not fit well into more traditional settings, and nourished each child's idiosyncratic gifts, helping him or her to thrive. Emory had promised her mother—who was a practitioner, not a writer, whose wisdom resided in the doing of things, not in the analysis of them—that she would write about the school; that the lessons of teaching and learning would be preserved through a rich narrative that educators would be able to learn from. But this project had been interrupted by Emory's personal and professional commitments; now was the opportune time to return to it. Now she had the space, the resources, the will, and the courage to dig through the boxes of letters, photos, documents, and begin to piece together the story—or at least the version of the story that only she could tell.

This was the best way to circle home, to fulfill her long-standing promise to her mother. And now—at the age of sixty-two—it was the best way to learn more about herself, looking backward into the future. Emory, the developmentalist, calls this stage "finding my stride": a stride forward that she probably would not have been able to navigate a minute earlier. It was work, she discovered, that required her full maturity, her devotion, her forgiveness, her commitment, and her restraint. It was work in which she was able to draw together the academic and autobiographical, the public and the private, the historical and the contemporary. In this Third Chapter, Emory looked into her mother's life and saw her own.

There are so many aspects of Emory's story that I find fascinating, so many ways in which she recasts the death-and-birth narrative that Anatole France speaks of in the opening quote for this chapter. First, she sees the natural inevitability of the "entr'actes" as times of confusion and incoherence, but also as moments for rest, reflection, and self-interrogation. They are built into the developmental cycle. She has experienced such moments throughout her life, and she has learned that they are life-threatening and life-giving, tortuous and exciting, restless and restful. Emory also expects that the developmental cycles will not unfold smoothly; that there will be moments of rehearsing old habits, regressing to past patterns of behavior and self-expression. She sees the unruly path forward. Second, she, like so many others I talked to, feels the need—after a lifetime of working intensively and relentlessly—to slow down, to enjoy the laziness, and to relish the idea of "wasting" time. She is able to exhale, to breathe freely, then to fill her days with the kinds of frivolous and aimless activities that she has never permitted herself to experience before in her life. Third, she takes control of her life by telling her story in several ways, offering up competing narratives about why she left the university and then choosing one that allows her to identify the developmental sequence that will ultimately lead to a satisfying conclusion. By the end of this story, she has found her way home and shaped and shaded herself into an "integrated whole." In fact, in painting the birthday portrait of her best friend, Emory is reborn. She seizes the opportunity to draw her evolving self: returning to the canvas each day, persevering over the changes, washing out the images she created the day before, and beginning again. It is a work in progress; even when she decides she is through with it, she knows it is not done. She looks into the unfinished, refracted images, accepts the imperfections, and discovers herself.

In her book *Composing a Life*, Mary Catherine Bateson describes the importance of framing the decisions we make about how we live our lives—both those forces and changes within our control, and those out of our control—as acts of "composing." Like Emory, Bateson uses the metaphor of painting to describe the agency and creativity that allow for the life composition. In another book, she writes, "One thing that you do in composing a life is to put together disparate elements that need to be in some kind of balance, like a still life with tools, fruit, and musical instruments."[2] This is particularly important when our lives are thrown out of balance—when we have lost our jobs, moved to a new part of the country, experienced the death of a loved one—and we are facing the treachery of transition, the chaos of discontinuity. Rather than conceiving of this transition as a process of surviving the death of the old and the birth of the new, however, Bateson claims that it requires bridging the old and the new realities; transferring aspects of our former identity into the new life that we are "composing." She focuses on the role of "analogy" as a bridge to the new learning:

> Much of the coping with discontinuity has to do with discovering threads of continuity. You cannot adjust to change unless you can recognize some analogy between your old situation and your new situation. Without that analogy you cannot transfer learning. You cannot apply skills. If you can recognize a problem that you've solved before, in however different guise, you have a much greater chance of solving that problem in the new situation. That recognition is critical to the transfer of learning.[3]

In composing the Third Chapter, then, we need to create a narrative that seeks to discover and then emphasize the connections, the similarities, the transpositions from one chapter to the next, rather than one that underscores the death of one and the birth of the other. Bateson even claims that the multiple narratives a person invents—like the four scenarios Emory replayed for leaving the university—are "empowering": they help a person feel in "control," remind her that she has "choice and ownership" of her life. In her focus on tracing the continuities from one life frame to the next, Bateson sees the role of memory as crucial. We must remember the ways we approached problem solving, adaptation, and skill development in the past—even how we felt when we first learned those things—and transfer that knowledge to the new situation.

> Unless you can find ways to relearn and recycle, you are left with the model of hitting bottom and starting over. This is the model where you reach a certain point and you are converted, you are born again, and you completely leave your old life behind. . . . What is important is to use the experience up to now, the skills, the learning, to approach the moment of transition with the memory of what has been learned before, and therefore the knowledge of what new learning felt like.[4]

DEATH AND REBIRTH

Most of the men and women I interviewed referred to the unease, discomfort, even panic of the time between leaving the old and entering the new, when they were often forced to question their choices and interrogate their motives, when friends and colleagues offered unsolicited judgments about their sanity, told them they were crazy or irresponsible or immature, while others seemed to envy their risk-taking and spirit of adventure.

All of the people I talked to spoke about their transition into the Third Chapter as being a time of great vulnerability—intense and difficult to navigate. "I've never felt more vulnerable," said one participant, his face grim, his voice choking back tears. "I've never felt my dignity so compromised, my self-respect so at stake." A former CEO who chose to leave his lofty position after carefully and judiciously planning his exit, spoke about his desperate feelings of "anomie." "Who I thought I was . . . it all got ruptured. Suddenly I was in the wilderness, with very little in the way of a fundamental core of selfhood." Interestingly, these feelings of loss are experienced whether the shifts in people's work and/or identity are of their own volition or not; whether the departures are carefully staged or completely surprising; and whether the changes in status and station are big or small, public or private. The sense of vulnerability—the feelings of being fragile, exposed, and assailable—takes various emotional forms, however. Some people feel an unfamiliar emptiness, a despondency; others, an unbridled rage; still others, a chronic anxiety.

Carolyn Chen, a seventy-five-year-old organizational consultant who has spearheaded large institutional reorganizations for governmental agencies, foundations, universities, and nonprofits, experiences the vulnerability of transition as a "lethargy and a listlessness" that still baffle and surprise her. When she stopped work a few years ago, she had no clear plan for what she would do next. After a demanding and strenuous career that required long hours, attention to deadlines, and global travel, she knew that she needed to rest awhile, but she also knew that she would soon need a "structure and a purposefulness" in her life. When she "slowed down enough to feel," however, she discovered that she was experiencing an inchoate yearning that she could barely describe in words, a wish to "create an environment for self-reflection and the courage for storytelling." But the yearning did not lead to action. It just produced an inertia that made her feel a "chasm of emptiness." She offers a contrast between the old days, when she was a single mother with a huge career, and her days now, which seem to be "running in slow motion." Before, she would come home from the office, make dinner, feed the children, help them with their homework, put them to bed, and stay up for another few hours finishing up work for the next day. Now she goes to the gym for strength training and yoga three days a week, and after that "the day just disappears." It used to be that when she blew in from work in the evening, she would rustle up dinner—a real, balanced meal—in fifteen minutes. Now it seems to take forever; she starts to chop the vegetables at four, and she finally sits down for dinner around seven. "I end up going to bed feeling I didn't do anything," complains Carolyn. She knows that at seventy-five she should not expect to have the same energy, the same fight, the same drive. But she also surmises that it is the emptiness (Carolyn describes the bodily sensation of feeling "hollow"), not her physical aging, that makes her weary. Until she has a new purpose, a clear direction—until she navigates the "abyss of transition"—she knows that she will continue to feel vulnerable and bereft.

Rather than the hollowness and yearning that Carolyn endures, Jerome Gunther responds to the vulnerability of transition with "raw rage." A distinguished oncologist at University Hospital, Jerome has a well-deserved national reputation and is admired as a compassionate clinician, a rigorous researcher, an expert fund-raiser, and a spokesperson whose advocacy for cancer research has moved donors and politicians "to do the right thing." At sixty-three, he is at the top of his game. He does not brag, but he has a strong ego and he works hard. However, even though he has met with enormous satisfaction and success in his work, even though his work life has encouraged his "lifelong learning," Jerome has always felt a chronic sense of not being fully appreciated by his colleagues at the hospital. "For a long time, I've felt more than typically taken for granted," he admits. "That arrogance is part of the institutional culture of the place, a kind of subconscious neglect, a being ignored. But recently I have felt it more personally, something directed at me individually." He contrasts his national renown and respect with the way he is regarded by his closest colleagues. His voice, which is very matter-of-fact at first, turns into a hurtful plea. "It is surprising, the extent to which I am unrecognized here. . . . I want to be come to, rather than be a supplicant."

Usually this latent lack of appreciation, "this sense of being taken for granted," is more than balanced by the public acclaim Jerome receives, and by the freedom and space he is given to choose and develop his projects. But a few months ago, a dispute over some contractual issues came up, and it really rattled him. He was not fired; the contractual change made almost no "substantive difference" to his income or his work. He is clear that the issue is not about the money, and that his response was "purely emotional." Jerome is now jabbing his hands through the air like karate moves. "It is the pain of being discarded. . . . It is about how I feel about all of this, not the loss of income or stature." He has spent the last several weeks "making up silly, stupid stories to make sense of it." Now he lets loose with a primitive war-cry—a response to the most "primal sense of powerlessness" this has made him feel. "I will get those fuckers. . . . The un-Zen-like me will be rejuvenated. . . . I am now the road-rage person!" Something about this experience has turned this normally strong, centered, and self-assured professional into a vulnerable and raging person. It has tapped into a part of Jerome that he knows is there but usually has no reason to express or expose. "I believe that we are each a series of multiple selves, particularly at this stage of our lives. We have lots of layers. With this, they will see the *me* who is the avenger." His voice sends out a warning. "Don't ignite that self. You'll find that you will be scared of the guy who is learning to breathe free. You'll like him less than I do."

We sit together silently and let the full measure of his pain and rage surround us. It is not that Jerome feels totally undone by all of this. Rather, there is this odd sensation that, at sixty-three, he is living a huge contradiction. He feels as strong as he has ever been, and he has never felt as powerless as he feels now. "I still feel as enfranchised, as authoritative, as credible as I've ever felt," he crows. "This is a narcissistic injury. . . . I'm offended, and the avenger in me has been triggered." Now Jerome looks both hurt and defiant, like a victim and a warrior. "I want to say to them, How could you not value me? Don't you know who I am?"

In his book *Managing Transitions*, William Bridges distinguishes between "change," which he describes as external, contextual, and public, and "transitions," which are internal, private, and psychological. He claims that change is relatively easy; we make a shift in the environment—the new boss, the new policy, the new project—whereas transitions are more difficult and emotionally demanding. "Transition is the psychological process people go through to come to terms with the new situation," he says.[5] It is these interior processes of learning and adaptation—not the external projects of change—that are the focus of the Third Chapter.

Bridges makes another observation about the psychological sequence people must follow to make successful transitions. He claims that, in our highly mobile society, where change and ambition are considered the coin of the realm, people fail to recognize that any transition process—in life, in love, in work—not only requires adapting to a new situation, but it also means letting go of old habits. Bridges lays out a three-step model. After the "ending" (step one) of something, a person must pass through a "neutral zone" (step two) before arriving at the beginning of something (step three). The "neutral zone" he defines as a kind of "no-man's-land between the old reality and the new," where the individual wrestles with issues of personal and professional identity. He regards the neutral zone as not only an essential passage to the new reality—to be seriously reckoned with—but also the most tortured and treacherous stage; a time when both opportunities and casualties present themselves. How a person manages the fears and inhibitions, the ambivalence and ambiguities of this period of "limbo" determines how productive and rewarding the transition will be.[6]

Although Bridges's model seems somewhat formulaic to me (not capturing the fits and starts, the circling back, the moments of retreat that I heard participants talk about as they spoke of exiting the old and entering the new, nor the pathos and passion I heard in their voices), I do resonate with the notion that people, particularly those who have led lives characterized by rapid ascent and external rewards, need to give themselves the space (the "neutral zone") to live with and really experience the loss before they can move on to the next stage. And I believe it is critical that we honor and recognize the rigorous emotional demands of letting go of the old and living in the "limbo" as a foundation for "composing" our Third Chapter. In exploring "Loss and Liberation," I was interested, then, in how women and men negotiate what Anatole France describes as the death of the old and the birth of the new; how they navigate the casualties and opportunities; how they move from the sadness of leaving behind the familiar and risk the learning that is required to embrace the Third Chapter. The narratives in this chapter capture the melancholy and the mourning of loss, the treachery and promise of the transition, and the forging of a new identity.

COCOONING AND FLIGHT

Lucinda Miller, a successful businesswoman in her early fifties who has recently returned to a part-time career on the front line as an international relief worker, regards the transitions between loss and liberation as signposts of three major developmental shifts in her adult life that she is able—in retrospect—to identify and name. The first, which she calls "venturing forth," reflects the adventurous, passionate, experimental life that she lived in her twenties, and her movement across a large and diverse landscape. It includes study and international travel: training in classical piano at a Paris conservatory; travel in Capetown, South Africa; getting her master's at a school of management; working for a refugee program in Thailand; entering the corporate world in New York City; and directing a hunger-relief program in the Sudan. This decade was a time of "risk-taking, experimentation, and adventure . . . a time of huge change and variety," when the landscape was "broad but not deep."

The next fifteen years (from her early thirties to her late forties) were a "radical departure" from the adventurous globe-trotting that had defined her twenties. Lucinda describes her next life phase as "pulled way in," as deep and narrow. This was the period when she was creating and growing her family and her corporate business, both endeavors that she shared and partnered with her husband, Max. During that time, she and Max had three babies and three miscarriages while also "birthing" a small company that struggled to survive through its early fragile years, almost closing down several times. Lucinda remembers, "Life was so emotional, so exhausting and difficult, as we invested everything we had—emotions and resources—in our family and our business." This second stage she calls "cocooning," to connote the intense focus, the intimacy, the boundaries that both protected and encased her. There were "wistful" moments of imagining the "roads not taken," of wanting "to take wings in flight," when Lucinda would occasionally dare to "peak out of the cocoon," but she was always conscious of her chosen path, and she purposefully did not allow herself other passions.

Lucinda wants me to understand how much energy and struggle went into these years—both within her family and at work—so she takes me back to the "most painful place" of losing her pregnancies. After each of her three miscarriages, she went into a state of "acute depression." Sometimes she could not see any reason to carry on, she was in such despair. "I think of that time as an era of great pain and struggle—trying to keep a pregnancy and not lose it, being thrown into despair when I lost it, and all the time keeping my head above water for my other children. It felt like we were fighting to survive." She sees clear parallels in the way she and Max had to work to protect and save their company: "always struggling so hard for the company to survive," trying to make sure they would not lose it through some "miscarriage."

By the time Lucinda reached her late forties—with her children nearly fledged and her business sturdy and growing—she was ready to "break out"; she was yearning to recapture her early passions. She tells me that whenever she has taken one of those personality tests to help determine the kind of career that would be best for her, she has discovered that she would be most in her element as a war correspondent. Her "most natural" inclination is to be attracted to adventure, travel, challenge, and danger; to be out there in the world on her own, investigating and reporting, all the while risking her life and living on the edge. She says this to underscore how much determination and restraint it took to "choose" the "deep and narrow life" of mothering and entrepreneurship, and also to let me know how easy and natural it felt to be pulled back to her earlier passions. Lucinda refers to this third stage—the one she inhabits now, in her early fifties—as a time of "recapturing her dreams."

Even though, to some extent, she is pursuing her ancient passions, this third stage feels very different, because this time Lucinda is able to build upon what she "has worked on before": she has been able to combine the substance, networks, strategies, access, and self-assurance that she learned and earned in her life of entrepreneurship with the maturity, balance, devotion, and wisdom that grew out of her mothering, and bring both of these realms with her into her new adventures. There is this feeling of combining all of these experiences into a "greater, more powerful whole"; not having a sense of either/or (passion or industry), but sensing the strength of "both and more."

Lucinda's favorite metaphor—for both growing her family and growing her company—is "building a cathedral." With this image, she wants to convey the creativity, the intentionality, the architecture/structure, and the sacredness of both these endeavors. She also wants to describe the beauty and the resilience: that the cathedral is built to endure, that it can be designed and inhabited by different generations of people. Lucinda first used this metaphor in a keynote speech she gave her staff in a company-wide annual meeting. "I wanted to tell them that we were about creating something beautiful and soaring, but that I recognized that there will be generations of architects that would come along later to build new spaces, that this cathedral would be built to outlive us." Although she saw herself as the "master architect" of the cathedral, she wanted to make it an organization that would be "something of singular substance that would not solely be dependent on me."

Lucinda feels similarly about rearing her children. In her family, she is the "master architect." When her children were young, she needed to focus her love, time, and energy on giving them the kind of attention and structure that they needed in order to feel safe and loved, and increasingly independent and self-confident. "They should always feel my unending devotion," she says with tears in her eyes. But now, as the oldest of her three children is about to go off to college, Lucinda has begun to feel the need to let go and pull back; it is time for their "launching." "Ultimately, it is up to them. As a mother you try to instill in them their own passions, their own vision . . . you try to help them go in their own direction. During that time, we provide them with unconditional love and support; we are a huge presence in their lives. But then there is the recognition that they will leave." Lucinda is as emotional as I have ever seen her when she talks about the twin feelings of liberation and loss, how pulling back from mothering and the leadership of her company feels both "liberating and heartbreaking." It has been—and continues to be—a difficult process of "explicitly trying to shed the bonds." "It is no longer my show at the company . . . and my child is going off to college," she says with sorrow and relief written all over her face.

Lucinda had anticipated this moment of heartbreak. As a matter of fact, about five years ago, she began a deliberate but "messy" process of "taking stock," responding to a deep "yearning for change slow burning" inside of her. She dared to "peak out of the cocoon" and began to admit to herself that she "needed something different." Her early explorations took the form of reading and rumination. She read a lot of Joseph Campbell and was moved by his ideas of "following your bliss and letting life develop organically." She found herself drawn again to her music, and decided to return to the Conservatory for piano lessons. She found herself thinking about becoming re-engaged in international crisis issues, yearning again for the risky, dangerous adventures.

Although she felt these "stirrings" for change, she had some anxiety about not knowing what was next. She did, however, feel clear about what she didn't want for herself. "I did have a few moments of panic and doubt," admits Lucinda. "It was not like I had the certainty and clarity of jumping into an all-consuming identity. I knew that I didn't want the ball and chain and entrapment of a big career position. I didn't want to jump in and be defined by one thing. . . . I wanted to be a free agent."

The "opening" came one day when Lucinda least expected it. She and Max were vacationing with friends at a ranch in Montana in a dreamy setting of gorgeous mountains and shimmering lakes. They were luxuriating, enjoying the stillness and the laziness of the day, paddling around in their canoes. The husband of the other couple—a friend from graduate-school days who is now the CEO of a large international relief organization—broke the spell by talking about his work in Kosovo. He described the violent, deteriorating conditions there and the decimated families and the orphans left behind. "It just hit me at that moment, like a bolt of lightning," recalls Lucinda: "I want to go!" She asked her friend—right then and there—whether "there would be any use" in her going to Kosovo to look at the "status of young children" and see what productive work the relief organization could take on there. Three months later, Lucinda was on her way to Kosovo. "I walked into the war zone of Kosovo and felt like I was home again!"

PROGRESS AND REGRESSION

Lucinda's articulation of her three adult developmental phases—from "venturing forth" in her twenties to "cocooning" in her thirties and forties to "flight" in her fifties and beyond, from living a life that was "broad," to "deep and narrow," to "both and more"—underscores what she defines as both the "ascendancy and deepening" of her learning in the Third Chap-

ter. As I listened to the story of Lucinda Miller and many of the
other men and women I interviewed, I was reminded of the
path-breaking work of Erik Erikson, a developmental psychologist who, a half-century ago, was the first scholar to chart the
sequence of life stages across the life span from birth to death,
the first to describe adult development as an opportunity for
growth rather than an inevitable loss of capacity, the first to see
the developmental shifts that Lucinda names as moments of
"crisis" between the old and the new, the familiar and the
strange, and the first to recognize the ways in which the cultural
and historical settings in which we grow up shape our learning
and identities.[7]

Like the "crisis" between "heartbreak and liberation" for
Lucinda, each of Erikson's eight life stages reflects a tension
between a positive and a negative force—between moving forward and being pulled back—that must be negotiated successfully if the person is to ascend to the next stage. It is not that the
positive wins out over the negative; rather, the manner in which
these crises get navigated and resolved influences the development of each individual. For example, in Erikson's stage one—
which he labels "basic trust and basic mistrust"—the baby must
begin to establish deep and trusting relationships with parents
and caregivers, but at the same time maintain enough distrust so
that he/she is not left completely unprotected and vulnerable. In
this way, across the life span, the productive resolution of each
developmental crisis determines whether we will experience
happiness and contentment, or discontent and despair.

Even though there is a downside to each of Erikson's turning
points, he sees each development crisis as potentially hopeful
and productive. In his view, the struggles, the contesting forces
of progress and regression, are inevitable and necessary for pro-
pelling growth. And even though Erikson claims that each stage

builds upon the previous one, he acknowledges that there is overlap between them. Lucinda Miller talks about this melding of developmental stages when she claims that, in taking on the new adventures of her international relief work in her fifties, she did not have to make an either/or choice ("replacing one set of values and experiences with another"). Rather, she could feel the strength and synergies of "both and more." And Emory Daniels refers to the fuzzy boundaries between stages when she admits to being pulled back, from time to time, to her old addiction: joining the motley crew at the online poker table, relishing the rare and seductive pleasure of "wasting time."

It is Erikson's penultimate stage—"generativity vs. stagnation"—that is most relevant to the learning and growth of people in their Third Chapters. By generativity, he is referring to the impulse within us to nurture and guide the next generation. Although his definition focuses on raising and nourishing our children and grandchildren, he broadens it to include teaching, writing, innovation, and artistic expression, activism, advocacy, and service. Certainly a common theme that resounded throughout my interviews was the urge among many women and men to use their Third Chapters for "giving back" and "giving forward," for "making an imprint," "forging a footprint," and "leaving a legacy." They no longer felt interested in, or inspired by, the lonely, solitary pursuit, making it to the top of the ladder of individual achievement, status, and success. Instead, they wanted to find a way to use their privilege, skills, networks, and access for the benefit of the broader community. Lucinda's story echoes many of the voices I heard that expressed a yearning to move beyond the boundaries, constraints, and "entrapment" of their former careers in search of ways to contribute more directly and more meaningfully to, as she puts it, "making the world a better place for all of the world's children."

Although Erikson does not talk explicitly about the expectation of reciprocity that often accompanies our "giving forward," he admits that "mature man needs to be needed"[8] and that people in their Third Chapters do, in fact, look to the younger generation for guidance, encouragement, and legitimacy. As I listened to people's stories, I heard their yearning for reciprocity. As teachers and learners, they wanted to establish relationships of mutual benefit, of give and take. They dispensed wisdom and experience to the next generation and expected youthful insight and perspective in return. They offered solace to the needy, but they also needed to be needed. In their Third Chapters, they wanted to feel useful, not used.

In their introduction to a collection of essays, de St. Aubin, McAdams, and Kim explain the dynamic of giving and receiving in the Third Chapter, linking it to Erikson's notion of "generativity."

> Generative adults are teachers, leaders, mentors, and what George Valliant has called the "keepers of meaning" (Valliant and Milofsky, 1980). They seek to pass on the most valued traditions of a culture, to teach the most valued skills and outlooks, to impart wisdom, and to foster the realization of human potential in future generations. As adults move into and through their midlife years, they may become increasingly concerned with giving something back to the world, perhaps in gratitude for the care and good fortune they have received.[9]

By contrast, if Erikson's seventh stage of development is not resolved productively, people in their Third Chapters will experience "stagnation," and "often begin to indulge themselves as if they were their one and only child"[10]—a self-indulgence that inhibits their full development in the later stages of their lives. This "stagnation" is what Carolyn Chen, at seventy-five, fears as she experiences the odd and ominous "hollowness" in her body, as she moves through her days "in slow motion." She knows that this "chasm of emptiness" will consume her if she doesn't find a way to navigate the "abyss of transition" between loss and liberation. She knows "deep in her bones" that she needs to discover "new ways of giving and contributing" so she will feel "worthy" and "filled up."

THE INDIVIDUAL AND
THE ENVIRONMENT

Even though Erikson's lens helped me appreciate the ascendancy of new learning in late adulthood, and allowed me to hear the tension between loss and liberation as inevitable and productive, his eight-stage model seemed too linear and predictable to match the messier, more unruly stories people were telling me; nor did it seem to reflect how we are all molded and influenced by the time and place into which we are born and raised. Beginning in the early 1960s, the work of an interdisciplinary group of scholars, calling themselves "life-span theorists,"[11] offered a refreshing perspective that built on Erikson's longitudinal framework but seemed to provide a somewhat more generous, more forgiving, and more improvisational view of development. They spoke, for example, about the "plasticity"[12] of learning throughout the life cycle: no particular time in our lives can claim primacy as the most developmentally vital and productive. Life-span theorists—including historians, demographers, sociologists, and anthropologists—projected a developmental scenario whereby individual differences prevail as people follow their own idiosyncratic path, whereby people born during different historical periods experience different realities and world views, and whereby particular life events—individual turning points—take on a unique importance and gravity.

Not only do life-span theorists claim that there is learning and growth throughout the life cycle, but they also urge us to see development as nonlinear and multidimensional, as layered and complex. Most developmental researchers, for instance, focus on forms of learning that are similar to the concept of "growth" in biology, a process that is conceived of as irreversible, and end-state–oriented. But the life-span group argues that development has myriad forms (growth and differentiation are just one of these), and that this complexity and variety are particularly prevalent in the second half of life. With this more generous view, researchers are able to trace changes and adaptations that do not have a straight, linear, or predictable trajectory. This framework, for instance, opens up the possibility of documenting the depth and character of wisdom. We are able to move beyond our central preoccupation with age-graded quantifiable measures of intelligence and achievement. As one of my interviewees said, in searching for a way to describe the "different texture and feel" of his new learning in the Third Chapter, "I'm interested in going slower and deeper, not faster and farther. . . . I want to become wise, not just smart."

There are other useful angles to this life-span approach that are related to our understanding of new learning in the Third Chapter and that framed the way I heard and interpreted the experiences of the women and men I interviewed. Significantly, this framework allows us to appreciate the ways in which the political, social, and historical periods in which we were raised shape our values and perspectives; and the ways in which we selectively respond to these broader social and institutional forces.

Growing up in the Depression, as my parents did, very much shaped how they envisioned their future, raised their children, saved their money, doled out our weekly allowances, and balanced immediate needs with future hopes. Their three children, all Baby Boomers, grew up at a time of relative abundance. Like our peers, we saw ourselves as powerful actors who could shape our futures, change the culture, and speak out against the cautions, rigidities, and injustices of society. We were change agents expressing a tricky blend of engagement, commitment, and bravado. The typical adolescent conflicts we experienced with our parents—around curfews, manners, music, virginity, drugs, and alcohol—were, I now realize, not only a reflection of our teenage impulse to move beyond our parents' shadow, break away from home, and establish our independence, but they were also related to the fact that we were shaped by a different history and set of cultural circumstances.

Likewise, the men and women I interviewed often began their stories of learning by placing themselves in the historical context that shaped their views and values. They pointed to powerful public events like the Vietnam War, the deaths of Jack and Bobby Kennedy and Martin Luther King, the passage of the Civil Rights Act, the March on Washington, and the murders of students demonstrating at Kent State. Or they pointed to the importance of major social movements like the civil-rights movement, the feminist movement, and the gay-rights movement. Or they simply identified themselves as children of the sixties, "Boomers," or postwar babies as a way of expressing a certain "attitude" about their place in history, a stance that reflected their collective belief that they "could make a difference," that they had—as a generation—a unique sense of empowerment and entitlement.

In her book of essays *Aging and Life Course Transitions* (1982), historian Tamara Hareven identifies "timing" as one of the critical aspects of the life-span approach that help us see the relationship between individual developmental transitions and the changing historical conditions. She reminds us that there are catalytic moments in our lives—events like marriage, childbirth, death of a spouse, major illness, career changes, and freak accidents, some of which are chosen, others thrust on us without warning—that transform our reality, require adaptation, and test our resilience. These events occur against a backdrop of societal expectations, timetables, and social arrangements that are, to a certain extent, prescriptive of the ways in which life stories are supposed to unfold. If, on the other hand, the timing is off, or out of sequence, our development may be altered or distorted. Hareven concludes that this "timing" not only affects our individual journeys, but it also has implications for the quality of our intergenerational relationships.[13]

The powerful influence of what another historian, Glen Elder, calls "publicly recognized stages and age graded beliefs"[14] is particularly intriguing when we think about people in their Third Chapters who—like the protagonists in this book—decide to take on the adventures, and submit to the vulnerabilities and uncertainty, of new learning, when the societal expectation and institutional arrangements signal a retreat into leisure and retirement. How do they navigate these challenges to public expectation about what they should be doing, when they should be doing it, and how they should be leading their lives? The gerontologists Neugarten and Hagestad hint at these shifts in timing that reflect not only individual choice but also changes in life expectancy and contemporary culture. They write that people "no longer move from adulthood to old age, but instead go through a relatively long interval when physical vigor remains high, when family responsibilities are diminished, and when commitment to work continues but specific work roles may change."[15]

Finally, life-span theorists broaden and complicate our view of the sources of influence on our development. Rather than the singular trajectory drawn by Erikson, they see a complicated web of institutions, state and social policies, and the dictates of the market, as well as personal choices and constraints, and an individual's sense of self-efficacy. In other words, they see interactions that influence our development taking place at the micro and macro levels and every layer in between; and they assert the critical role of human agency. Glen Elder articulates this last important ingredient by underscoring the ways in which people initiate, as well as respond to, the historical narratives of which they are a part: "People are influenced by opportunity, but they also make opportunities."[16]

The stories and frameworks that fill this chapter provide useful perspectives and intriguing metaphors for understanding and negotiating the space between loss and liberation. Emory Daniels's theatrical illusions light up the stage on which the path to liberation is played out, by rearranging the scenery, recasting the actors, and composing a plot that twists, turns, and circles back home. It is a journey of progress and retreat, of inhaling and exhaling, of wasting time and surging forth, of losing faith and hitting her stride. Lucinda Miller's story imagines the patient and protective gestation of a caterpillar plotting her emergence as a butterfly. In her thirties and forties, she is committed to "cocooning"; she "pulls way in" and lives "deep and narrow" as she births her business and nurtures her family. By the time she reaches fifty, she is ready to burst forth, spread her wings, and take "flight."

Anatole France's refrain about dying "to one life before we can enter another," and Bridges's three-stage construction about how people can successfully move from death to rebirth, help us honor the vulnerability and loss we experience in leaving the familiar—how hard it is to let go and take the leap of faith. Bridges also helps us to recognize the inevitable feelings of ambivalence and confusion that mark the "neutral zone"—how learning to tolerate the "limbo" is a prerequisite for productively moving forward.

Challenging the concept of "completely leav[ing] your own life behind" as you move on to the next stage, Bateson emphasizes the role of analogy: the transition is made easier and smoother if we search out continuous learning; the skills and qualities that we honed in the past might be transferred to the new problems and situations that we face in the present and future. Recollection—the deliberative plumbing of our memories—supports the new learning in which we are embarked and gives us courage to endure the anxieties and fears of passing through the "neutral zone."

Erikson and his colleagues help us see as productive the longitudinal perspective, the inevitable tug between the positive and negative forces—of progress and regression—at each stage. His work allows us to view the "crises" we face with each developmental leap as inevitable and strengthening, even redeeming. There is worthiness and optimism in the struggle. Finally, lifespan theorists help us listen for the more complex and layered learning that happens in the second half of life, for the ways in which developmental changes in the course of aging reflect biological, social, psychological, and historical events, and in which people—like Lucinda and Emory—are architects of their own lives, designing their own cathedrals and writing their own plays.

TWO

Constancy and Change

I am what survives me.   —Erik Erikson[1]

RETREAT AND ENGAGEMENT

At about the same time that life-span scholars were drawing out the themes that would constitute their interdisciplinary theory, a noticeable cultural and institutional shift recast the roles and status of older people in our society; the idea of retirement as a life of leisure and retreat emerged. Both movements—one academic and scholarly, the other defined by popular societal views and shifts in the market—developed in the 1960s and, put side-by-side, they offered a paradoxical perspective on people in their Third Chapters. On the one hand, life-span theorists urged us to view learning as lifelong; their optimistic work suggesting that people between the ages of fifty and seventy-five should continue to be actively engaged in the world around them, seeking out opportunities for continued growth, challenging definitions of elderly decline. On the other hand, "leisure entrepreneurs" forged a view of people in the second half of life that emphasized their need for rest and entertainment, and began to build institutions that would protect them from the complex, overly stimulating, and unwelcoming communities that no longer wanted or needed them. This latter view—a short "history of aging"— offers an important backdrop for considering the challenges facing people in their Third Chapters who have chosen engagement over retreat, labor over leisure, and reinvention over retirement.

In agrarian times, people worked until they were no longer healthy. There was intergenerational interdependence, in which older Americans "carried their weight in the community by helping out . . . whether it was taking care of their grandchildren, teaching kids to read, or being of use in whatever way they could."[2] At the same time, older Americans depended on the loyalty and dedication of younger generations, especially given the realities of their declining health and the home-based nature of elder care. In his masterful book, *Prime Time*, which documents the historical and cultural shifts in the views and status of older Americans, Marc Freedman identifies a major transition in the second quarter of the nineteenth century—during the religious and social movement of the Second Great Awakening—when elders were not given the reverence and respect that they had enjoyed in earlier times. With intellectual, religious, and political leaders placing an emphasis on youth and progress, "the old were portrayed as leftover relics from an outdated and regressive world—a past with little to teach the present."[3]

In the latter part of the nineteenth century, the position of older Americans deteriorated further. Professionals such as social workers, management experts, and physicians characterized aging as an incurable disease that required a new set of institutions: old-age homes and mandatory retirement. I. L. Nascher, the founding father of the field of geriatrics, for example, expressed an infantilized view of older people: "The old man does not know what is best for him. . . . He cannot accommodate himself to new conditions brought about by civilization."[4] This shift in perception—from viewing elders as wise, experienced, and resourceful to seeing them as childish and diminished—showed up in costumes and dress. Whereas Americans used to powder their wigs to appear older and cut their clothes to imitate the sloping shoulders of the elderly, the twentieth century gave rise to articles such as "The Quest for Prolonged Youth" and "The Art of Not Growing Old."[5]

By the 1960s, Americans were marveling at the expansion of the elderly population, a shift in societal perspectives on aging that reflected both ambivalence and confusion. A 1962 *Time* article presented a list of statistics on the elderly in staccato fashion: "Between 1950 and 1960, the over-65 population increased about twice as fast as the total population. Between 1920 and 1960, the number of people 75 or more increased by 79%, and the number 85 and older increased by a phenomenal 92%." At the time of this article, a sixty-five-year-old could expect 12.7 more years of life.[6] The language of the article makes clear that living to sixty-five and beyond was a new phenomenon, of which the social, economic, and psychological implications were just in the beginning stages of being understood. Even in the mid-1980s, Frances FitzGerald said that "the aging" or "senior citizens" were a category of people in the act of becoming, much like the category of "child" developed in the last century. "That the name of these people has not yet been agreed upon shows that their status is still transitional," she said.[7]

By the 1960s, not only were Americans living to be older, but also they no longer needed to spend all of their lives working. This possibility of retirement had only come with the New

Deal. FitzGerald wrote that the Social Security Act of 1935 "created a presumption that American workers had the right to retire—a right to live without working after the age of sixty-five."[8] The expansion of government and company pensions made the exercise of this right economically feasible. Yet, though Americans may have been economically ready for retirement, many were not socially or culturally prepared. The 1962 *Time* article described Americans as feeling "too old to work and too young to die"[9]—a depressing and discomforting limbo. In a 1964 *New Yorker* piece, Calvin Trillin described one retiree's despair at facing a retirement that felt like death:

> A retired pump mechanic, apparently deranged, had gratuitously wounded a Phoenix policeman with pellets from a shotgun and held six more policemen at bay in his front yard for twenty minutes. According to the newscast, when the former mechanic was finally talked out of his house by the police captain, he offered a simple explanation of his unusual behavior. "You can't retire and live," he said.[10]

This feeling seemed to be common. The Boston gerontologist Natalie Cabot commented on the shocking change in status and identity that happened with retirement: "Nobody suddenly becomes a Negro or Jewish, but people do suddenly become retired. They become a minority almost overnight, and it hits them hard, usually within the first three weeks."[11] This new experience was difficult and demeaning for some, unbearable for others.

By the late 1960s, retirement communities had emerged in response to the anomie and despair of elders who were feeling displaced and useless. In a 1970 *Life* article, Paul O'Neil described retirement communities as "a compensatory social phenomenon,"[12] creating conditions in which older Americans would not be ignored and ostracized the way they were in the larger society. He wrote that, "for those who are psychologically and financially equipped, a retirement community is a good bet for security, congenial company and what elderly people really want most—independence."[13] O'Neil's view of retirement communities as "compensatory" institutions was certainly influenced by a gerontological theory spawned in the 1950s—"disengagement theory"[14]—that saw older people as needing to lead quiet, sedentary lives, avoiding excess and overexertion.

Thomas Breen, vice-president for development of the Del Webb Corporation, however, thought otherwise. After doing a small amount of market research, he was convinced that older Americans would welcome more active lifestyles, and he proposed an age-segregated retirement community organized around the principles of "activity, economy, and individuality."[15] The elderly would abandon lives of rejection and inactivity for this new alternative. Housing prices would be kept low, there would be an abundance of shared facilities including a golf course and recreation center, the opportunity would be created for volunteer work, and the restriction age would be fifty. On New Year's Day 1960, Breen's vision became a reality, and the first retirement community, built in Arizona by the Del Webb Corporation—called Sun City—opened for visitors. It was expected to attract ten thousand visitors on opening day, but some one hundred thousand showed up, eager to tour the first age-segregated, gated community explicitly designed around the lifestyle, rituals, and routines of retired people. The sign erected on the third birthday of Sun City advertised the insular, contrived environment, the safe asylum that would serve as a model for many more Sun Cities and other, similar age-segregated communities to open over the next several decades. It read as follows: "Del Webb's Sun City, Arizona. Where Active Retirement Originated. Population January 1, 1960: 0. Population January 1, 1963: 7000. Total Clubs and Organizations: 90. Total States Represented: 50. Motel. Shopping Center. Medical Building. Two Golf Courses."[16]

By 1970, Sun City included four golf courses, three shopping malls, a hotel, four swimming pools, four lawn bowling rinks, a 33-acre artificial lake (with a 28-foot artificial waterfall) and a community center with stone polishing rooms, woodworking shops, therapeutic pools, and illuminated outdoor shuffleboard courts.[17]

One interesting aspect of this Sun City retirement community (and the many others that opened later) was its stated egalitarian approach. Freedman observes, from historical record, that in Sun City "all the status and achievement anxieties of midlife were set aside."[18] He writes that this "egalitarian climate seemed to appeal particularly to individuals tired of all the jostling for position and status associated with midlife, as well as the sudden decline in status in mainstream society that accompanied retirement."[19] Mabel Meade, who had moved to Sun City from Mason City, Iowa, exclaimed, "It's wonderful having everybody on the same level. Here they're not interested in your financial status the way they are in most communities."[20] At the same time, says Freedman, residents also felt as if they were living a life of luxury, able to afford a retirement on a golf course. Del Webb was indeed selling "a way of life. The homes [were] secondary."[21]

Interestingly, even though Sun City provided an "oasis" for people who felt out of place and underappreciated in society, it also perpetuated prejudice. The gates kept out anyone who was different from the white middle-class mainstream inhabitants.

In his 1970 article for *Life*, O'Neil wrote about one such community: "The town has no hippies, no smog, no race problems (since, in fact, it has no Negroes), no riots, no bombings, no LSD, and no relief rolls. It is a rare inhabitant who is not ('by God') against them all."[22] These retirement communities also reinforced—in fact invited—generational conflict, an adversarial distance between the residents and their progeny. Residents were, for example, fined or summarily thrown out for defying the age ban by illegally housing a grandchild. These policies of exclusion still prevail today in many retirement enclaves. Just this week I heard a report on the evening news of a couple in their mid-fifties living in a community in Florida who were being forced to sell their property and move elsewhere because they had taken in a four-year-old grandchild whose mother—their only daughter— was a cocaine addict and could no longer care for her child.

Sun City is just one incarnation of the retirement culture, but it has been described by Frances FitzGerald as "a prism on the broader culture of retirement as leisure that has evolved over the past half century."[23] Yet, given the consumer culture of the United States, Sun City has been as much a catalyst as a prism, creating and propagating this culture of retirement. Rather than envisioning these institutions as a kind of cultural undertow, a "structural lag," Del Webb provided what sociologist Phyllis Moen has called a "structural lead"[24]—"his invention got ahead of society, providing a glimpse of what retirement could be like and helping to make the vision real."[25] In 1997, nearly four decades after the first Sun City opened its doors, the vice-president of the Del Webb Corporation observed the already discernible shifts in the cultural landscape, in definitions of old age, and in the hearts and minds of the elderly—shifts toward more activism, engagement, and new learning. Witnessing the changing scene, he remarked that the current audiences of retirees "may want to learn, volunteer, or try an experience that may not be related to recreation."[26]

These recent shifts are also the result of significant changes in the lifestyle, longevity, and educational attainment for people in their Third Chapters. The statistics tell the story of what many are calling the "Boomer Burst": a major spike in the demographic landscape for people between fifty and seventy-five. The 2000 U.S. Census figures offer compelling data on the population bulge, an increase that results both from larger numbers of people in the Boomer cohort and from greater life expectancy. People born during the early years of the Baby Boom (1946–50), for example, fueled a 55 percent increase in fifty- to fifty-four-year-olds, the largest percentage growth between 1990 and 2000 of any five-year age group. In raw numbers, in 2000, there were 37.7 million people ages forty-five to fifty-four, and 13.5 million ages fifty-five to fifty-nine.[27]

The greatest number of people within the Boomer cohort is combined with greater longevity among older Americans: the next generation of Americans age sixty-plus is expected to be the healthiest and longest lived in history. Between 1970 and 2002, life expectancy for Americans increased dramatically: for white females, the life expectancy increased from seventy-six to eighty years; for black females and white males, it increased from sixty-eight to seventy-five; and for black males, it rose from sixty to sixty-eight.[28] Whereas, as recently as 1980, young people made up a much higher percentage of the population, now older people make up similar proportions of the overall population.[29] Further, the National Center for Health Statistics reports that the likelihood that an American who reaches the age of sixty-five will survive to age ninety has almost doubled over the last forty years (from 14 percent of sixty-five-year-olds in 1960 to 25 percent in 2000, to a projected 40 percent in 2025).[30]

Not only have the numbers of older Americans increased dramatically, but they are also more highly educated than any previous generation. Again the most dramatic increases are among the Boomer cohort, whose high-school graduation rates—according to 2004 figures—range around 90 percent, compared with about 70 percent for people ages sixty and older. The difference between Boomers and slightly older cohorts in terms of bachelor-degree attainment is even more striking: 28.6 to 31.5 percent of Boomer cohorts graduated from college, whereas 16.7 to 25.6 percent of the older cohorts did.[31] In addition, recent data from a 2002 AARP study called *Staying Ahead of the Curve* show a surprising number of respondents—60 percent—between the ages of forty-five and seventy-four who say that they plan to work during retirement: 34 percent of those plan to work part-time for their interest and pleasure, and 19 percent for additional income; 10 percent plan to start their own businesses, and 6 percent expect to retire but work part-time doing something else.[32]

I present this brief history of the "retirement of leisure," and the institutions that were spawned by it, as a way of contrasting the segregation, isolation, and recreation that retirees sought and relished "back then," and what I—and many others—regard as major shifts in the statistical profiles, attitudes, and behaviors among people in their Third Chapters, many of whom are yearning for lives of active engagement, purposefulness, and new learning. This book tells the stories of men and women who are part of this growing, thriving population, who are "neither young nor old," and who have chosen to leave the worlds they know and have conquered, the institutions in which they have made their marks and left their imprints, the work in which they have become expert, to venture into new domains, develop new skills, take on new vocations, learn new fields, and contribute to society in new ways. "Retirement" is not in their vocabulary; they do not want to retreat from their engagement in, or contribution to, society, even though they are eager to develop new kinds of activity, new daily rhythms, new habits of conduct, and new sources of motivation and reward. In order to take on these new life adventures, then, they must challenge two primary cultural assumptions: first, that aging leads to a deterioration of mind, body, and spirit, and that productive and creative new learning rarely takes place after the age of fifty; and, second, that there is a social, psychological, and economic benefit in the segregation of older people into communities where they will be able to enjoy lives of safety, leisure, and recreation.

THE OLD AND THE NEW

After living for twenty-five years in Syracuse, New York, Grace Clark, an emerging playwright, resigned from her job in publishing at a university press, packed up the house in which she had raised her family, said goodbye to her friends (several of whom were "furious" that she was leaving and "abandoning" them), and moved to Philadelphia, a place where she had few connections, no friends, and no work. She decided (she saw this as her "choice") to make the move because her husband got his dream academic position, allowing him to collaborate with the best colleagues in his field. And now that both of their daughters were grown and had their own children, Grace and her husband were able to be more mobile; they felt, for the first time, that they were free to fashion a new reality for themselves. Grace recalls her first response to the move. "I had what I initially saw as a problematic transition. I left a place where I was comfortable, settled—where I had been a leader, an organizer, an activist—on the school board, involved in social and political movements, founder of an arts festival. . . . When I went to the supermarket, seven people would greet me, and they might be from seven different worlds. . . . I lived a life of layers and density."

In a presentation that she made at a theater conference a year or so after moving from Syracuse to Philadelphia, Grace talked about her move, referring to the ways in which place, work, and identity seemed to converge, and how she experienced the distance between the familiar and the strange, the old and the new.

"I am new to the community where I live. . . . In Syracuse, I was an insider. I served on the school board and the community-theater board, and endless committees, advisory councils, and caucuses, started an arts festival, stayed married, raised two wonderful daughters, organized in the downtown community, and worked for years at the university. If you stay in one place long enough, people remember somewhat vaguely all the things you did, the ways you looked, the friends you shared, the books you wrote, the caucuses you supported, seeing in you the much younger person who originally caught their attention. But in Philadelphia, I arrived as old as I am, an outsider, for whom there were no particular expectations because there was no particular history or identity. I have been reinventing myself these last many months, surprised by the energy and excitement of my fresh start."

Even though the impetus for her move seemed to be the needs of her husband and his career, Grace soon discovered that it allowed her to admit that she had outgrown her vocational life, that her work no longer felt creative or energizing. She had worked at the press for over a decade in several capacities, doing a variety of jobs. "I was a floating competent person," Grace says modestly about the way in which she learned and then taught almost every aspect of the business. "I was in charge of exhibits, marketing, direct mail, building the website. . . . For the last five years I was in charge of publicity." Over the years, mastering each one of these publishing tasks had made it interesting for Grace. But in the last couple of years, she had begun feeling the redundancy of the work; things were beginning to feel routine and devoid of excitement and challenge. "I found myself getting too old for this work," she recalls about being surrounded by people who were half her age. "I was the mentor to a slew of people, but there was no new learning for me. Work was not as engaging or revelatory. I spent a lot of time writing letters of reference for young people. And I also got tired of dealing with the office culture—you know, the press was no more immune to the pettiness and gossip that besets any institution."

In a sense, following her husband's work to Philadelphia helped Grace recognize that her own work was no longer satisfying or interesting; it forced her hand. Certainly it felt like a "loss," a "letting go." But even as she felt the sadness of leaving, she could feel that "the larger part was liberation." "I had thought that leaving Syracuse was a sacrifice. In fact, it set me free." It offered her the chance to start again, unencumbered by the responsibilities and obligations of community, by her deep commitments to friends and colleagues, and free from well-worn views of her place and identity. "I retired, moved, reinvented myself, all in one swoop. In Philadelphia, I reset the meter."

Forcing her hand and resetting the meter opened up the space for Grace to pursue work that she had been putting off for decades. For the first time in her life, she had the leisure to focus seriously on writing plays, and she had the opportunity to take herself seriously as a playwright. She had always loved the theater and had spent most of her adolescence involved in acting and directing in high school and local community productions.

Grace wrote her first play in college: a short play that won a one-act-play contest and was performed to great reviews. Even then, she had felt bitten by the bug of playwriting. But after college her life never allowed her time to pursue it. Instead, she spent a great deal of her energy building the structures and opportunities for other young playwrights to make their work public. She was the orchestrator, the manager, the midwife—but not the creative artist.

Moving to Philadelphia allowed her to leave the full maturity, experience, and responsibility of her adult world in Syracuse and enter an arena where she was "not exactly young" but where she was "psychologically and professionally a baby." Shedding the mantle of comfort and maturity was difficult, but much easier than it would have been if she had remained in Syracuse, where her identity as convener and activist had been so completely forged. Resetting the meter to become a neophyte was both terrifying and exhilarating. Grace recalls, again, her presentation on the panel at the theater conference when, at sixty, she was the oldest speaker but the least experienced playwright. She remembers thinking to herself, "I am the gray-haired adolescent" on the panel. "Old is what I am. I am an outsider by virtue of my age. In this way I feel marginalized. But I am energized and committed." It was exciting to feel the sensation of being both "old and new," which offered a "pragmatic disadvantage" but a "spiritual advantage." When Grace's turn came to speak on the panel, she talked about the advantages of her outsider status. "I have lived a profoundly privileged life that, in itself, creates a self-consciousness, a reason not to speak. Being sixty and being new gave me enough of an outsider status to startle me, goad me into a stronger commitment to write and to be heard."

Just before she left for Philadelphia, Grace had actually completed her first play (that is, the first since her prize-winning one-act in college): a children's musical, a collaboration in which she had written the libretto and her old friend from childhood, a famous Broadway composer, had written the music. It was the story of a young girl who was moving from her hometown to a strange new place. The first half of the play was all about how much she loved her life in her hometown; it celebrated being happy, comfortable, and safe surrounded by friends and loved ones. Then there was the sadness, fear, and anger that she felt when she was forced to move with her family to the new town. In the second half of the play, the young girl feels the awkwardness and isolation of her dislocation, but she also begins to make new friends and feel more and more at home in the new place. Along the way, she is guided by the appearance of a Fairy Woods Creature who helps her discover a "magic tree" that can set her free; the little girl begins to understand that it is she who has the power to find happiness within herself in this new place.

Amazingly, as Grace wrote this play—on the eve of her departure for Philadelphia—she did not see the connections to her own journey. She had written it as a children's play, seen from a child's point of view. (As a matter of fact, the play was originally based on a journal Grace had kept when she and her family had moved across the country from Kansas to Syracuse, when her daughters were very young. In her journal notes she was trying to capture her "kids' perspectives.") She had decided to write a children's musical—rather than an adult play—because she believed that it would be easier for her to get it performed, and because she thought it would turn out to be a modest effort—a good place to get started. In retrospect, Grace recognizes how this children's play actually turned out to be her story. She was the little girl in the play, frightened by leaving her home, so terrified to make the move, so worried about what she would find in a strange new place. Grace shakes her head, still wondering how she could have missed those obvious connections. "If you had asked me before I wrote the play, I would have told you it was focused on children. But really I discovered that the play was a way of dealing with my sadness, my ambivalence, and my excitement about the move. The play, in fact, is unbalanced toward the sadness of leaving—I don't do justice to the arrival. I was the scared kid!"

Grace's journey—from a place where she was well known, respected, and deeply engaged, a place where her layered "life had a density," to a place where she had no history, networks, or reputation—underscores the power of place; the shift in geography provokes new learning. First she feels the sting of loss—of status, identity, of all things familiar—and then, right on the heels of her sorrow, she sees the edge of her liberation from the routines, rituals, and responsibilities of her old life. Extricating herself from ancient relationships, community expectations, and a life of service, she is transformed from being the mature mother nurturing and guiding her children, her younger colleagues at the press, her fellow activists, to being a "gray-haired adolescent" making her way in a new town and beginning to find her way in a new career. Interestingly, the freedom of not being known in her community and the infancy of her new vocation move her from the center of the action to the margins—a "marginalization" that, in her eyes, gives her artistic voice legitimacy. Even though she was unaware of it, Grace anticipated the move from Syracuse to Philadelphia, coping with the inevitable fear by writing herself into the children's play. As she wrote the libretto, from the child's point of view, she was beginning to create her own narrative, one that would help her make the psychological and spiritual journey from the old to the new.

THE TREACHERY OF TRANSITION

Rachel Middleton admits to me that transitions have always been hard for her—a confession that surprises me. Born in South Africa, raised in Detroit, educated in fancy colleges and universities in the United States, Great Britain, and France, she has, at fifty, become practiced in swift environmental and cultural shifts. Unlike Grace, she does not feel the change of place, the shift in geography, as an assault on her identity, but it replays a "psychological loss" that she experienced at age three, when her beloved father died. She relives this primal loss every time she makes a major life change—particularly when she decides to leave a career that has brought her both status and stature, an organization that she has "birthed and mothered."

So it was exceedingly hard for Rachel to make the decision to leave Work Alliances (WA), the nonprofit policy organization that she had built, "the child" that she had nurtured for two decades. The transition was painful and protracted as she tried to figure out the next stages of her journey. She had known for quite a while that it was time to move on. She had loved the challenges and creativity of developing the organization, and she had relished the opportunity to make the "translations" from theory to practice, from research to advocacy. She had also put in place large national networks and programs focused on helping poor minority kids make the transition from school to work, and she had learned how to take these model programs and "scale them up."

It was actually her success as a leader of WA that helped her know it was time to leave. "I was a leader who let the organization grow up," says Rachel. "As the organization matured, it became less interesting to me. I began to feel that I was growing too far away from what gave me passion, which was learning,

which was my commitment to educational and economic justice. You see, I love, and am drawn to, new ideas . . . and I love
creating new structures and institutional forms. But by the time
I left, WA was a highly functioning organization, great for training young people and launching their careers, but not in need of
the innovative mothering that I had done in the early years."

Even though she knew it was time to leave, it took her a
very long time to admit it to herself, and even longer to begin to
announce it to her staff. She could feel that she was "growing
restless and frustrated." But her restlessness, she discovered, was
related to more than her wanting a new challenge, a new venue,
another place to make her imprint. She wanted actually to
change her way of working, to use a different paradigm. After all
of these years of translating "evidence into advocacy," Rachel
began to realize that "facts, research, and data" don't, in fact,
"change people's hearts." She acknowledged that she was more
interested in "working on values"—"the ways in which difference and fear of difference is threatening." Getting a glimpse of
how she wanted to change her work and her purview, Rachel
got "panicked." Her first step was to take a sabbatical from WA
and spend a year at the university, studying public policy; but
this academic setting, it turned out, felt removed from the
action and the passion that she was seeking. The discussions
among students and professors felt hollow and humorless, competitive and opaque. "I learn by doing," Rachel says again, "and
this reflective, academic environment never felt good to me.
And, of course, it was not a place where people seemed to care a
lot about 'working on values.'"

The panic was always there, lurking around the corner, making Rachel feel lost, confused, directionless. She tried therapy as
a way of unraveling her jumbled emotions, and as a way of dealing with the loss of leaving WA, as a way of "letting go of the

child." And slowly but surely—it took four years in all—she extracted herself from her leadership role at WA, found a way of tolerating her colleagues' anger and feelings of abandonment, and took the leap of faith that landed her in divinity school.

Therapy helped her deal with the "terror and the panic" and find a path, helped her discover and name the origins of her fears, and helped her "forgive" herself for her uncharacteristic inertia and reluctance. But she was also shielded by the full support of her husband. A man whom Rachel describes as "secure in his own person," he watched her tentative/determined moves and cheered her on. He is not threatened by her new growth; he feels proud of her. "I am very lucky, actually blessed," says Rachel with great relief, "to have a partner who knows me in my adult self and loves me in my passions. . . . He accepts the fact that you do not have to stay in one career."

Even though Rachel had her husband's full and uncomplicated support, most of her friends could not understand why she chose to leave WA, where she was making a powerful impact and had earned a huge reputation as a national leader, and go back to graduate school to study something that seemed to them far away from the world of politics and policy. Divinity school seemed to her colleagues and friends to be a strange choice, an odd detour. Rachel admits, "Eighty percent of the people I know feel like I've gone off the deep end and done something real crazy, and the other twenty percent see me as making an important, courageous change—one that even inspires them to think about a transition in their own lives." Rachel had been raised a Lutheran but had not attended church regularly since her childhood. She did not decide to go to the divinity school in order to become an ordained minister, or even in order to become more deeply knowledgeable about theology or church history. She was searching for spiritual renewal, for a place in her life "where the spirit could reside." "I was desperate for the chance to integrate my life . . . to weave together the threads of my life . . . to be my values," whispers Rachel with great intensity.

Rachel was also searching for a way to participate in the justice movement by "speaking to people's hearts" rather than by using the tools of analysis and objective evidence to appeal to their minds. In the personal statement that accompanied her application to divinity school, Rachel spoke about this shift in her lens. "Over the past five years, I have found myself increasingly called to a different kind of work whose outlines are not clear to me. After a career using analysis, demonstrations, and public policy to try to improve access to opportunity, I have come to believe that effective leadership, or 'ministry,' on the issues I care about needs to come from a different place than the analytic and policy work in which I have spent two decades. While I am not certain what this work might look like, I am convinced that the answer will come from a place of faith, 'discerned' from turning into my own spiritual questions and opening myself up to new ways of learning." Her statement, a beautifully crafted, revelatory piece, reflected both Rachel's searching and her determination, her turning inward, her deep questioning, and her guarded optimism.

Even though the divinity school seemed like the right place to cast her net and practice "discernment in a community of faith," it was actually a mixed bag, both fulfilling and disturbing to Rachel. It turned out to be a place—like so many institutions of learning—where the rhetoric often seemed distant from the practices and pedagogy; where, for example, all the talk about collaborative learning often played itself out as fierce competition among students. "On the one hand," says Rachel, "it is a community, a relational place; and on the other hand, it is full of arbitrary things not aligned with what I came there to do. . . .

On the one hand, it is a place that abhors the abuse of power and inequalities; and on the other hand, it is full of bullshit power relationships."

When Rachel arrived at school, she found herself spending a good deal of her energy trying to decipher these contradictions in the institutional culture, to unravel the text from the subtext, to discern the differences between the overt and the hidden curricula. This "reading of hidden agendas and mixed meanings" not only required time and attention, but it also made Rachel feel "infantilized." Here she had come from an organization where she was a respected, experienced leader, a mature and responsible adult, into a place where she was made to feel like a child. These feelings of infantilization would probably be true for most adults who have enjoyed a good deal of autonomy and authority in their former work lives, but whose student status, in their Third Chapters, made them feel suddenly impotent. Here at the divinity school, it seemed exaggerated by an institutional rhetoric that explicitly decried the hierarchies of power and knowledge but in practice seemed to abuse them.

By far the hardest part of Rachel's socialization into the culture of the divinity school had to do with "owning" her new "minority status." As a middle-aged, blond, blue-eyed, diminutive white woman from an upper-middle-class background, she was the outsider. Suddenly she found that she had to explain and defend her "positionality"—a new word she learned to use as she mastered the school's liberation lexicon. Rachel describes the scene: "You see, this is a place where everyone is focused on race and gender and power, and I was perceived as an elite, as the enemy, as the one who was implicated in the oppression of others. I was constantly put in the position of always questioning my own motives and behavior. Do I keep my social location or do I renounce it? What does it mean to be perceived as an ally of the oppressor class?" Rachel's response to her feelings of "marginalization" was mixed and provocative. She both loved and hated the chronic discomfort, the feeling of being off balance and overly self-conscious about every move she made. "I met people at school that I would have never known otherwise—a large proportion of gay and lesbian people, for example, who have a deep humanity. The challenge and marginalization I felt were always double-edged: powerful and beautiful, and very fractured and destructive."

Certainly the difficult process of naming and claiming her "elite" status in the community was very charged for Rachel. It harked back to her early-childhood years in South Africa, where her white privilege and "positionality" were explicit and unquestioned, where her warm and loving relationships with her family's black African servants reflected a complicated entanglement of intimacy and distance. Here she was at fifty living with these ghosts from her childhood—trying to figure out the dynamics and boundaries of these old relationships, to claim some responsibility for her part in them.

At the same time, Rachel was also experiencing a kind of "schizophrenia" between her new, unsettling world in the divinity school and her old comfortable place at WA. In order to pay the tuition bills at school, Rachel hung on to parts of her old job, continuing to do consultant work, give speeches, and sit on boards, while she was taking graduate courses. The switch from one world to the other was hard, disjointed. She draws the schizophrenic contrast vividly: "I was trying to bridge two worlds. At WA, I was unaccountable, privileged, and I enjoyed access to a global network; and at school, I was marginalized, feared, and prohibited entry to the important conversations."

As Rachel offers the troubling comparisons, she is reminded of her anger: a rage that sometimes erupts when she feels as if her work at WA is being diminished or dismissed, a fury that defends her deep and steady commitments to justice. Now her voice is heated. "A lot of this pointing of fingers at school makes me angry. I did a huge amount of work on race at WA. Half the organization is people of color. We purposely created a diverse organizational culture." As soon as the fury escapes her lips, however, Rachel takes a step back and recognizes that there are even lessons embedded in the accusations, things that she needs to pay attention to and learn from. Maybe even her fury is a sign of some blind spot that she refuses to acknowledge. "I know too much to just write it off, to say that it is all about them. There is a lot of stuff—hard, useful stuff—I'm learning from just living in the community."

Almost a year into the school experience, Rachel is still unsure and uneasy. The learning is deep and hard; the lessons are so challenging and complex. She sums up the mix of feelings exhausting just to think about. "This has been a very challenging year. I haven't figured it all out yet. I chose a high-risk path. Many times I feel exhilarated by the learning. I even have moments of feeling successful and productive in my learning. . . . But much of the time, I just feel panicked." Since so much of what Rachel describes sounds like deeply introspective work, relational and emotional work, I ask her whether her experience at school feels like therapy to her, or something different. Her response is immediate and adamant. "It is much deeper and harder than therapy," she claims. "In therapy you are in an incredibly self-centered, privileged environment: you get to talk about yourself, and the relationship is with someone that you are paying to listen attentively. At the divinity school, there is a community of belief that demands to be heard, that pushes toward authenticity. It is about how you are in the world."

The treachery of Rachel Middleton's transition, then, echoes with an early and devastating loss—the death of her father—that gets replayed when she decides to leave an organization that she has "mothered," the "child" she has raised. Her feelings of guilt, ambivalence, and loss are amplified by the cries of her colleagues at WA who feel abandoned, by her friends who express bafflement and disapproval at her choice, and by her tough entry into a strange new community that feels confusing and inhospitable, a move that takes her from the center of the action to the margins, from being at the top to being on the bottom. The old and the new often feel to Rachel as if they are warring realities—incompatible and unsettling.

But I believe that one reason the transition from the old to the new seems to take longer and cut deeper for Rachel than for Grace is that it is about a change of heart, not a change of place. In making the shift from the world of advocacy and policy to "working on values," from an activism driven by evidence and data to a commitment to "changing people's hearts," Rachel is shifting paradigms. She is working to change the structure of her thinking and feeling fundamentally; she is redrawing her "life's terrain"; she is seeking to plumb the depths of her interior, spiritual world. The decision to enroll in divinity school was not about learning new skills, developing new aptitudes, or moving on to the next career; it was part of a larger search to become a more "integrated person," to enter a place where she could practice "being my values." This shift of paradigm Rachel is forging feels especially "treacherous" because it rocks her core, disturbs her rhythms, and requires a new learning defined by a private vigilance, not by public affirmation.

THE BERRY PICKER'S DILEMMA

The template Matthew Gladstone lays out for me is about neither changes of heart nor place, psychological loss, or spiritual searching. Rather, it is about the rational calculations that he believes people make when they are considering leaving the work that has sustained them for most of their lives; the positions that have given them stature, status, and resources; and the places where they have been known, rewarded, and respected. It is about calibrating the costs and benefits between constancy and change. He sees these as tangible decisions: they can be visually represented, even drawn on a graph.

Matthew sits across the table from me and talks with his hands. He draws the graphs in the air (of "marginal costs" intersecting with "marginal benefits") and sounds like a professor who is used to making difficult material understandable. This, after all, is Matthew Gladstone's work as a journalist and television commentator: the translation of obtuse, theoretical, and technical material from the field of economics and business into usable knowledge connected to people's real lives. It is his capacity to make the obscure understandable (to "make it plain") and to make the dull interesting, even intriguing, on which he has built his professional reputation. This is why he has won national and international prizes for his reporting. (It also helps that he has a wonderful sense of humor that comes through on camera, as well as an offbeat, creative way of presenting material.) But his real secret of success, I am sure as I sit across the table from him and listen to his soliloquy, is that he can explain things in a way that makes you feel smart. So many teachers do the opposite: they make you feel dull and dumb, as if you will never truly be able to grasp the esoteric material that they are presenting.

So, before I can even ask my first question, Matthew has begun his pedagogy: his "formulation on the economic insights into this stage of life, this Third Chapter." He presents the competing economic concepts that create a "particularly perplexing bind" for those of us between the ages of fifty and seventy-five. The first is the idea of the "division of labor"; the second refers to "diminishing returns." The first one was first explained and examined in the work of Adam Smith; the second in the classic text by Alfred Marshall.[33] The first concept refers to the idea of the specialization of labor on which our postindustrial economy is based. We divide up the labor, and we become expert in doing what we know how to do. Matthew explains, "As I do it more, I'll learn more, I'll get better at it. The longer I go, the better I'll get, the more I will be worth." Matthew uses himself as an example. "I would of course add more value if I studied business than if I were training to be a chef." He also cautions that his analysis only refers to that class of people who have abundant resources, and who, therefore, have "some choice."

Though one line on the graph travels upward—indicating the division of labor that yields "marginal costs"—another one comes down, indicating the second economic principle of "diminishing returns": the more of something you have, the less additional return it will give. "When you hit sixty," says Matthew, "you are now very expansive, dependent on the income that you have amassed." He uses an example taken from the beginning of Marshall's book—a story about picking berries—to explain this second principle. As the berry picker gathers his harvest, he is faced with the question of whether the additional effort is worth the pleasure of having and eating more berries; whether the satisfaction he'll get from each berry picked will be sufficient. Marshall points out that the return—the satisfaction and pleasure—is least for the last berry picked. Matthew's hands draw the graph in the air again: the line traveling upward representing "marginal costs," the one traveling downward reflecting "the marginal benefits." You stop picking the berries at the point where these two lines intersect. When we are in the Third Chapter, we face a "fundamental tension" that we try to resolve in the life choices that we make. "We try to find ways," says Matthew, "of staving off the diminishing returns with new learning and exciting adventures." But then we face the fact that the quality of our lives, the resources that we depend upon, require a continued commitment to specialization of what we know how to do well, to the division of labor. Matthew offers up two additional caveats that mark important contextual shifts in the economy, and that influence the way this "fundamental tension" is resolved.

First, there is the rise of "globalization," which tends to threaten people's sense that their jobs are secure and safe. "It all feels much more unstable and precarious," claims Matthew, "and this provides an element of anxiety." Sensing the insecurity and the threat, people begin to ask themselves how long they will be able to hold on to their jobs. This mixes with their feelings of the "diminishing return" they get from doing their jobs over a long period of time, and the whole thing is further complicated by the vulnerabilities and anxieties that go along with aging.

The second complicating contextual factor that Matthew identifies has to do with the "general perception that you need more money rather than less" during the Third Chapter, that it will take more resources to maintain your quality of life. There is also the recognition—"the prospect"—that we are all living longer, and we will need more income to support the welcome longevity. Quoting Juliet Schor, author of *The Overworked American*, who has written persuasively on this conundrum of living longer and remaining prosperous, Matthew says, "You feel that you can't afford to downshift."

I find Matthew's analysis fascinating. Of course, I knew that he would bring his rigorous understanding of economics and business to the interview, and that some of his examples and stories might be related to his experiences and insights in those domains. But somehow I am surprised by his use of economic models—which I remember puzzling over when I took micro-economics as a freshman in college, and that seemed to me, even then, to bear little relationship to the realities of human behavior—as a way to frame the discussion about the motivation for "new learning" in the Third Chapter. I suspect, of course, that people rarely make consciously the economic calculations of which Matthew speaks. (He is the only one of my interviewees who explicitly refers to the economic models supporting their professional and personal choices.) But I do think that the "fundamental tension" that Matthew addresses as he shows me the lines on the graph does show up in the anxiety and risk-taking that often accompany new learning. I suspect that the subtext of people's conscious deliberations about choices and options, and responsibilities and accountability to themselves and others, may in fact be related to the berry picker's dilemma.

Using the classic lenses of economics, Matthew Gladstone graphically describes the "perplexing bind" that we face in our Third Chapters: the tension between continuing to pick the berries, even though each one tastes less pleasurable, and moving on to something strange and unfamiliar that may provide the excitement and adventure but may not offer us the resources we need to survive and prosper. Both Rachel and Grace articulate this tension when they say that their work at the university press and at Work Alliances was no longer compelling for them. They had ceased learning and growing; they faced redundancy and boredom in their daily routines; they had "hit the wall."

The berries no longer tasted sweet. But in facing the loss of leaving the work that had defined their identities and brought them renown, they trembled at the idea of seizing upon something new.

Another thread that weaves through the experiences of people who successfully navigate the terrain between the old and the new, is the power of storytelling. We see how the act of composing a narrative—even offering up competing narratives—helps us feel less vulnerable, gives us a sense of choice and agency, and permits us to feel some measure of control. Each of the protagonists in this chapter offers a narration. Grace surprises herself when she recognizes that the young protagonist in the children's play that she authored is actually living her story. Through the character she has created, she composes the next chapter of her life; she works through all of the emotions and fears she is about to face in transplanting herself to Philadelphia. It turns out that Grace is the "scared girl" moving to a strange place. Likewise, Rachel uses the essay that is part of her application to divinity school as an opportunity to name her emotions, examine her motives, and begin to fashion a new narrative. And Emory Daniels, whom we met in the preceding chapter, paints her story on a canvas. For months she struggles over a true representation of her best friend, reworking the image over and over again, until she discovers herself "as an integrated whole" in the painting that emerges. Each layer of paint on the canvas, each feature and gesture that she draws, represents another version of who she is becoming—another chance to narrate her own story.

One of the reasons that finding the balance between constancy and change strikes so many of us as uncomfortable, even treacherous, is that in our Third Chapters we tend to be working on dimensions of our identity, character, and values that are fundamental and core. Each of the people I spoke to talks about the new learning of this chapter as requiring a "paradigm shift"; many refer to the work as being integrative, a time to bring the pieces together and make ourselves whole, to align our professed values with our actions, our rhetoric with our behaviors. Others are explicit in uncovering the spiritual subtext of their narratives, discovering that the real struggles and insights during this transition are deeply spiritual. Rachel says of her choice to enroll in divinity school that she was in search of a place "where the spirit could reside." And when she speaks about the terrifying and exciting experience of being a "gray-haired adolescent" learning to be a playwright, Grace compares herself with her much younger peers. The sensation of being both "old and new" offers her a "pragmatic disadvantage" but a "spiritual advantage." The searching agendas of our Third Chapters—often experienced as confusing, risky, and passionate—are likely to be more difficult and demanding than the learning we have experienced at earlier stages in our lives, making the journey forward feel more hazardous. The stories we compose are our only map.

THREE

Healing Wounds: The Journey Home

The commonplace now is shot through with new glory—
old burdens become lighter, deep and ancient wounds
lose much of their hurting. A crown is placed over our
heads that for the rest of our lives we are trying to grow
tall enough to wear.   —Howard Thurman[1]

When people in their Third Chapters prepare to engage in new
learning, and take on the risks and vulnerabilities associated
with life transitions, they often discover that they must "journey
home" and confront the ancient traumas of their childhoods.
They do not want to live any longer with the hurts, the remorse,
the guilt connected to their childhoods or their own flawed
parenting—twin guilts that have weighed too long on their
consciences and burdened their emotional well-being. "Going
home"—metaphorically, psychologically, literally, spiritually—
to face the ancient impediments becomes a way of moving forward with their lives, and it requires courage, resolve, patience,
and new learning.

In her brave and revealing autobiography, *My Life So Far*,
Jane Fonda writes about an epiphany brought on by facing her

fifty-ninth birthday. Anticipating the big-age-marker of sixty, she felt compelled, she says—using the theatrical metaphor—to enter "Act Three" of her life. Having endured the first two acts—so filled with pain, chaos, self-loathing, and guilt—she now faced the denouement, the chance for reckoning and reconciliation with her roots. Here was the chance to "return home" and face the anguish of her mother's death to suicide, her father's emotional remoteness, the abandonment by her three husbands, and the wounds she inflicted on her own children. Returning home required that she learn a new way of being, that she learn to face her demons and, for the first time, tell the truth. Her book, she claims, is a reclamation project, a healing journey. And her decision to make her story public—at this moment in her life—reflects a recognition that she is not alone in her struggle. Even though she is a rich, sexy Hollywood star who has lived a controversial, very public life, her quest for self-understanding in the third act is, she believes, a universal quest. "For me," she writes, "discipline, liberation, means acknowledging my demons, banishing them to the corner, seeing my past and excising the old patterns and baggage to make room for the stillness."[2]

Many of the men and women I interviewed spoke passionately and longingly about how the Third Chapter is a time when they have finally been able to face the deep injuries of their childhoods—assaults that they have ignored, repressed, or fled from for most of their lives. They find that confronting these early injuries allows, in the words of one person, the "ancient wounds to lose much of their hurting." Revisiting these "old burdens" allows them to move on to the next chapter in their own lives, and allows them to recognize and try to repair those hurts that were—wittingly or unwittingly—passed on to the next generation. Some of the people I interviewed find a safe place to "visit these ghosts" in therapy; others just feel a "readiness to throw off the shackles of guilt" that have distorted their relationships with their parents, spouses, and children; still others feel with a new urgency the "finiteness" of life and say to themselves, "If not now, then when?"

Occasionally, people discovered the source and site of their early injuries during the course of our interviews. All of a sudden, in the retelling of a story they had told many times before, they would stumble upon a detail, a metaphor, a sign, or a symbol that would unlock feelings and open up a floodgate of tears. Or they would begin to replay an experience from childhood—say, a conversation with a parent or a teacher—that they had always seen as positive and uplifting, and discover the dark underbelly; the reinterpretation of a practiced story would suddenly bring forth the pain from the long-ago injury.

Steven Fox had this kind of surprising revelation when I interviewed him. At sixty-seven, Steven is a public-health doctor who has spent his professional life doing epidemiological research in the lab and working in the rural regions of West Africa to eradicate malaria. Before going to medical school, he was a Peace Corps volunteer in Sierra Leone, an experience that etched in him a lifelong commitment to international relief work. From an upper-middle-class African American family, he has lived his life simply and with great humility, working behind the scenes to fight disease and oppression all over the world, always joining his professional engagement and expertise with his personal and moral commitments. He believes in "thinking and acting, locally and globally." In a decision that "snuck up" on him, Steven decided to sign up for voice lessons at the local community music school. This was a "radical departure" from his "workaholic life," which had never left him the time or energy to pursue pleasurable avocations, never left him any time to play. As he began to recount to me the story from his childhood that motivated his "new passion" for singing—the "big adventure" of his Third Chapter—he discovered the subtle hurt carried in his mother's glance one Sunday afternoon when he was about six.

Steven's favorite memory of early childhood is sitting on his mother's lap listening to the radio when the Metropolitan Opera broadcast their weekly performances. He had "an immediate love affair" with opera and begged his mother to let him take voice lessons. She did not refuse him permission, but there was something in her eyes—a subtle dismissiveness—that made Steven withdraw his request. "Somehow, she made me feel like opera singing was something for sissies," he recalls sadly. Then, when Steven became a young adult, he himself decided that opera was both too frivolous and too aristocratic for someone who was devoting his life to changing the world. But a few years ago, he decided that he had denied himself long enough, and he secretly began taking voice lessons. "This was the hardest, most exciting work I've ever done, simply thrilling," he says about his first year of study, in which he never produced a note that even "vaguely resembled" the luscious tones that he had heard across the airwaves some sixty years before. The sound does not matter to Steven, however. What matters is the chance he now has to live his dream—that is "the big turn-on"—and the high that comes with "a freedom he has never known" when he sings. What began as a benign and gentle story about being wrapped in his mother's arms listening to opera, in the retelling during our interview turns into a painful encounter with her disapproval of him. His tears catch up with him as he traces the connections between his recognition of the injury and his opportunity—in his Third Chapter—to "heal the hurt" with his voice.

Likewise, Jasmine Jones, a sixty-two-year-old graphic artist, recalls a devastating sentence spoken by her junior-high-school art teacher that changed the course of her professional life: "a sentence that almost turned into a life sentence," and one she found a way to challenge during her Third Chapter, finally reclaiming her "artistic identity." Jasmine, who has made a handsome living directing a small-niche graphic-arts firm, has recently turned to painting large watercolor canvases whose wild bursts of color and imagery are a striking contrast to the linear, exacting, practical art that has consumed her work life. Exploring the new medium of watercolor feels like a journey back in time, recapturing a childhood dream that was stolen from her one day when her eighth-grade art teacher frowned on her "unruly, experimental, and courageous" painting, and told her in a dismissive voice that she would "never be a real artist." She was devastated and humiliated, taking the hurt inside and never doubting his judgment of her. But now, after living with "the curse" for a half-century, she has thrown caution to the wind and is teaching herself to paint again, resisting the harshness of her overly critical inner voice, and discovering how the recovery of her painting is linked to "finding her voice in so many other realms." "This is a reclamation project," Jasmine says to me with fire in her eyes. Returning to the site of the injury and confronting the hurt allows her to "move forward."

Almost every one of the women and men I interviewed found it necessary to begin their stories of Third Chapter learning with flashbacks to their childhoods. For some, their autobiographical references captured only fragments of a story, gestures, or images that reverberate with broad and deep meaning: a mother's frown of disapproval, a teacher's cruel one-liner, a competitive sibling's fierce determination to earn better grades, a humiliating moment forgetting the practiced prose of a valedictory speech. For others, the narratives were detailed and sequential, embedded in a context, and rich with emotional texture. Interestingly, for most participants—people who have led successful and productive lives by most people's standards, lives rich with resources and adventures—the stories they recounted focused on traumatic and painful experiences, not memories of triumph or achievement. And it is the former tales that needed to be unmasked and confronted before people could take on the risks, and tolerate the vulnerabilities, that would allow them to live fully in their Third Chapters.

As with Steven Fox and Jasmine Jones, the ancient traumas usually occurred at home or in school—the most intimate and public spaces for children. People recalled searing moments of disrespect and humiliation, indifference and cynicism, the harsh and insinuating judgments from a parent or teacher. They told stories of trying to please, of reaching out for love and feeling dismissed, of being confused by mixed messages, of feeling misunderstood. And they recounted the silence that often surrounded the injury, the hiding out that followed the hurt, with everyone pretending that things were normal, cheerful, that everything would be all right.

Here, then, I will explore the ways in which people in their Third Chapters often return to their childhood haunts to visit the ghosts from their past. These visitations may be literal, geographic excursions: a man drives cross-country, arrives at the house in which he was raised, climbs the stairs of the front porch, knocks on the door, and greets his elderly father face-to-face. Or the visitations may be psychological and emotional: the parents and teachers are long gone, and a woman confronts their ghosts in her therapy sessions, reliving the ancient traumas through storytelling, analysis, and catharsis. Or the visitations may be metaphoric: "going home" does not mean physically returning to the places of our childhood, or reconstructing our childhood stories in therapy sessions; rather, it means a journey defined by symbols and signs that capture the refracted, often spiritual feelings of circling back to the source. "I am returning to the well," said one woman about a childhood in which she always felt "parched and dry."

LIVING INTO THE CONTRACT

Luther Brown grew up in an upper-middle-class academic community, the oldest son of a professor of literature at the university. His father, who had come from a wealthy, aristocratic Southern family, was a distinguished literary scholar, an academic star, and a generous philanthropist. He was also an alcoholic, an addiction that was widely known but never talked about—a family secret that everyone was complicit in trying to preserve. His mother, who grew up in Dublin, came from a working-class background and was the first in her family to go to college. Luther claims that he spent his youth being a "superachiever": the "good kid," the rescuer in his family. "I had an understanding that if only I was good enough people would see my family as successful. They would not see the trouble, the alcoholism, the pain. My achievements would mask all of that." Luther calls this unspoken responsibility that he took on as a child "living into the family contract."

His elementary-school years were spent at a snazzy all-white private school, followed by the local high-achieving public school full of the progeny of the rich and learned. As the "superachiever," Luther studied all of the time, lived the straight and narrow life, and "didn't take any chances." He was drawn to the theater, but he did not dare to take on anything in which he might risk exposure, or might have to be open to scary and unpredictable emotions. "A whole lot of me did not get expressed," he recalls sadly, "and I had a whole lot of anger at having committed myself to this unconscious contract." Luther remembers a "stunning moment" when he was fourteen years old and having a conversation with his school guidance counselor. She had asked him about the things that he enjoyed doing, the times that gave him the most pleasure, and Luther had responded that he most loved reading Yeats with his father. The words that came out of his mouth expressed pleasure, but his face was grim. The counselor surprised Luther by saying, "Oh, how sad!" He had expected her to be approving, even amazed by his precocious devotion to learning at the knee of his father, the great intellect. Luther recalls that her comment did not sound disapproving, she just felt sorry for him. "I was a kid," he says, flaring up in defiance, "and here I was dutifully being my father's student!"

There are so many ways in which Luther's eagerness to be the perfect student and son, to make things right in his childhood family, now get imprinted on his relationship with his wife, Sasha—a troubled marriage that has survived with a "fierce love" for twenty-five years. In the past several years, he has learned "the hard way" that here again he finds himself "living into the original contract." "In my relationship with Sasha I'm caretaking, trying to make things okay, as I did in my own family, and I have loads of anger about taking on that role. The anger is like a toxic-waste dump that doesn't explode, it just sort of leaks out."

Luther Brown's ghostly journeys home combine psychological, spiritual, and metaphoric dimensions. When he refers to "the dark night of my soul," Luther points to a moment of crisis he experienced a few years ago, when he turned fifty—the age his father was when he died. The anniversary of his father's death hovered like an ominous cloud for months before the birthday. Memories of all the unresolved conflict, all the silences and lies between them, all the tortured attempts to connect with each other, converged into a "frightening turning point" for Luther. Suddenly he felt—with "unnerving urgency"— compelled to break out of the rigidities and constraints that had dominated his life. "There was something in me that was so constricted, so bound up," he recalls, gazing out at the gray day and the still waters of the lake in front of us as we sit talking together. Pain is written all over his face. "I had been a frozen-over pond. The ice cracked after the winter freeze, and shattered the shell I had been inhabiting all my life. This was my introduction to the spiritual life."

As Luther speaks about the "crisis," he relives the drama, the rage, the pain; he feels the discomfort and the rawness. "This was not a gentle process," he says, "it was like childbirth." Throughout our interview, Luther frequently uses the metaphor of childbirth to describe both the pain and the joy of new beginnings, the darkness and the light of self-discovery. His awakening, he seems to be saying, held all of the excruciating anguish of a woman in labor, and all of the exhilaration of hearing a newborn baby's cry of arrival. His "dark night of [the] soul" required that he discover the feminine, long-suffering side of his nature, demanded that he endure the pain in order to experience the joy. Expressing his awe at the terror and triumph of this "awakening," Luther says, "I honor midlife crises." In his case, Luther's midlife crisis took the form of an affair, a liaison that he describes as "intense, passionate, and short-lived, but long enough to shatter the foundations, to break the ice cover."

Couples often come to counseling in the midst of a crisis, but that is "just the tip of the iceberg," says Luther. There is so much going on underneath, so many layers that have built up over the history of a relationship, so many habits that have become ingrained and invisible, so many lies spoken and unspoken. The counselor helps people discover ways of speaking the truth and being heard. For several years, Luther and Sasha have been in counseling with a couples therapist. "At first," says Luther, "it felt clunky and artificial" to begin to try to tell the truth. It was, of course, difficult to face his wife with truths he had never told her, but even harder to tell those truths to himself. The counselor worked to create a safe place where love—not judgment—would flourish. "He shined the light" into the darkness and tried to help Luther and Sasha not be so judgmental of each other or themselves. "The therapist doesn't reinforce the inner judge which is yammering all of the time," says Luther. Rather, he helped make space for compassion to flow in two directions, which allowed the couple to take some responsibility for what they had done. Luther laughs at the treachery that he often feels as he tests out the safe spaces of compassion in these sessions. "I'm able to take responsibility for what I have done and the pain that I have caused if I know that I won't be hammered by Sasha when I try."

What Luther has discovered, in this "vulnerable-making and revelatory" experience of marital counseling, is the way in which intimate relationships—particularly those with a long and arduous history—are the best way to get to know oneself more deeply. "One way I have come to understand relationship," he reflects, "is to see it as the most powerful vehicle for learning about myself." He makes an even stronger claim: "Relationship is the key to my becoming a full human being. It is such a great test tube for all of this." When he looks back on his relationship with Sasha, he realizes that he chose her precisely because she provoked in him the exposure of his vulnerabilities. Of course, his choice of a mate three decades ago (when they were both undergraduates) was "totally unconscious"; he had no idea that she would be the most adept at discovering all of his "blind spots." It was sort of like "cosmic radar," he recalls with a smile. "I chose someone who always brings up for me the things I need to work on. She has always pushed the buttons about what's driving me."

Through his work in therapy, Luther begins to see that his relationship with Sasha—his deep devotion to her and their enduring struggles—all have "antecedents" in the role he played in his family of origin, and most particularly in the relationship he forged with his father. He is better able to hear the generational echoes; he can feel the ghosts hovering. He can identify the emotions, name them, and begin to extract himself from the constraints of the ancient "contract." But the understanding and naming of anger and pain is not enough; though it is a necessary first step, it does not get you very far. Luther quotes his therapist, who often says, "Understanding is the booby prize; it can often get in the way of doing and acting."

It has taken a long time for Luther to come to terms with his family history, but he now feels "very at peace" with his parents. It is a "precarious peace," he admits—one that occasionally, for instance, gets assaulted by still-difficult encounters with his younger brother, Jonah. Within the family, Jonah was always seen as the family's bad boy, the screw-up. Nobody could be as perfect as Luther, so why should his brother even try? Luther is now laughing at the ways in which the roles that they each played distorted their individual development and their relationship to each other. He muses, "What did it mean to be my brother? A pretty horrible lot, I guess. But my role as the good guy was not a total gift, either."

Having survived—"with scars"—this striving for a perfection that tried to mask the family wounds, Luther has been intent upon not passing along these injuries to his two sons. His now adult children are both very intelligent and artistic (both having graduated with honors from fancy universities), and he believes that they have been able to live more fully and more freely than he was able to when he was their age. He even believes that his current work in couples therapy with Sasha will yield benefits for them as they create their own families and raise their children. "I believe that cleaning up our acts now will help them," says Luther with certainty.

Luther's devotion to "cleaning up his act" so that his children, and their young offspring, will be liberated from the painful family legacy—what he calls the "antecedents"—that he has lived with his whole life, reminds me of a famous essay written by Selma Fraiberg. A psychoanalyst, Fraiberg traces the ways in which early-childhood experiences—primarily formed within the intimacy and potency of parent-child relationships—not only shape adult personality and temperament, but they also get replayed in the next generation. She speaks about the unwelcome and unconscious presence of these "ghosts" hovering in the nursery, establishing residence at the baby's side, casting a spell on the way the parents relate to the child. "These are the ghosts in the nursery . . . visitors from the unremembered pasts of the parents, the uninvited guests at the christening."[3] Although the ghosts to whom Fraiberg refers are invisible and intangible, they are very real in the emotional lives of the parents. The images and stories of the ancestral figures from the parents' families make a claim on their unique view of the child and on their hopes and dreams for who he/she is and will become. If—through the penetrating work of therapy—Luther can identify and expunge the "ghosts in the nursery" who have claimed him, then they will no longer haunt his children. The harsh generational echoes will be silenced.

In searching out a way to heal his wounds and move forward, Luther is not seeking to carve out a particular career or path. There are lots of things about which he is deeply curious, lots of things he is eager to learn. His ambition for his Third Chapter learning is both broader and deeper than any particular set of skills or any discrete body of knowledge. He is able to list many of the areas where he hopes to make progress. He wants to take voice lessons, join a theater group and try acting, he wants to be a more effective "peace builder" around the globe, and become better and more effective with the immigrant children who are in the English as a Second Language classes that he teaches at his local public school. And he hopes to learn to be a "more present and attentive" grandparent and discover ways of "redefining what it means to be a good husband." But he sees all of these things as vehicles for self-discovery—overlapping efforts, joined by their common goal. "They all flow through an evolving understanding of who I am," he admits. "I want to learn to express myself as freely and joyously as possible. . . . I want to be who I am. . . . The doing of these things, the learning of these things, all flow out of the being." This is a quest that will never have a conclusion. It is an ongoing, dynamic process—difficult and promising, painful and plentiful.

As Luther describes this search for his "essence," this effort to challenge the rules and constraints of the "family contract," he uses the imagery of nature and the metaphors of childbirth, and refers to qualities usually associated with womanly wisdom and experience. Breaking through the ice cover of the frozen pond, shattering the shell of his inhibitions, is excruciating work: unbearably painful and terrifying, and incredibly mysterious and hopeful. Likewise, when he speaks about getting to know himself through relationship ("Relationship is the key to my becoming a full human being"), his language reminds us of the central themes and rhetoric of feminist psychology that point to the contrasts between men and women in how they define the boundaries of their identity. Men tend to see themselves as separate, their identity defined by the lone pursuit, whereas women see themselves in relationship, knowing themselves through their connectedness to others.

In her classic book, *In a Different Voice* (1982), Carol Gilligan vividly portrays these gender distinctions by describing the contrasts in the ways in which men and women (who were college students at the time of the study) responded to the images presented on a projective instrument called the Thematic Apperception Test. Interpreting the pictures that were presented to them, men consistently saw violence in the images of intimacy. Women saw less violence overall than men, but more violence in the images of achievement and competitive success. Gilligan concludes that "men and women may experience attachment and separation in different ways and that each sex perceives a danger which the other does not see—men in connection, women in separation."[4] Interestingly, as the people were brought closer together in the pictures, the images of violence in the men's stories increased, whereas when the people were set farther apart, the violence in the women's stories increased. Gilligan concludes that women most often projected violence onto the picture of the man seated alone at his desk (the only picture portraying a person alone), whereas men most often saw violence in the picture of two acrobats on a trapeze (the only picture in which people touched). Certainly, in the past twenty-five years, the principles and preoccupations of feminist psychology, and our societal views of sexual identity, have become more nuanced and layered, but Gilligan's analysis of gender differences has prevailed as a central framework—deeply imprinted in our culture's perception of gender, enacted in our behaviors, and woven into our daily rhetoric.

Luther Brown's soliloquy—so full of the relational language of feminist psychology—however, defies these gender classifications that have been so firmly planted in our cultural imagination; and he is not alone among the men I interviewed. There must be huge developmental differences between the responses of Gilligan's college students and the Third Chapter protagonists to whom I spoke (although it is interesting to note that these college students who spoke to Gilligan in the late 1970s would now be in their Third Chapters). And, Luther stands out as distinctive in his explicit references to the metaphors of childbirth as part of his "healing experience." But several men spoke to me longingly about their yearning for "meaningful and authentic relationships" and about wanting to find ways of "nurturing intimacy and connection" with friends and loved ones. They saw "learning to be vulnerable" and "learning to express empathy" as central goals of their Third Chapters. They saw themselves as disadvantaged by their "masculine masks," by the difficulties they experienced in getting in touch with their "feminine side." These male laments seemed particularly true for those whose stories revisited the early wounds of their childhoods—those who had chosen to confront the "ghosts in the nursery" and liberate themselves and their children from the painful ancestral legacies. Taking the journey home seemed to require being in touch with the feminine path. One corporate lawyer—who disparagingly described himself as a "caricature of the macho male" but who looked much more gentle and reflective to me—summed up his feelings at the close of our long interview: "There is a lot of gender bending that goes on at this time of life. I look to women—my wife, my daughters, my women colleagues—for wisdom and guidance."

Not only does Luther use the womanly metaphors of nature and childbirth to signify the hard labor of his Third Chapter, but he also, by contrast, uses mechanistic, male imagery—whose "combined poisons" do violence to nature—to describe the ways in which he had, for too long, let the rage build up inside of him: his seething, unexpressed response to being "the good kid living into the family contract." When he speaks about it, he sucks in the air through his clenched teeth.

BLAMING THE VICTIM

In facing the ghosts and the ancient traumas, Pamela Stein does not return to her early childhood—a time she remembers as nourished by her parents' "unending devotion and love"—nor does she, like Luther, describe years spent playing a family role that left her feeling constricted and contorted with rage. Rather, Pamela can point to a specific moment in her early twenties when the injury occurred, when she was thrown off her course, when powerful men tried to destroy her dream. Her memory of "the incident" is "sharp, palpable, specific"—not shrouded by ghostly appearances, not covered over by dust or distance. In revisiting that moment, Pamela discovers the impetus that has shaped and inspired her professional work and identity, particularly in her Third Chapter.

A psychologist by training, Pamela Stein has spent her professional life working in many domains and from a variety of venues. She has been an academic scholar and researcher, founding and directing programs in feminist psychology and women's studies at the university, and developing programs that seek to draw the connections between research and activism, and between academics and community service. She has written scores of books about women's psychology and public policy that have reached both academic and lay audiences. She has been a "public educator," speaking out frequently about political and cultural issues in the press and in the media. She has been a clinical psychologist doing individual therapy with private patients, and she has served as an expert witness in court cases. In all of her roles—as activist, scholar, author, clinician, and court psychologist—she has lived by one mantra: "Don't let people pathologize you." Don't let people give you labels: ADD, ADHD, learning disabled, dysfunctional, deviant, bipolar, psychotic.

As a feminist scholar, Pamela has spoken out about the ways in which the traditional scholarship performed by white male researchers has often "pathologized" womanly traits and characteristics, labeling healthy responses to abuse, for example, as mental illness or emotional frailty, and causing women to blame themselves for their pain. As a public educator, she has tried to help people understand the ways in which cultural priorities, scientific "data," and institutional values conspire to victimize and marginalize powerless people, and lead to a "blaming of the victim." Most recently, for example, she has written articles and editorials about the military men and women who have returned from Iraq, ravaged and scarred by the violence and horrors of war, rendered fearful and depressed by the haunting images of mangled and dead bodies, unable to explain their pain, feeling isolated from their friends and loved ones. In her interviews with the vets, Pamela not only listens to their stories of devastation, their list of physical and emotional scars, but she also questions the assumption that these wounds can be helped or healed through individual therapy. After you've watched your best friends get killed, are sadness and anxiety an "abnormal" response, a sign of maladjustment? Does sending these vets into therapy shield our society from really facing the ravages and casualties of war? Does it mask not only the profound damage done to an individual soldier or marine but also the real harm done to an entire generation?

Pamela takes all of her professional roles seriously and sees their interconnectedness—the ways in which research can inform thoughtful policies, and in which some use research "findings" to justify prejudicial views or condone injustices. But among the many roles she plays, serving as a public educator is the one that allows her to join her scholarship, her clinical acumen, and her activist inclinations. It allows her work to go public; it is where she often feels she can "make a difference." In 1989, when Pamela was on the faculty of a Canadian university, a man woke up one morning, sipped a cup of coffee, walked over to the university, through the corridors, classrooms, and cafeteria, and went on a shooting rampage, killing fourteen women in less than twenty minutes. As he splayed the bullets, he kept screaming, "You're a bunch of fucking feminists." It was called the Montreal Massacre, and it shocked and terrified people across Canada, a country, Pamela says, "that does not think of itself as a violent culture."

Pamela, who already had a public profile as a thoughtful, outspoken feminist because of her many published books, was asked to come on radio and television programs to talk about the massacre. She welcomed the opportunity to reach out to an audience that was "grieving and raw from this horrific event." This, she discovered, was another form of teaching, a way to cross the border from the university to the broader public, and both to help assuage people's pain and to challenge their values. "On the radio show," she recalls, "we received phone calls from people across the country who just wanted a place, a community to share their outrage and their grief. . . . I wanted to help people grieve: How do we feel about this? What can we do? I also wanted to give the event a context, recognizing, of course, that this man was either seriously disturbed or evil. I wanted to say that this is a manifestation of ongoing sexism in the country. . . .

I wanted to help people look at some of the underlying causes."

The urgency and adamancy that Pamela always feels as she works to "repair the world" is rooted in a searing experience she had in graduate school. At the end of her first year as a Ph.D. student in clinical psychology, the faculty—all white middle-aged male professors—decided to throw her out of the program. Her dismissal was shocking: her academic record was superb, and her relationships with her professors and peers seemed comfortable and unstrained. If anything, Pamela had been a student who bent over backward to work hard and not make waves. When she asked them why, her professors refused to give her a straight answer, hiding behind their "natural authority" to make decisions that they deemed best for the program and the profession. Finally, one of them caved and told Pamela that the faculty had decided to dismiss her from the program because she had problems with "ego boundaries": they felt that she would not be able to be a discerning or effective therapist.

Pamela—who had grown up as an "all-American girl" from the Midwest and been socialized to "do the right thing" and "fit in"—had no idea what her professor meant by "ego boundaries," and he was not willing or able to give her a clear definition, just a whole lot of opaque psychiatric rhetoric. He did say that his colleagues worried that Pamela was not able to "take criticism," but that was all he would say; the rest was shrouded in mystery, never disclosed, a harsh judgment seemingly based on nothing except, perhaps, a vague discomfort with her presence. Despite her dismissal from clinical training, Pamela's excellent grades allowed her to transfer to another Ph.D. program in social psychology the next academic year. Many years later, Pamela wrote an article about this horrible event, about how she absorbed her professors' labeling and blamed herself for her failure, how she was wounded by their "pathologizing" of her, and about how she hoped that her story would help to warn others facing simi-lar experiences. "I tell this story," she wrote, "not just because it happened to me but because I know that such appalling things still happen to women. . . . At my age, I don't feel inclined to guard the dirty little secrets of the men who mistreated me. Obviously I hope that hearing about my experience will reduce the isolation and self-blame of those who have had similar ones."

As I listen to Pamela tell this story, I cannot help thinking that part of the injury she experienced has to do with the word "boundaries." Here is a woman for whom the crossing of bound-aries has been a lifestyle, a good thing, part of the reason for her creativity and productivity. And here is a tale, now almost four decades old, of her professors using the word pejoratively, as if crossing boundaries were wrong and dangerous—a tale that shows how powerful people can ruin other people's lives by using labels and rhetoric that appear to be based on fact or data but are really just a justification for their personal preferences and prejudices. In her autobiographical essay, Pamela makes the con-nection between this graduate-school event and her lifelong professional commitment to question authoritative views based on "fact." Her books, one after another, replay the trauma she experienced in graduate school when she tried as hard as she might to follow the rules of the game, only to be told later—based on who knows what—that she lacked the character, the muscle, the grit to do what needed to be done. Her books chal-lenge the abuse of authority, the lack of transparency, the misuse of data, and the legitimacy of labels.

Unlike Luther Brown, who sees therapy as a safe space—a site for loving, compassion, and forgiveness—Pamela Stein, who is herself a psychotherapist, sees it as a potentially dangerous place, full of obfuscation and minefields. She is suspicious of the psychiatric labels and categories that have "no basis in fact or evidence." She is wary of the "pathologizing" of emotions and behaviors that are actually healthy, normal reactions to pain or abuse or oppression. She challenges the asymmetry of power between the therapist and her patient. She believes, then, that a therapist's office may not be a safe place to heal wounds and journey home. In fact, several years ago, she stopped working as a clinician because she "hated to be possibly implicated" in therapeutic relationships, so distorted by the "subtle abuses of power."

Pamela believes that the best way to heal the wounds of early abuses is to get active, get busy, and get even. It is not that she thinks it is wrong to identify the old hurts and uncover the roots of the pain. That is a necessary first step, a prerequisite for moving forward. She just does not want to languish in that ruminative place, and she does not trust that the rhetoric and categories of psychology are, in fact, benign strategies of exploration. Pamela wants to resist the ancient haunts through activism, not by "navel gazing" and intense analysis of life's "antecedents." Hers is a strategy of active resistance, challenging the academic institutions and professional hierarchies that create the categories, write the labels, and declare some people impaired or diseased. Her experience and training allow her an insider's perspective. She knows the theories, the data, the evidence, and the proofs; she can see when a psychiatric label, for example, becomes a self-fulfilling prophecy; when a diagnosis becomes an act of "blaming the victim."

As she revisits her own experience of abuse and manipulation at the hands of her male professors when she was only trying to be "a good girl," Pamela is moved to create a "counternarrative": one that would expunge a category like "ego boundaries" that has dubious basis in evidence, and challenge the powerful people and institutions that have invented the label. "In my work, I want to listen to the authenticity of ordinary people's stories, and I want to listen without preconception or judgment," she says thoughtfully. "But mostly I want to be engaged in a critical dialogue with the powerful professional voices that would exclude the wisdom and experience of ordinary people." Her voice rises to a crescendo. "This is about rearranging the dynamics and structures of power." Pamela's Third Chapter work, then, is more political than personal—steeped in the politics of persuasion and confrontation, not in the examination of the psyche.

AN ORPHAN IN THE WORLD

For Luther Brown and Pamela Stein, their journeys home put them in touch with the early wounds inflicted by judgmental and powerful parents and teachers. Moving forward in their Third Chapters—through therapy and activism—requires that they identify and name the injury, confront the pain, and then get busy. But sometimes in journeying home people discover that their parents were actually the ones who spared them injury, who watched their backs, who were their great protectors. The loss of the parent/protectors in their Third Chapters makes them feel exposed and vulnerable; it adds "insult to injury." This was the case with Meredith Travis, a successful entrepreneur and publisher, who experienced an "overwhelming darkness" when her beloved mother recently died. "I was an orphan in the world," she says with tears rolling down her face. "I was completely bereft, really depressed. . . . I couldn't find any meaning in life. I felt that the good stuff was over." Meredith's mother had died after a courageous struggle with ovarian cancer. A year and a half before, she had survived surgery, but her health declined precipitously after that. Meredith, who had always been close to her mother, visited with her frequently during those last months, and they were able to have deep and meaningful conversations.

They had grown so intimate by the time her mother died that something in Meredith died as well. There were moments when Meredith did not see any use in carrying on. Every day was a struggle. "There was plenty of weeping. I would do something or hear something that would remind me of her, and I would fall into a funk of sadness . . . or I'd be driving along in the car, and just start sobbing for no reason. . . . I simply could not figure out where you find happy." There was also anger. She could almost not help lashing out at the people closest to her, those who were surrounding her with embraces and love. "I admit it," she says remorsefully, "I was horrible, sometimes even abusive. I'd come home and want to kick the dog, or I'd blow up at my husband, who was spectacular and loving during this whole awful time, and say, 'You're such an asshole,' when what I was really feeling was that I was such an asshole."

Meredith's father had died twelve years earlier, and even though he was the parent with whom she most closely identified, his passing was not as devastating. She was sad, and she missed their conversations and his guidance and mentoring; his death had left a large hole at family gatherings; but mostly she had felt appreciation for his experience and his example (and his belief in her), which had allowed her to become an entrepreneur. All through her growing-up years, she had watched how her dad "had gone against the tide," building businesses that his colleagues thought were losing ventures, taking calculated risks; sometimes his ventures brought great profitability, and at other times they went belly-up. The family got used to the inevitable cycle of abundant periods followed by fallow ones, although they were never anywhere near destitute. "When things weren't going so well, we ate Spam or macaroni and cheese," remembers Meredith, smiling. Her father's adventurous spirit, his entrepreneurial acumen, and his willingness to risk failure rubbed off on his daughter and made her "unafraid" to become a businesswoman. His experience also left her with an urge—that has remained—to "run my own story."

As her father was off in the world making money (and losing it), her mother was holding down the home front and doing volunteer community work. She was on the town's school committee, and, to her young daughter's great embarrassment, she would ride her bicycle to the meetings every Wednesday evening. (All the other mothers were driving their station wagons.) Meredith's mother believed that it was "the responsibility of those who were privileged to give back to those who had less," and she did that in her daily life with uncommon grace and humility. But when Meredith tries to understand the profundity of the loss she experienced when her mother died, she talks about her mother's unerring support and advocacy.

As a child, Meredith struggled with a learning disability that was not well understood at the time, and one that teachers often confused with a lack of intelligence. By the time she reached third grade, her teachers were telling her mother that she was "retarded" and needed to be placed in a special residential school. But Meredith's mother would not hear of it. She did not believe or accept their diagnosis or their remedy; she knew her daughter was bright and could be a learner, an achiever, and a success in the world. So she spent all of her energies resisting the school's views and fighting for her daughter's place in the "regular" school curriculum. Meredith remembers her mother's fierce advocacy when everyone else was giving up on her, and she thinks that at the root of her own determination and ambition as an entrepreneur is a desire to prove all of the naysayers wrong. "When all those educators and tutors were telling my mother that I would never be able to read, she prevailed—and the underpinning of being told I can't do something has left me with a need to prove all of them wrong."

Somehow, in the last year and a half of her mother's life, as Meredith sat on the edge of her bed and watched her health decline, she knew with great clarity that she was losing her protector; that she was saying goodbye to the one person on earth who never left her side or stopped believing in her. In those last months, in fact, she was able to tell her mother how much she respected and appreciated her love and unyielding belief in her gifts and capacities, and that she would not have been able to make it without her. In the midst of all of the anguish and the chaos of her mother's final weeks, there were sweet and tender moments; there was time to "trade love stories."

Only recently has Meredith begun to feel that "there is life after death." Each month feels a little less sad than the month before. She is not overcome by weeping whenever something reminds her of her mother, and she has begun to recognize that a part of her mother is growing up in her, making her less lonely for her. In her Third Chapter, then, Meredith—who for most of her life identified deeply with her father's "very male entrepreneurship"—discovers her mother's power. She now sees and appreciates how her mother protected her from the injurious labels applied by educators and doctors during her growing-up years; how her mother believed in her intelligence, her ambitions, her dreams. She now knows that her mother's legacy—of intimacy, nourishment, constancy, and fierce protection—will guide the ways she nurtures her own children. "To be able to sustain more loving kindness in the world would be a tribute to the way my mother lived her life," she says.

Howard Thurman's beautiful words that open this chapter offer us compelling images to soften our view of the hard healing work of journeying home. He reminds us that visiting the ghosts in the nursery and confronting the ancient wounds is not a one-time event, accomplished efficiently and completely. The recovery is ongoing and imperfect, the path rocky and unruly; we stumble and fall, we stand up, move on, and forgive ourselves. But in circling back to the source, "old burdens become lighter," and "the commonplace now is shot through with new glory," giving us the energy and allowing us the space to imagine and compose the new adventures of our Third Chapters. The journey home helps us to see things differently and newly; helps us release the rage and banish the fears; helps us see the beauty in the ordinary, the universal in the particular. And it helps us to know that part of the labor of learning in the Third Chapter is found in the intention and determination to keep on "trying to grow tall enough to wear" the crown.

FOUR

Looking Back and Giving Forward

Your vocation is that place where your deep gladness
meets the world's great hunger.   —Frederick Buechner[1]

One of the ways in which people are able to endure the melancholy of loss, the death of the old, is to envision, actually to begin to picture, their new life. Ironically, the pictures that they construct are often shaped and shaded by a return to their childhoods, to the values and rituals into which they were socialized in their own families of origin, to the historical and cultural moments in which they were embedded. In other words, just as there is a paradox in the dynamic of loss and liberation that characterizes their transition to the Third Chapter, there is also a paradox in the ways in which the women and men I spoke to look backward into the future. They look to their origins, to the lessons they learned at home—about service, charity, justice; about collective responsibility and citizenship—and feel—often for the first time—compelled to find a way to enact those values and principles. They feel at a point in their lives when they can take the time to look back and "journey home." By this stage, they are likely to have accumulated a rich array of experiences, resources, and skills that they are yearning to use wisely and well. Over the years, they have developed patience, learned restraint, grown in wisdom. They have honed their expertise, identified their gifts, and learned how they learn. They have built professional networks that allow them access to resources and institutions. What seems to surge up in them—like a compelling imperative—is the wish to "give forward," to be useful, to make an imprint. They want their lives to have meant something. For the first two chapters of their adult lives, they have worked to succeed in the world of entrepreneurship and profit; they have been personally ambitious; they have amassed wealth, privilege, resources; they have "made it." In the Third Chapter, they want to turn the tables, rewrite their priorities, reinvest in their relationships, recalibrate the meaning of success, even re-envision their concept of work.

In his important book *Prime Time*, Marc Freedman speaks about the growing imperative among people in their Third Chapters who want to contribute to society in a new way; who want to find a way of working and living that is active, generous, and altruistic; and who want to bring their wisdom and resources to their new projects. They want to preserve their dignity and self-respect even if they are ready and willing to relinquish their status and seniority; they want to be useful, not used; engaged, not isolated. Rather than the "retirement of leisure" that might separate them from the world, they want to be actively engaged and making a difference. (We might even shift the language from the "retirement of leisure" to the "re-engagement of activity.") In Buechner's words, there is new passion and "gladness" in discovering, and responding to, the "world's great hunger" with open hearts and plentiful resources. Freedman sees this impulse to give back as a "great adventure," an "opportunity for continued learning and growth in later life."[2]

PLANTING GARDENS

A couple of years ago, I noticed my down-the-street neighbor go through a costume change. A tall, erect, patrician-looking gentleman with a square jaw and a silver mane of hair, he would glide up the street each morning, heading to the subway stop, on his way to his office in one of those gleaming, glass downtown buildings. A senior partner in a corporate law firm, Charles Watson would gaze out on the city landscape from his perch in the corner office on the thirty-seventh floor. At sixty-three, he had worked at the firm for all of his professional life, entering right after completing Yale Law School, and rising to become partner when he was thirty-six years old. It had been a lucrative, mostly satisfying career until about the last decade and a half, when his days began to feel stressful and boring—"a deadly combination." In the last several years, from his point of view, the practice of law had lost its purposefulness, dignity, and moral edge; now it seemed like pure hustle for the big deals and big bucks, and senior partners were not spared the "dog-eat-dog action." So, in his heart of hearts, Charles had been ready to leave the practice—in fact, to leave the field of law entirely—in his mid-forties, when the professional climate had begun to deteriorate. But he had hung on, continuing to enjoy some of the perks of his high status: the lofty salary, the splendid view, the daily habits he had grown used to. And he had wanted to make sure that his financial house was in order before taking off. When, three years ago, his firm—one of the oldest and most prominent in the city—facing a fiercely competitive landscape, was forced to merge with another firm, Charles decided to call it quits. As his colleagues jostled for position in the merged company, he felt only relief. He was thankful for the chance to make a graceful exit. "I was so ready to walk," Charles admits.

As he packed up his office—taking down the big, heavy law

books from the shelves, the paintings from the walls, and clearing his desk of the precious artifacts that had kept him company for almost four decades, he noticed the photograph that used to greet him each morning, the one that always caused longing in his heart. Among the family pictures of his wife, his three children, and two sweet granddaughters, it was the oldest photograph on his desk. There he was, age eight, with his mother, standing in the garden behind their house in North Carolina with shovels in their hands, smiling into the camera, faces happily smudged with dirt. Looking at the photo always reminded Charles of his greatest childhood pleasure: planting the gardens—flowers in the front yard, vegetables in the back—with his mother. When he was a very small child, his mom would let him sit on the edge and dig in the dirt, or run up and down the rows of corn and cucumbers. When he got to be school age, he would run home from the school-bus stop, quickly change his clothes, grab a snack, and join his mother in the garden. By the time he was a teenager—in high school, and an athletic and academic star—he had no time to work in the garden, or to hang out much with his mother, for that matter; he missed both.

As Charles packed up his law office, and carefully wrapped the photo, he knew where he was headed: he was getting ready for a costume change. No longer did I see him striding down the street each morning in his sleek corporate suit. Now he was always in his worn jeans and sweatshirt and big, heavy boots (which he called "shit kickers"), his hands covered in topsoil. Charles began very modestly, fixing up the tiny plot in front of his brownstone, designing an elegant Japanese-inspired garden with beautiful smooth stones and rare miniature trees. But within months, he had offered his services to the neighborhood association, clearing and planting the narrow park in the middle of his block, painting the big planters and filling them with unusual combinations of bright flowers. Then he was on to volunteer at a newly renovated children's art center, where he started from scratch: digging a new foundation for brick patios, wooden benches, handsome shrubs, and flowering-magnolia trees. I could look out my window at dusk and sometimes see Charles returning from work, his gait weary, but his face beaming, as he must have looked in the childhood photo with his mother in the garden.

During the last year, he has found, as he puts it, "a regular gig" close to Chinatown, working in a large city garden where folks—all Chinese—grow their crops. One day, Charles, who had passed by this garden for years and looked longingly at the people bent over in their labor, decided to walk over there and see what they were planting. He loves flowers, but he had missed planting vegetables—missed the exquisite pleasure of tasting in his salad the luscious tomatoes taken fresh from his garden. The folks—mostly grandparents themselves; some with their young grandkids twirling, as he had once done, up and down the aisles of vegetables—at first looked a little skeptically at him, wondering what this tall white man, who looked for all the world like a corporate lawyer dressed in overalls, wanted from them. They didn't talk very much: there was a language barrier. But soon one of the men beckoned for him to come over and see his row of bok choy, and Charles gladly sauntered over to admire the healthy crop. The next day, he came back to watch; several days later, he came to work. Now, almost any day, you can drive by the garden and see one tall man in a Red Sox baseball cap in the midst of a bunch of short Chinese elders in their broad, flat straw hats, bent over, tilling the soil, working away silently in the hot sun.

Even though Charles approached his work with his mother's

garden tips still clear in his mind (and heart), he quickly discovered that he had a lot to learn. This time round, he learned to learn by carefully watching and witnessing, not talking and explaining. He learned how to plant economically and strategically on narrow strips of land, and he learned some new tricks for irrigating the city soil. He learned the Chinese names for produce he had never tasted before. He learned to love the slow pace, the sun on his face, even the physical weariness after a day of digging. Charles suspects that in the next several months he may begin to feel the urge to expand his horizons a bit, maybe even find a way to use some of his legal expertise. He might, for example, volunteer his services doing pro-bono legal work for one of his favorite community-service organizations, or he might explore the possibility of taking on a part-time management role at a small organic farm just outside the city that has asked for his help. But in the meantime, laboring in the Chinese gardens is Charles's chosen vocation, and it echoes with the deepest pleasures from his childhood. Each day feels like "looking back and giving forward."

As he contemplated his Third Chapter, Clark Clayton also heard the echoes of his mother's voice urging her five sons to "fulfill the responsibilities of our privilege," although the gardens his mother planted were in the "ordinary middle-class altruism" of community service. Clark recalls, "I grew up with a sense from my mother that the ultimate responsibility is yours. She would say, 'If you see a problem, fix it.'" Her lessons were not just about the responsibilities of "service." They were about "making a difference that was observable, measurable—a difference that made an impact." Clark took her admonitions to heart, fulfilled a promise that he had made to his family thirty years ago, and retired at sixty, so he would have the time and space to follow through on his mother's lessons.

As a CEO and COO of several start-up companies, Clark had had an ambitious, fiercely competitive, and lucrative career. He had made more than enough money to live a life of genteel luxury and leave something substantial for his children, enjoying the status, abundance, and privileges of a successful senior executive. Now he was looking for a way to make a contribution; he wanted "to do good" and "to give back."

Clark surmises that it is easier for him to feel "that change is possible" than it is for someone who has not lived the same kind of privileged life. Abundance, he believes, offers you the resources, the space and energy, maybe even the optimism that is required to imagine a different reality. Says Clark, "I am a white male, highly educated. I grew up in a family with two parents who were educated in the Ivy League. . . . It was time for me to find a way to do something useful." He reflects back on his parents' sense of belonging in the community where he grew up. "They were not social or political activists," he says. "My father was a volunteer fireman, not someone who signed up for Meals on Wheels." When his mother spoke to her sons about "giving back," she meant very "ordinary," nonprogressive, nonconfrontational things: volunteering at the library, working as a Scout leader, reading to the elderly at the old-age home. Her brand of generosity and service were woven into her weekly routines, and were very "nonflamboyant," never calculated to bring her visibility or acclaim.

But by the time Clark reached college and then business school, the political context had changed radically. The campuses were on fire. In 1970, the year the United States invaded Cambodia, Clark was in business school, attending classes with "officers who felt betrayed by their country and were the most outraged people in the school." During that time, students were allowed to take the term off to do activist work and get course credit on their transcripts for doing so. Clark did not become an outspoken activist, something he now seems to regret wistfully. Instead, he remained steadfastly focused on his studies, determined to carve a smooth path into the corporate world. But he does remember that the tenor and ethos of the late sixties and early seventies felt both energizing and tantalizing. "I hated, and still hate, confrontation," says Clark, explaining why some of the activist tactics turned him off.

As he looks back on those heady, provocative times thirty-five years ago, a part of him yearns to re-create the energy and excitement that he missed the first time around, when his cautious pragmatism compromised his full participation. But he also feels fortunate ("truly blessed") that there has been a clear shift in the arenas of activism, that the action is no longer on the streets. "The political activism of the early seventies is now in the social sector," says Clark. He remembers that when he was in business school, for example, there were no courses focused on nonprofits. Now business-school curricula always include reference to the nonprofit sector, and some minority of their graduates, who hope to change the world and make a difference, choose to work in that sector. Clark seems thankful and relieved that his eagerness, at sixty-two, to become a consultant to nonprofits, and his decision to bring his business acumen and strategies to that sphere, come at a time when "most of the action is there"—when the activism and advocacy have migrated to the social sector.

As he has tried to learn how to be useful translating what he knows to activists, advocates, and social-service entrepreneurs in the nonprofit world, Clark has had to become a "student," a "new learner." He has had to look to his much younger colleagues—mostly women—for guidance, instruction, and criticism. Not only is he aware that they are more "in touch with the contemporary scene and cultural context" than he is, and more conversant with the perspectives and values of "the people working on the ground," but they also seem to have developed a broader repertoire of ways to engage the people with whom they work. They are better at "relationship building," at giving voice to people who have been largely unheard, and advocating for their best interests. Clark is a watchful witness of this generation of young entrepreneurs, learning lessons from them each day, soaking up the energy and passion they bring to their work. "They are my teachers, my mentors—they are the wise ones," he says about his youthful colleagues. He contrasts his thirty-five years as a savvy business executive with his "still-young and naïve" work consulting with nonprofits. "In my former jobs, my energy usually got consumed by others, but in this work, there is a huge chance for amplification. For the first time in my professional life, the place and the people create energy in me!"

I am talking here about "giving forward" (rather than "giving back," which is the term Freedman uses) as a way of reflecting how people in their Third Chapters must develop ways of engagement and service that point toward the future, and not get stuck in the nostalgia and anachronisms of the past. In order to be useful, they—like Clark Clayton—must respond to the contemporary context and envision a future into which their altruism might make a contribution. They need to listen to the voices and views of their children, and their children's children, for lessons on contemporary culture, and for clues about how they might serve and be useful.

In her wonderful book of essays, *Willing to Learn: Passages of Personal Discovery*, Mary Catherine Bateson argues that, given the speed of change today, not only is learning necessarily a life-long process, but it also requires major and continual adaptations. In order to cope with the challenges—and, I would add, in order to "give forward" in a way that is meaningful—people have to continue learning. Bateson equates the experience of living in our ever-changing world to the experience of immigrants. She quotes from a lecture she gave to a group of university alums—most in their Third Chapters—"Every one of you in the room today is an immigrant in the sense that you do not live in the country you were born in. . . . It changed you. You've got the same passport, you might even have the same address, but you live in a different world."[3] Emigrants from overseas usually have a difficult time adapting because everything changes for them at once, Bateson argues. People who have always lived in the same place, while change has taken place, have it a little easier, because they have "been able to adapt piecemeal."[4]

Several years ago, when my daughter was in the throes of her "operatic" adolescence, I remember confiding in Bateson, who is a colleague and friend. I was asking her for her wisdom (she is the mother of a strong and beautiful daughter several years older than mine), anticipating that she would offer me what I have come to know as her long and generous view on mother-daughter struggles. She listened to my stories—filled with melodrama, miscommunication, awkwardness, frustration, and weariness—and said, "You must listen to your daughter—she is from another planet, and she has a great deal to teach you." With the metaphors of immigrants and visitors from another planet, Bateson conveys the rapidity of change in our culture, so that we must keep learning all through our lives and value the lessons our children teach us. If, in our Third Chapters, we were to "give back" in our efforts to be useful, we would miss the mark. We must "give forward" in order to meet the needs of the changing environment around us and to continue to grow and learn ourselves.

Here, then, I am exploring the dynamic of looking backward

into the future, examining the notion of "giving forward," and searching out the ways in which our childhoods often anticipate the ways we choose to give forward. I will trace the motivations and aspirations, the frustrations and vulnerabilities voiced by my interviewees as they learned new ways of being useful, as they planted new gardens, as they worked through the "responsibilities of their privilege," and as they searched for more effective, more lasting ways to "repair the world."

EMISSARIES OF THE SIXTIES

As Clark Clayton's recollections demonstrate, his family story is embedded in a context: a historical and cultural moment when the seeds were planted for "giving forward," producing a generation that would reverberate with bravado and activism. The fact that he "hated conflict" buffered him somewhat from the waves of political and social upheaval and muted the fierce calls for peace and justice. But he was still left with a lingering nostalgia for those exciting and tumultuous times, when folks in their twenties and thirties could feel the impact of their actions, the imprint of their advocacy.

The political context of Rebecca Fleishman's coming of age seems to define how she both sees the past and envisions the future. A judge for the past decade, known for her bold and carefully reasoned decisions, Rebecca at sixty reflects on her youth—in college and law school—as a time when people of her generation believed that they could "make a difference" and change the world, when people felt a sense of responsibility and accountability to work for justice and equality. She recalls, "We were the generation on the leading edge, we felt a public obligation. When we were younger, we believed that we were emissaries. We believed that we actually stopped the Vietnam War. As feminists, all of us were every woman." The younger generation today does not feel the same sense of "public responsibility." Says Rebecca, "They believe in purely private choice, without the public implications." It is a mistake, she believes, for her generation to look to young people to take up the mantle, because they have not been shaped by the kinds of historical and political forces that gave her generation "voice."

Rebecca feels, therefore, that those of us in the Third Chapter have a responsibility to take on our "public obligation," once more with feeling, and that we are in a better position now—with more resources, networks, influence, wisdom, and experience—than we have ever been. But she worries that the tendency of many of us, who were activists in the sixties, has been to "turn inward" to become much more "cautious," to live a life of gardening and fly-fishing, as you see in all of those retirement commercials. "I cannot imagine going off to the garden," says Rebecca with exasperation. "The notion of withdrawing from the public stage feels like an abdication of my responsibility. Surely I want to travel, but not just for my own pleasure and adventure. I want to travel for human-rights work, to join the international criminal court, work on the war crimes in Kosovo."

Rebecca tells me of a recent experience trying to get her fellow law-school classmates to participate on a panel at their fortieth reunion. The proposed panel she titled "60 and the 60's," and the idea was to shape a conversation that brought together reflections on age and politics, on how the developmental themes of the Third Chapter intersect with our historical and current political engagement. "I hoped for an intensely political conversation," says Rebecca earnestly. "After all, our generation was into feminism, race relations, the cultural wars, progressive politics, and I hoped that the panel would address who we are now, who we were then—what animated and animates our generation?" Although over the years she has kept in touch with many of her classmates, even collaborated with some of them professionally, Rebecca's call for participants on the panel has received almost no takers; and those who have come forward did so reluctantly. This reluctance both puzzles and frustrates Rebecca as she considers "the mush and the caution" that seem to have drowned out the activist voices and impetus of her peers. "I'm sick of everyone trying to engage the younger generation," she says. "Every organization I know is looking for the new energy from youth. I want to engage our generation to become activists now. If not now, when?"

But it is not only that her embeddedness in the tumult of the sixties makes Rebecca feel doubly responsible for being actively engaged in "meeting the world's greatest hunger," a responsibility that she demands of herself and her Third Chapter cohort, not one that she seeks in the younger generation. It is also that her "giving forward" is motivated and shaped by her family origins, by her upbringing in a working-class Jewish household in the Bronx, and by the great contrast between the way she grew up and the way she now lives. One of the reasons, for example, that Rebecca feels she was so successful appearing before old white male conservative judges as a civil-rights attorney fighting for justice for the marginalized and indigent was that it felt very much like her growing-up experience talking to her father. "My relationship to the judge replicated my relationship to my father," she says simply.

Rebecca's father was a high-school graduate, her mother never finished high school, and she was the first in her family to go to college. For her first two years of college, she commuted from the Bronx, a change in culture that was much greater than the distance in miles. Rebecca loved the academic life. She relished devouring the books, enjoyed the intellectual discourse, and the mentoring by her professors. She was also intoxicated by the campus radicalism—"swept up in the sixties activism." The travel back and forth from the Bronx to Manhattan required that she become a "translator" of her experiences. "I was raised with ordinary people," says Rebecca respectfully. "I learned early, when talking to my family, the process of taking complex issues and translating them into simple language."

This process of explaining and making things plain, but not "talking down," served Rebecca well when she moved to the public arena of the courtroom and tried to win over the hearts and minds of the jury, or when she presented her case before a judge who was at first skeptical of her gender and her politics. "The judge would be an older white man who I charmed like I would my father. It was very natural for me to do the translator-and-educator part." Still deeply identified with her working-class roots, Rebecca says, "My success—first as an attorney and now as a judge—comes from the combination of Harvard and the Bronx."

Rebecca has felt another kind of translation in her personal life, reflecting a dimension of "giving forward" that has grown deeper and more complicated in her Third Chapter. Married in her late thirties, Rebecca did not become a mother until she was thirty-nine, when her first of two sons was born. Becoming a mother was the biggest change that she had ever experienced in her life, especially the feeling of "not being in control," and the feeling that her boys "were alien creatures who bounced in their own direction." In so many ways her sons seemed like strangers; she couldn't see herself in them. "They were so much the other for me," says Rebecca, shaking her head. "It was a huge challenge, for example, for me to understand how my children learned. It was so different from the way I did."

Rebecca was also surprised by how much parenting consumed and shaped her life. Somehow, before having children, she had imagined that her busy and public professional life might keep her from becoming overly preoccupied with her sons. "I thought, with all of my work, I'd have all of these layers that would inoculate me and keep me at some distance. I was astonished that I couldn't resist thinking about them—there were no layers between us. I just realized that I had the ability to multitask, to always think about them and do everything else." She tells a story about recently attending the baby shower of a young colleague where each of the women spoke about her experiences in mothering—words of wisdom for the new mother. Rebecca had told the gathering about her emotions following her younger son's departure for his freshman year of college, a response that she actually experienced as a painful physical sensation. "I felt like someone took my entrails and put them on my son's feet," she said, tearing up.

Rebecca's deep, protective involvement with her own children was surprising in another way. For the first time, she began to identify with her own mother. She found herself turning to her mother for guidance, not so much in the sense of asking her directly for advice, but, rather, in the sense of feeling parts of her mother grow up inside of her. "We are so different," says Rebecca. "My mother didn't work, didn't go to college. We had homemade blintzes; she was a throwback to another generation. I had even resisted marriage for so long because I thought that I would have to do it like my mother did—a total, huge commitment that left me no space for myself. I was seeing marriage the way my mother saw it." But now, late at night, when Rebecca has come home from the court, she feels her mother's presence, particularly in the kitchen when she finds herself making pot roast at one in the morning. The smell and warmth of the kitchen make her appreciate her mother more and more, and marvel at how she was there for her children.

The familiar smell of the roast also reminds Rebecca of the ways in which mothering has called her home. Even when her work takes her to the other side of the world, she feels the pull to home. She will be preparing a speech at her hotel in Oslo, and she will realize—calculating the time difference—that it is time for her son's dentist appointment. And she remembers traveling to China and receiving a call from her son on her international cell phone asking her where he could find his socks. "I am my mother," says Rebecca about how natural and appropriate this long-distance request felt to her; and about how—in her Third Chapter—she has inherited her mother's deep devotion to this "all-consuming" role. Just as her conversations with her father have helped her make the "translations" as a lawyer in the courtroom, so, too, the nourishment from her mother's kitchen has helped her translate the needs and desires of her children, helped her hear and heed the call "home."

Rebecca Fleishman's return "home"—to the family in which she was raised, and to the cultural and historical scene of the sixties, which shaped her values and activism—and her issuing of a "call to action" to her cohort of Boomers, remind us of two of the important lessons captured in the work of life-span theorists, which we reviewed in chapter one. First is the appreciation of the power of context—the ways in which the political, historical, and cultural settings shape our perspectives and behaviors—and second are the ways in which individuals selectively respond to these broader social and institutional forces. Not only has Rebecca absorbed the energy and passion of her generation, but she has also done something special with it. She has hung on to it, clung to its principles and imperatives, remained steadfast to its mission and goals, and brought her hard-earned wisdom, experiences, and resources to the way she "gives forward" through her work and family today. When she urges her law-school classmates to sign up for the panel, she hopes that they will bring their sixties drive and commitment, but also that they will develop a discourse that "takes responsibility for now" and begins to articulate what animates the work that they must take on in their sixties.

This "cohort effect" that Rebecca Fleishman exemplifies has been observed by social scientists and activists who for decades have been following the national trends in civic engagement. At a 1995 White House Conference on Aging, Ralph Nader—himself an iconic advocate for citizen rights and civic engagement—offered a clarion call to Third Chapter Boomers. He noticed a new awakening of their commitment to service echoing the political engagement into which they were socialized forty years earlier. Said Nader, "A generational stirring is rumbling among those who grew up in the 50's when America was number one in just about everything and who now find their land in deep trouble on almost all domestic fronts. With their children raised and some financial security achieved, more of them are looking outward to help solve the country's problems."[5]

GOING HOME AGAIN
TO A STRANGE PLACE

Lucinda Miller, whose clear depiction of her three life stages we were introduced to in chapter one, enacts and embraces the reawakening of passion and the reengagement in activism that Rebecca Fleishman urges on her peers, and that Ralph Nader welcomes and applauds, although her commitments extend beyond our domestic borders to the world stage. At fifty-two, Lucinda's return to international relief work in war-torn and devastated countries around the world feels like both "going home" and a "new adventure"—both ordinary and exotic, routine and revelatory. Now, twenty-five years after her first efforts to "feed the world's hunger" in the Sudan, she approaches her work—on the Gulf Coast, in Kosovo, and in Darfur—with so much more to "give forward." This time she brings a complex blend of passion and restraint, purposefulness and patience, optimism and realism. She also brings with her years of experience, vast networks and alliances, and her access to governmental and nongovernmental organizations, foundations, and social-service agencies.

"I walked into the war zone of Kosovo and felt like I was home again!" exclaims Lucinda about her initial return to the "front" after two and a half decades of building a business and raising a family. "I'm the ultimate rationalizer. Whatever direction I take, I embrace—and believe in it fully." Now there are tears in her eyes. "Once I did that, there was no going back. I had unleashed my passions!" In many ways, Lucinda felt she was reclaiming her individual identity, "shedding the bonds" of the life that had intervened. "I remember arriving in Kosovo feeling, I'm free. It was a powerful feeling of liberation. I'm not here as wife or mother or CEO—I'm here as Lucinda Miller. All these other identities pull me and bind me." Liberation was one part of how she felt entering the war zone; the other was a sensation of being in a place that felt both strange and deeply familiar. She experienced a mixture of feeling both young and old, like a novice and a veteran, with butterflies in her belly and a sturdy self-confidence.

Sometimes Lucinda felt this blend of the old and the new in her "body," in the ways she experienced her sexuality and womanliness. "You know," she explains to me, "these relief organizations are full of these young cowboys—these sexy, strong iconoclasts. When I was in my twenties I was part of that excit-

ing, sexy scene." Now, at fifty-two, Lucinda sits across from me
looking slim and sexy in her deep-purple suit, her narrow
straight skirt hugging her hips, her shiny black hair pulled back
with tortoiseshell barrettes, her curvaceous legs ending in high
heels. I think to myself how completely this woman exudes a
sexiness that is full and natural.

She admits somewhat sheepishly that her first-blush
response to arriving on the war front in Kosovo was to imagine
herself as a thirty-five-year-old woman. "There is some inner
core in me that still thinks of myself as young and sexy." But the
response of the "cowboys" put her in her place and brought her
back to reality: "They were treating me with such respect and
deference." To them, she was a mature, experienced mentor who
had a lot to teach them. There were no flirtations. What she discovered almost immediately was that her own "sexuality and
desire" had to do not with being young, but with being comfortable in her own body, secure with who she is. "I feel very sexual
and comfortable in my own skin," she says self-confidently. She
suffers some "age-related symptoms," like a torn kneecap that
occasionally flares up and causes her discomfort and pain. But
for the most part, aging is not on her mind. Lucinda regards her
fifties as the "best decade" of her life so far and holds a very optimistic view of her strength and authority. "I have this hopeful
feeling—the world is my oyster."

Lucinda's hopefulness about returning to her old passions—
"going home again"—reflects a new sense that this time she is
returning with much more to offer. The youthful energy, commitment, and passion that defined her activist work in her
twenties are now scaffolded and supported by the experience,
maturity, networks, skills, and wisdom she has acquired since
then. "Now I'm standing on the platform of my decades of work,
building on my investment, reaping all of the gains from those

years of blood, sweat, and tears," she says. "I have all of that at my disposal this time. I can use it and build on it."

When she went to Kosovo the first time, for example, Lucinda found a way to "share the journey" with her company. The large network of company affiliates followed along by satellite as she wrote a daily journal about her travels. Using the resources of her company, she was also able to initiate several maternal-health programs in some of the most devastated areas. This joining of resources and information was good for both the relief organization and her company, breaking down some of the mysteries and misunderstandings across geographic and cultural boundaries. Lucinda worked out the same kind of organizational collaboration when she recently joined the board of an international relief organization as she put together—in cooperation with her corporation—a joint response to help some of the family-service organizations in the Gulf Coast that had been devastated by Hurricane Katrina. She loves being able to "double the impact" of her giving forward by creating alliances, building bridges, and convincing organizations to work together to provide relief to those who are suffering in the world. "I have been able to negotiate major deals and mergers across groups," she says proudly, "using my business skills and experience."

In the last year, this approach—of using all of her resources, connections, and skills to create connections and mergers—has translated into her work in Darfur, Sudan. During her twenties, Lucinda codirected a major hunger-relief program in the Sudan. This past year, she returned to the region twice. The first time was to speak with women in displacement camps in western Darfur who had been gang-raped during the attacks by the Janjaweed militias. For ten days, Lucinda traveled to the camps and heard the anguished and horrific stories of scores of women. In a piece that she wrote on Valentine's Day, Lucinda quoted a mother of eight children (ranging in age from two to nineteen years) from the farming village of Turu.

When the sun rose, the planes came with shooting. Then the men with guns came in on horses and camels. . . . They quickly surrounded our village. They collected all the men and boys, shot them, and cut them up. I tried to run away. But I had too many children and the Janjaweed came in all directions. I carried one child and put another on my back. The soldiers pulled my children away from me and put me in the hut. Four soldiers held me down and raped me. They beat me with rods. They put the rod in the fire and then burned me on the shoulder. They raped my twelve-year-old daughter. . . . As soon as the Janjaweed left I pulled my daughter up and carried her and we ran. We ran barefoot carrying nothing. The attackers had torn off our robes so we were not able to cover ourselves. We ran and found my eldest girl. She was pregnant. Soldiers shot and killed her. All the people in the village were running. Some people stopped to help me bury my daughter, and the soldiers shot three of them. We ran a very long distance. We had no shoes, clothes, or food. The sun was very hot. We finally made it to the refugee camp. Relief workers gave us food and oil, and our people gave us some clothes.

For hours and days, Lucinda sat on the parched land under the burning sun, huddled with women, listening to their stories about the carnage and brutal violence they had suffered— tales about the murders and rapes of their sisters and daughters, the dislocation from the land their families had lived on for generations—painful stories that Lucinda absorbed and recorded so that when she returned home to the States she would be able to speak the truth about the horrific conditions in the Sudan. When she returned from her trip, she made the rounds, speaking at colleges and universities, community forums, churches and synagogues. She published editorials in major newspapers and made appointments to speak to policy makers in Washington. "This time I was able to use my passion in a more substantive and strategic way," Lucinda says about how she was able to take advantage of her "new layer of skills." "I am more confident, able to open more doors. . . . I have more access and influence—more networks and contacts. I'm able to meet with the undersecretary of state and function strategically at much higher levels."

INTIMATE INEQUALITIES

One of the fascinating aspects of "looking back and giving forward" in the Third Chapter is that it is often a time of deep reflection and self-discovery, a time when we are—sometimes for the first time—able to see the "true origins" of our passions, the authentic roots of what motivates our renewed commitments. For example, in the first two chapters of our adult lives, we may have created a narrative that saw our activism—our giving forward—as growing out of witnessing the larger societal injustices surrounding us when we were children, only to discover in the Third Chapter that our motivations have different, more intimate origins. For most of our lives, we may have been telling ourselves a story that was easier to digest, that wouldn't make us feel the sharp edges of guilt and remorse, that might not make us feel personally implicated. This was the case for Rachel Middleton, whom we met in chapter two, as she experienced the excitement and the panic connected to her decision to shift the paradigm from her work in public policy to the "sacred work of the spirit." In struggling with her decision to leave her executive position at Work Alliance and enroll in divinity school, Rachel uncovered the "real roots" of her commitment to justice work. Her discovery made the act of giving forward feel more "grounded, more authentic, more integrated" with the rest of her life. Unmasking the "real story" in her Third Chapter unleashed new energy in Rachel, a deepening commitment to make a difference in the world.

Following her father's death, when Rachel was three, her family moved from South Africa back to the United States and settled in Detroit. Even though she left South Africa as a young child, Rachel still considers it home—her "touchstone, source, family"—and she travels back there every three or four years, now taking her three children with her. As she reflects on the "lost strands" of her life, she thinks about the heavy imprint of apartheid, a fact of life she was unaware of as a child, but a condition that in many ways has defined and shaped her life journey ever since. "I didn't know how wrong it was and how implicated people I loved were in it," she recalls, her voice laced with guilt and sadness. "It was my response to apartheid that spawned my interest in social justice, education, and eliminating poverty. The politics of justice is my journey."

When the family moved to Detroit, young Rachel experienced another kind of apartheid—"de-facto segregation"—and a reality of race relations that felt deeply familiar. Once again, the black people were on the bottom and the white people were on the top. But the inequalities did not always get in the way of the intimate—even loving—relationships between the races. Rachel, for example, remembers the black people who worked as servants in her maternal grandparents' home, and how as a child she looked to them for nourishment and comfort. Lucy, the cook, was a huge figure in the little girl's reality. "Lucy's kitchen," recalls Rachel with tears in her eyes, "was the heart of the house." But it wasn't only that she "owned" the space where the food was prepared, it was that she seemed to warm the entire household with her "softness and strength." "Lucy was an extraordinary moral force, a humanist. My family was much more brittle," says Rachel. The irony and contradiction embedded in the tangle of deep intimacy and "positional inequality" have become the focus of Rachel's current intellectual and spiritual studies in divinity school. The emotional bedrock of the questions she raises now, at fifty, had its origins in these early relationships.

When Rachel traces her lifelong commitment to "the politics of justice," she begins with the early unconscious imprints of apartheid in South Africa, her birthplace, and then follows with the stories of her conscious awakening to its meanings when she experienced de-facto segregation growing up in Detroit. The structural inequalities, these stark divisions between the powerful few and the powerless many, between blacks and whites in both South Africa and North America, were part of her up-close reality as a child and the source of her motivation to "make a difference" as an adult.

But as Rachel thinks about her commitment to erasing inequalities, her heart reaches back to another place—a deep division, an unfairness in her family. This is when her tears come; this is a part of her story that she has only begun to recover and reveal. As Rachel excelled in school and went off to elite colleges and fancy graduate schools, her sister struggled to complete the special-education classes at their public school in Detroit. Her sister has major learning disabilities that have required that she stay at home under the supervision of their mother. Even now, in her middle age, she lives with their mother, and works as a nurse's aide in a position that she has held for almost thirty years. This is, perhaps, the most searing injustice of all, the one that has caused Rachel the greatest guilt and grief. How could she be bestowed with a brilliant mind and endless opportunities, how could she have traveled all over the world, when her sister has been forced to live such a limited, meager existence?

As a matter of fact, the pain around their different realities has been so intense that most of Rachel's life she has just buried it, hidden it away in some deep place, knowing that it would hurt too much to give it any thought. Perhaps her efforts to challenge the structural injustices through her policy work, and even to challenge the inequalities related to job opportunities, has been the best way she could figure out to redress the pain of her own sister's impaired mind and poverty-level salary. Only recently has she begun to talk openly about her sister and consider how the distance between her sister's reality and her own has shaped her own choices and actions, defining the ways in which she has chosen to "give forward."

Rachel even links the uncovering of her sister's story to the birth of her youngest daughter, to a moment when she realized that her "hiding out" had been holding her back and not allowing her to be the "evolved person" she wants to be. She remembers, "In the period after my third daughter was born, I tried to integrate better who I was with what I did." She decided for the first time to talk about her sister publicly, and to embed her story in a major speech she was giving about educational inequalities and work opportunities. For the first time, she began her public speech with a very personal example. Her apprehension and anxiety were huge as she mounted the stage. "When I finally did talk about her in my speech, I cried," she says about the public/intimate revelation. This is what she read from her carefully, painstakingly prepared speech to a rapt audience:

> My work is very much influenced by the experiences of my sister, who has significant learning disabilities. As a child with learning disabilities in the late sixties, before mainstreaming, she was enrolled in the Special School District in Detroit, Michigan—a pretty grim place. I watched my mother single-handedly create a set of learning opportunities for my sister that got her out of a dysfunctional high school and into a rich series of internships and work-based learning at a large teaching hospital in Detroit where she could participate in a professional community and earn a certificate as a nurse's aide. . . . Yet despite the hard-won victories for which my mother and sister fought, there is a huge disparity between the life chances that my sister and I have received. She works as a nurse's aide paid $7.00 an hour after thirty years' experience and I stand before you as an "expert."

In the first paragraph of her application to divinity school a few years later, Rachel linked South African apartheid with the experience of witnessing her sister's limited life. Both realities— inside and outside of her family—shaped her awareness of the damage and distortions resulting from inequalities. "My experiences with my sister's struggles and in South Africa as a child and through repeated visits in my adult life gave me an early and sharp awareness of the consequences of unequal opportunity. They also made me angry and this anger propelled many of my educational and career decisions over the next twenty years."

REPAIRING THE WORLD

Each of the people whom we have just met find ways of "giving forward" in the Third Chapter, a generosity of service that energizes and enlarges them, that takes advantage of the skills, temperaments, and perspectives that they have accumulated in the first two chapters of their lives. Charles Watson speaks about how working on the "local landscape" gives him a new feeling of connection with, and accountability to, his community, a new sense of civic responsibility that is "grounded and real." Clark Clayton refers to the "huge amplification of energy" that he discovers in his "new learning" about the nonprofit sector as he is mentored by his "young and wise" colleagues. Lucinda Miller finds new power in "returning home" to the places where she did international relief work a quarter-century earlier. She is no longer the sexy, brash young cowgirl who impressed everyone with her risk-taking and passion. Now her giving forward is scaffolded and enriched by maturity, savvy, patience, and restraint; by her access to networks, resources, and power; by the knowledge and confidence she carries in her body. And, in discovering the real source of her rage against societal inequalities and the roots of her lifetime "journey for justice," Rachel Middleton feels more empowered and more whole. Her giving forward is enlarged by her decision to "out" herself in a public speech. For the first time, she speaks about the deep residues of pain that she still carries for her sister's plight in life, for the huge and unfair disparities between them. This is the real injustice, and it hurts the most.

Each of their stories reveals the ways in which these people resist and challenge pervasive cultural caricatures that focus on the diminished power of people in their Third Chapters, stereotypes that would cast them as weaker, anachronistic, and irrelevant. Instead, they find the opposite: that their energy and imagination are not diminished, that their activism has grown stronger and deeper, that their giving forward is intensified, that their sense of urgency is greater. Not only do these people resist the cultural stereotypes, but they also find ways of adapting to new institutional contexts that allow them to be learners and teachers, imitators and models, followers and initiators; and that honor their maturity. Into these new settings they bring the wisdom of their years and the depth of their experience, but they also feel compelled to learn new lessons, strategies, and methods of working from younger people who are closer to the edge of cultural change, closer to the action.

For some people in the Third Chapter, it is fair to say, their experiences in discovering ways to "give forward" are not so positive or fruitful. They find it harder to move against the waves of negative cultural regard, and they have a harder time finding organizational contexts or social arenas where they can grow in their learning and make an imprint. In his book *Prime Time* Marc Freedman writes about the ways in which our society tends to not support the respectful engagement of older people, and in the process we miss the richness of their contributions, their insights, and their service. The pejorative cultural regard of people in their Third Chapters often diminishes and demeans them, infantilizes and isolates them, and does not take full advantage of their wisdom, perspectives, and experience. These negative views are amplified by institutional arrangements—both structural and legal, formal and informal—that do not encourage or welcome their full participation.

Freedman argues for developing structures, institutions, and arenas where people in their Third Chapters will be able to become involved in public service; a "win-win" dynamic that will enrich both individuals and communities. Freedman's hope is "to expand opportunities and options, not obligations; it isn't to promote an endless grindstone, or to uphold giving back as the only legitimate route to aging successfully." Rather, he writes, "what we need to do is to widen the range of compelling pathways available to individuals in later life. Specifically, I believe, to uphold and develop the option for public service that constitutes the greatest potential 'win-win' combination for individuals and society. We have failed to do so. It is still much easier to disengage or focus on leisure in later life than it is to make a significant investment in the common good."[6]

Pamela Stein, the psychologist and activist whom we met in the preceding chapter, expresses disappointment and frustration as she struggles against a cultural inertia and "stagnancy" that will not allow her to give forward fully. She invents a role for herself as "public educator," a role whereby she combines her new learning as an emerging playwright with her long experience as an academic. As a public educator, she hopes to bridge scientific knowledge and artistic expression, a stance that will allow her to speak to broader and more diverse audiences, a place from which she will be able to commune with the "heart and the head." In her presentations—in theaters and lecture halls, on radio and television, at political demonstrations and public forums—Pamela joins the realms of aesthetics and empiricism; she combines theater and public policy in an effort to make a larger, more profound impact on her audiences. Both her art and her social science are designed to "make a difference" in "repairing the world." She uses the Hebrew term Tikkun Olam (meaning "repairing the world") to speak about the values and purposes animating all of her work—an urgent and inclusive call to action, a responsibility that she believes we must all collectively embrace.

Pamela traces her commitment to Tikkun Olam to her

childhood in a small Midwestern town, where her family was one of a handful of progressive Jews surrounded by a conservative majority of born-again Christians. Her parents stood out— especially her mother—for their outspoken views on civil rights and racial equality. "I was raised with a very strong sense of how evil racism was," she says. Pamela recalls her first job, working for the local paper when she was sixteen, when she produced copy for the society column. One Sunday afternoon, she did a piece on the wedding of a couple from a prominent Negro family, and took a photograph of the elegant event. When her publisher saw the article, he explained to her that the paper did not run "pictures of the coloreds" in the society pages. "At that moment, something hit me in the gut—a feeling that has never left me," recalls Pamela. She immediately sat down and wrote a letter of resignation to the editor. This was the beginning of a lifetime of "quiet and persistent" confrontation and resistance, working against the biases and prejudices that marginalize and exclude poor people, women, and people of color. Now, on the eve of her sixtieth birthday—forty-five years after her resignation from her small-town newspaper—Pamela's determination to "repair the world" continues unabated, but feels compromised.

In a meditative letter that she wrote me after our interview, Pamela talked about the opportunities and barriers that she faces today in trying to "get things done," and the odd sensation that, now that she is at the top of her game, she feels the most impotent, the least effectual.

"When I have written books or done public education, I have always been surprised and gratified if anything improved in any way, because I have certainly never felt like a very powerful person. But it is hard to know how to put that together with seeing how much needs to be done and knowing that it could happen if only the forces of fear were not so pervasive and impenetrable. I have always wanted to work with people rather than against them. I have never understood competitiveness nor the enjoyment of fighting. I suppose I still cling to the perhaps naïve belief that if people could only listen, really listen to each other, much of the mess of getting set up against each other as opponents, even enemies, would fall away, that it would be so clear what really matters. I think I still believe that, but too often (at least with regard to the things that mean the most to me), it seems that the steps toward mutual listening and respect are too hard or too scary for people to take."

Pamela feels the urgency, the challenges, and the disappointment even more deeply as she anticipates the end of her life. As the years grow shorter, her hopes for enlarging the scope and depth of her work become more ambitious. She is keenly aware of the finiteness of life, the large and the small casualties of aging, and the time that she has left. "I know that only very recently have I viscerally felt how limited my remaining time might be. My uncle, to whom I was very close, died just before he turned sixty-six. His mother—my adored maternal grandmother—died at sixty-eight. But my other three grandparents lived into their early nineties. I feel, though, the need to assume that I will not by any means necessarily live beyond my sixties, so, yes, that certainly intensifies my despair of repairing what I'd like to repair in the world."

The problem, as Pamela sees it, is not just a matter of limited time, not just a question of death looming large. It is also related to the size of her ambition, the scope of the agenda that she sets for herself. In her Third Chapter, her determination to repair the world has only increased, and the public-policy issues that she is working to change seem increasingly challenging and unreachable. Pamela draws the contrast between the tangible, manageable work that shaped and consumed the first two chap-

ters of her adult life—where she could see and feel her impact—
and the bigger intractable issues that concern her now.

When I had a regular job and was raising my kids, there
was a great deal in my life that I was able to accomplish,
because, even though I was often taking a more radical
approach to many things than were most people, it was
still the case that a lot of my time and energy went into
things for which I could actually see some effect, make
things happen—from making a meal for my kids or seeing them laugh to giving students feedback on a draft of
a thesis, etc. . . . But now I find that there is much less
opportunity for doing achievable things. The changes
that seem to me profoundly important, potentially
extremely helpful to people, are things that the world
calls "radical." As you know, most Americans consider
"radical" to be bad. I have often said in lectures that
"radical" is a good thing, because it is about change
"from the root," exactly what is needed when people are
being devastated because radical changes are required
and nobody is making them happen.

Pamela believes that we as a society know what to do—
about universal health care, about domestic violence, about
unmasking the "pathologizing" within psychiatric diagnoses,
about offering emotional and pragmatic support to the damaged
veterans of war (all public-policy efforts on which she has
labored long and hard). We have the knowledge and the tools.
But we don't have the will or the courage to do the right thing,
to do the "radical" thing. It feels deeply discouraging that at this
point in her life—when she is poised to give her all to get things
done, when she brings wisdom, experience, and a sense of ur-

gency to the task—the solutions seem out of reach; it is even harder to rally people's sense of collective responsibility. This makes the Third Chapter feel "especially sad," "almost tragic" to Pamela. In a long, passionate missive, she writes me the words that are probably too hard for her to say in person.

The upshot is that as I am about to turn sixty . . . I have spent an increasing amount of time on issues that have the potential to improve the lives of enormous numbers of people but I know it is virtually impossible that I will ever be able to do what needs to be done on the scale on which it needs to be done. It is all the more troubling because I know how little time it would take to do it right. So increasingly, the time and energy I invest in direct social and political action goes where I increasingly know that these important changes will never happen. And facing my own mortality and thus the limited time I have in which to make anything good happen, I find this sad. I feel as though I am somehow outside the Earth, sort of orbiting around it, seeing the tragedies happen, but being unable to do much about them except, sometimes, one person at a time. And that is far from enough.

The sadness and disappointment, and the feeling that time is evaporating, converge with Pamela's sense of urgency and the largeness of her ambitions. Her activism grows more radical; her yearning to make a difference intensifies just as she realizes that our cultural priorities and institutions—both governmental and nongovernmental—are not designed or prepared to embrace her mission and hear her truths. Throughout her whole life, she has prepared for this moment of maximum impact, and now that she has arrived, ready to give it her all, she feels compromised and inhibited.

☙

Pamela Stein's frustration and sadness, her despondency about how little time she has left to "give forward," point to a major undercurrent that flowed through all of the stories in this chapter: namely, the tension people experience between patience and purposefulness, between urgency and restraint. Patience grows with maturity and experience, as people in their Third Chapters take the long view and recognize the casualties of daring and risk-taking. Patience also grows with age itself—the need to take things more slowly, the development of rituals and routines that respond to the slower pace that our bodies and psyches require. Freedman sees this patience as a "major gift of age,"[7] and recognizes the down-shifting as life-giving and life-sustaining. He writes: "How they [people in their Third Chapters] are doing the work that they do has a great deal to do with the qualities of patience and perspective and with the virtue that can best be described as slowness. These individuals have an understanding that some things in life—ranging from mentoring to medicine—are best done slowly, and that efficiency, expediency, and productivity have a way of undermining those endeavors."[8]

But the gift of patience often flies in the face of the impatience and urgency people in their Third Chapters feel as they search for ways to make a difference and repair the world. They see the years closing in on them; they appreciate that every day counts in a life that will inevitably end sooner and sooner. Just as Pamela Stein rails against the institutional and cultural barriers that slow her movement forward, so, too, Rebecca Fleishman urges her peers to re-enter the fray: "If not now, when?" I believe that part of the challenge facing women and men in their Third Chapters is figuring out how to navigate this tension between slowing down and speeding up, between mining the privileges of a well-earned patience and responding to the imperatives of time racing by. Discovering the "deep gladness" in giving forward means finding a precarious balance between these contrary pulls of energy and time.

FIVE

Crossing Boundaries and Embracing Contradictions

The borders are our natural sites of creation . . . the
places where we invent, transgress, and create.
—Toni Morrison[1]

The Third Chapter is not a continuation of where we have
been. It means moving into a different dimension, crossing the
border into new territories. Several of the women and men I
interviewed claim that their experience of "boundary crossing"
instigated new learning. They speak about boundary crossings
in many ways—crossing disciplinary boundaries, crossing the
boundaries between art and science, crossing generational
boundaries, crossing geographic boundaries, crossing the boundaries of race and class, crossing gender boundaries, and crossing
the boundaries between work and play. As they navigate the
borders, they are forced to learn new skills, take on different
temperamental styles, try on new personas, learn how they
learn, and reinvent themselves. In navigating these boundaries,
people begin to enlarge their repertoire, their range of choices,
perspectives, and frameworks—their ways of being in the world.
They become more layered and multidimensional. In the end,

boundary crossing often leads to a surprising and paradoxical result. Rather than living and learning on one or the other side of the border, forsaking one to join the other, people speak about resisting the either/ors, and finding a way to incorporate both realms. Ultimately, they do not have to choose between divergent paths; they can decide to embrace both. The new learning involves synthesis and integration; the border crossers travel far but never leave home.

Roma Wolfe, the fifty-seven-year-old physicist we met in the introduction, who has cut back on her laboratory research in order to teach in an after-school program for low-income black and brown middle-school students, admits that her new learning has forced her to "venture forth" into places "formerly forbidden," places she used to consider "ominous and dangerous." Even though she has lived in Chicago for the past thirty years—first as a graduate student, then as a research professor—Roma had never traveled far from the shadows of the university. She had never even dared to drive through "the mean streets" of the West Side with her car doors locked, never had a "real conversation" with an adolescent (she is single and without children of her own), never experienced being the token white person in a crowd of black folks, never felt so far outside her element. These were all new experiences that felt both exhilarating and terrifying to her. The hardest part of "venturing forth," she claims, was losing her fear, being willing to face the unknown, and ridding herself of the deeply ingrained prejudices that had contained her life and restricted her movements. Now, after almost a year of working with the kids, after months of awkwardness and many missteps, she has begun to feel a little bit more comfortable, a little less foreign, and a lot less afraid. Now when Roma teaches them astronomy, the subject that she loved the most when she was their age, she looks into their faces and occasionally recognizes herself. She can begin to see in them the curiosity and eagerness that she once felt. "The kid in me has been sparked!" she exclaims, looking amazed at the familiar sight she sees in this still-strange place.

Jock Raymond, a sixty-two-year-old successful entrepreneur, jets all over the world scoring big deals. He has always believed that, never mind the new technologies that he uses every day—cell phones, teleconferencing, a BlackBerry—the best deals are made face-to-face. There is no substitute for gazing into someone's eyes, watching someone's body language, and feeling someone's handshake. But recently Jock decided to take a university course online in music theory, something he had wanted to learn since his days playing trombone in his high-school jazz band. He had always been curious to know the "logic and design" behind jazz music, the "basic structures" that allowed for the improvisation. So, even though he is a "face-to-face kind of guy," he decided to "cross the border into cyberspace." Now he finds himself, after a high-powered business meeting at the Taj Mahal Hotel in New Delhi, racing back to his hotel room and logging on to his computer, in order to complete a homework assignment. Not only does the learning online require a "different kind of discipline" and a "private kind of accountability," but it also seems to combine the odd sensation of intimacy and anonymity with his long-distance professor. In cyberspace, he experiences a new creativity, a new way of learning. He feels freer to ask "dumb" questions, freer to pursue his peaks of curiosity, freer to take risks, freer to fail. He says, "Cyberspace is my new frontier." Grinning, he shifts metaphors, "I feel like a kid in a candy shop!" Work crosses over into play. The distance between New Delhi and New York City disappears into nothing. "The border becomes the natural sight of creation."

THE NOMADIC LIFE

Katrina Adams, a successful, internationally renowned portrait painter, whose Third Chapter career was launched ten years ago, when she was in her early fifties, sees her whole life as a series of border crossings. "My first two chapters," she confesses, "were completely nomadic." By far, the most important move was "geographic and psychological." Right after she finished high school, Katrina made her "great escape" from the Midwest to the Northeast—from a family "steeped in conservatism" where she had always felt like "something of a stranger," to a place where she knew no one but felt more "at home." "It was like I had been born to the wrong parents, at the wrong time, in the wrong place," she says with resignation and sadness.

Katrina remembers spending most of her youth feeling deep-down like an artist, but always having to battle her parents' pejorative view of artists and their suspicions of the art world. "I grew up in Minneapolis, in a family of teachers," she says, in discussing the limited career options that her parents thought appropriate for their daughter. They let her know, in no uncertain terms, that she could be either a teacher or a nurse. Katrina did not like either alternative, so she chose the one that was at least a little bit different from her parents' vocation, and went directly from high school into nursing school.

For the first three years, she managed to tolerate the classroom instruction, although she was very suspicious of Western medicine and knew even then that "doctors and nurses rarely carefully observed or listened to their patients." She felt that medical professionals had an arrogance about them that did not allow patients any authority or insight in finding ways to heal themselves. "My personal belief—and I knew it even as a young girl—is that our bodies tell us what we need to fix ourselves." By the time Katrina reached her clinical rotation, she was completely fed up with "traditional medicine" and turned off by nursing. Not only did she object to the way that medicine was practiced, but she also could not stand the hierarchies in the hospital, the way the nurses took orders from the doctors although they were often closer to the lives and needs of their patients, and the way the nurses often took out their frustration and rage on the nurse's aides, or even on the patients. The hierarchies and symbols of status got in the way of delivering good medicine to, and building relationships with, patients. So, six months before she was to graduate, Katrina quit. "I walked out. I didn't like taking orders."

It was clear to Katrina that she could no longer endure nursing school, but she felt lost as soon as she left: she had no plan, few skills, and no clear purpose. She spent the next two years traveling around, doing odd jobs, and trying to survive. Wherever she landed, Katrina was always carrying a sketch pad and drawing what she saw around her. Drawing kept her company; it was something she knew she was good at, and a way to chronicle the chaos of her life. At one point, when she had landed in Wellfleet, on Cape Cod, she got a job caretaking an old aristocratic alcoholic lady ("No one was ever allowed to talk about the fact that she was alcoholic"). Whenever she had a few hours off, Katrina would escape down to the ocean's edge with her sketch pad and take in the gorgeous coastal scene. Pretty soon she began to draw the parade of people walking by the water, and soon after that, she decided that she might be able to earn some money drawing their portraits. So she began a little business, charging the tourists five dollars for a portrait. There was a fellow down the beach who was doing the same thing, but he was charging his customers fifteen dollars. He did not appreciate the new competition (particularly since Katrina's portraits were superior to his), so he got the local police to chase her away. Katrina is laughing as she recalls the scene. "The guy had me arrested. All of a sudden there was a policeman bearing down on me, grabbing me by the scruff of my neck." She remembers his gruff, dismissive voice. "All of you artists are the same," he said.

Rather than being frightened or alarmed, Katrina felt a sudden surge of gratitude. "It was a discovery moment for me!" she says, her voice still filled with awe. The policeman could not have said anything more wonderful. "I said to myself, 'Yes, I am an artist.'" The police didn't even take her down to the station; they just gave her a tough warning, told her to stay away from the harbor, and sent her on her way. The epiphany—for that is what it was—that, yes, she was an artist, made her feel immediately happy. She knew that she had found her calling, her purpose, her dream. But, at the very same time, Katrina could sense her parents' dismay and disapproval. She knew, without even talking to them, that they would not like the direction she was about to take. "My family would rather that I was a prostitute," says Katrina, only half joking. "When she found out, my mother actually lied to people. She told them that I was a secretary."

Only hours after being picked up by the police, Katrina had found a pay phone and was calling an art school in New York City, the Institute of Design, to see if she could enroll there. It was lunchtime, and the secretaries were not at their desks, so the president picked up the phone himself, and was captured by the urgent, charming voice at the other end of the line. Before the end of the day, he had told Katrina that she was admitted, given her a scholarship, and found her a part-time job. "Bless him," says Katrina three times in discussing the "miraculous string of events" that began her journey into the world of art.

Katrina tries to tell me how unprepared and innocent she was in approaching art school, how out of her league she felt among her teachers and peers. She knew for sure that she could draw concisely and beautifully, that she could figuratively reproduce everything she laid her eyes on. But beyond that she knew nothing about art. "I didn't know that paint came in tubes. When I talked to the president, he had asked whether I had a portfolio, and I had no idea what he meant. I had never been to a museum and seen a painting." It was all a strange new scene, exciting and overwhelming, and Katrina approached it hungrily, wanting to devour every bit of information, every shred of insight.

The day after she arrived at school, Katrina walked the several blocks over to the museum, her first time entering these hallowed halls. She could feel her heart quickening, her pulse racing. She found her way to a gallery where many of the portraits by the "old masters" were hanging—Titian, Raphael, John Singer Sargent, Winslow Homer—and she stood there awestruck. She had simply never seen anything as breathtakingly beautiful, or anything as emotionally moving, in her whole life. Katrina recalls the moment as if it were yesterday, with tears shooting to her eyes. "I saw the old masters' paintings—the luminosity, and the extraordinary light on the surface—and I burst into tears." And once her crying began, she couldn't stop the floodgate of emotion. When one of the guards approached her and asked whether anything was wrong and how he might help her, all she could do was give him a sign of reassurance. These were tears of joy, not sadness. Right then and there— standing and weeping before the luminous paintings—Katrina decided that one day she would become an artist in the tradition of the old masters. There was no doubt in her mind; she could see it all so clearly.

The art school that Katrina was attending ("the only one that would admit me"), however, was not a school for the fine arts; it was not a place to study the old masters. The school's curriculum was focused on the graphic arts, on teaching the commercial side of the art world. So, when Katrina dried off her tears, returned to school, and asked her teachers to introduce her to the work she had just seen at the museum, they could only laugh. "They told me to draw a mayonnaise jar," Katrina says, smiling. Now, forty years later, Katrina applauds her graphic-arts training, and says that she is glad that this was the place where she got her start. In fact, a central part of the curriculum was life drawing, which they did three days a week for three years. But beyond teaching how to capture the human body figuratively, the school also turned out to be a place where students received very disciplined training in the "craft" of art production, and for that Katrina feels doubly grateful.

After finishing art school, Katrina got married ("to the first man who walked down the street and said he wanted children"), had two sons in quick succession, got divorced, and barely scraped out a living over the next couple of decades doing commercial art—painting signs, designing books, and decorating yachts. "At least I had a brush in my hand," she says gratefully about the work, which, though often tedious and physically strenuous, allowed her to hone her graphic skills and make a modest living. All along she knew "deep-down" that she was developing the craft, the discipline, and the work ethic that would one day allow her to "paint like the old masters."

A second marriage, to a generous and strong man who loved her "artistic soul," allowed Katrina the space and resources to follow her dream. "William was not threatened by what I could do," says Katrina with gratitude and admiration. "I had never experienced that before. He is a guy who is confident and comfortable inside himself. My success didn't diminish him." His appreciation and support have "liberated" Katrina, allowed her "to reach for the stars," to "take the lid off" of any former inhibitions or constraints. After all of those border crossings—from Minneapolis to Cape Cod, from nursing to art school, from the fragility of single parenting to a strong partnership, from a life of struggle to one of "abundance"—in her Third Chapter, Katrina finally has the resources and the "emotional space" she needs to "return home" to herself. She believes that each of these border crossings has helped to make the homecoming "that much sweeter."

BOUNDARIES OF PLACE:
PRIVATE AND PUBLIC ART

I make my way to Fiona Featherstone's studio, a wooden storefront space, on a tiny back street in a working-class neighborhood in Waltham, a suburb of Boston. The outside of her studio matches the weathered gray buildings on the street, which seem to crouch modestly close to the ground, but everything inside her space is saturated in rich and radiant colors. Magenta and deep-orange pillows are there to lean on; bright mobiles hang from the ceiling; sculptures of clay and metal are placed in corners, on ledges, and on windowsills. There are bowls of fruit to eat. Miles Davis's *Sketches of Spain* is playing softly in the background. The back door of the studio opens to a huge green backyard that seems to go on for miles. An old rowboat sits in the midst of the trees. Fiona leaves the door open, and the sound of the rain falling feels soft and soothing. The whole environment is intensely busy and peaceful, rigorously organized and improvisational, like a work space and a playground.

We sit together in her studio, surrounded by the beauty of her quilts, gorgeously hung on one large wall. There are a series of pieces representing changing water levels, the idea inspired by Al Gore's film, *An Inconvenient Truth*. On the back wall of her workroom there are hundreds of fabrics from all around the world, neatly organized by color and texture. There is a long worktable for drawing, cutting, and composing; another table for sewing and putting the pieces together. There is a window seat, on which Fiona sits with her legs folded under her; her hands carve shapes in the air as she talks.

I perch on a painted chair facing her, trying to take in the beauty of this Fiona-created scene. I think to myself that I can learn so much about this artist's "new adventures in learning" by taking in the setting that she has designed—the place that has always been, as she says, a "place of retreat" and has now become the "site of the action." This is the space, the asylum, where Fiona Featherstone, a seventy-year-old quilter, gathers her energy and ideas, the place where she creates her art. It is also the space where she has recently invited groups of people in to work together on "public art."

Fiona then walks around the studio to show me her work, picking up pieces that trace the process of the collaborative, community work that she has launched, called the Mandala Project. I listen, trying to get used to the rapid cadence of her voice, words and ideas swirling around in patterns—like a quilt—that only become apparent after I listen for a while. She is a visual thinker; her language is full of imagery. The idea for the project was spawned soon after the shocking and devastating 9/11 attacks, which catapulted Fiona into a state of chronic anxiety and terror. Each night, she would find herself waking up from ugly nightmares of death and destruction, unable to get the bloody, mangled bodies out of her mind, unable to erase the sounds of children crying for their lost parents, or firefighters weeping for their brothers crushed under mountains of debris.

Her terror lingered for days and weeks after, demanding a response, an action.

Like so many other times in Fiona's life—a life that has been committed to art and healing, art and justice—she called together six or eight of her artist friends from around Boston and invited them to dinner. Gathered around the big round cherry table in her home, they ate and talked; they grieved and raged; they spun out ideas and fantasized scenarios; they challenged one another, their serious, urgent dialogue punctuated by laughter. Many potluck dinners followed, during which the conversations lasted late into the night. Ideas sprang up in such a way that it was hard afterward to pin down who had authored them. The round table is always the place where projects are conceived and take shape; something about the mix of food and friends and good talk releases the imagination and nourishes the soul.

The Mandala Project grew out of these soulful exchanges—a local, city-wide activity designed to be a response to the global despair that everyone was feeling so acutely. It is fascinating that one of the first responses to violence, to fear and despair, is often not words, not argument, not analysis. When we feel desperate, words will not do. They do not seem cathartic or productive; they will not carry our complex emotions. The New York City public-school teachers from District One, who could see the fiery destruction of 9/11 from their classroom windows, knew this intuitively. When they were looking for a way to help their young students rage and grieve, they turned away from the formal curriculum and turned not to words but to art. They asked their students to draw their fears, paint their pain, dance their anguish, and rap their rage. The raw emotions got channeled into art when words would not do. The stories got told through poetry and murals and hip-hop. The teachers knew to begin there: the vulnerable place where intense and inchoate feelings can be splashed out on the canvas. And, of course, the magnificent AIDS quilts—sewn two decades ago, that honored the thousands of lives lost to the AIDS virus, traveling around the country in a solemn procession of love and mourning—were also an act of communal outrage, an anguished collective memory.

I imagine that the folks who came together around Fiona's table must have intuited the same thing as the New York City teachers, and they must have felt inspired by the exquisite example of the AIDS quilters. They knew that words and arguments would not do, that analysis was not enough, that the project would have to be built on emotion, and that art would have to be the medium, the center of a collective response to our fragile and troubled world.

But even art did not seem to be enough to capture the feelings. Fiona and her friends searched for a communal response—one rooted in human connection, carved out of culture and tradition, "animated by the Spirit." Quilts seemed the perfect artistic and collective medium, the apt creative metaphor for mending and healing. For hundreds of years, quilt makers—almost always women—have been the community builders, gathering in their living rooms or around the kitchen table, telling stories, sharing news, providing support, offering comfort to one another. Quilting has always been as much about creating community as it has been about making art; as much about collaboration as about individual expression. The folks gathered around Fiona's cherry table began to envision the ways in which the traditional art form of quilt making—generous, organic, and communal—might be a beautiful antidote to the violence and devastation enveloping our world.

As they began to concoct the idea of the Mandala Project, Fiona happened to see a documentary on *Frontline* called "Faith and Doubt at Ground Zero," which got her thinking about the rich diversity of faith traditions in the city, and about the complex history of institutionalized religion that has been the site for exclusion and oppression as well as liberation and justice. Could quilt making become the site for communities of faith to come together for spiritual nourishment? Could quilting be the medium for collections of believers to explore their traditions, rituals, values, and beliefs, and in the process discover their connections to people from other faith traditions? "I am a lover of exotic opportunities," says Fiona. "Quilts became the vision, the goal for this anthropology project."

Women gather in groups of eight to ten in their living rooms, in schools, in church basements, in synagogues and mosques, in Fiona's studio. A few are quilters, but most have never had any experience making quilts, and some have never even sewn a stitch. The facilitators, all experienced quilters, come from the original dinner guests at Fiona's table; each takes responsibility for leading three or four groups. Fiona keeps a guiding hand on the entire project, overseeing the architecture of the whole—serving as the leader for some groups, a cheerleader for others, a mediator and firefighter when conflicts arise that need an outside, experienced voice. Tibetan women and children meet each Monday night at a Tibetan restaurant in Watertown where, at the end of their session, they are treated to a luscious meal. Muslim women gather with their daughters in a large basement room at their mosque in Dorchester. Quaker women sit together in a circle at the Meeting House in Cambridge, lighting scented candles and talking in low voices. The Unitarian women from Concord, all quilters, come together in their homes and studios, and chronicle their process with video cameras and journals.

In the end, there are as many as fifty quilting groups—with

close to four hundred participants in all—scattered across the city of Boston and reaching into the near suburbs. They are from every faith tradition: Muslims and Mormons, Jews and Hindus, Pentecostals and Episcopalians, Catholics and born-again Christians. Fiona recalls, "At first my thought was that the people would reach out beyond their churches, mosques, and synagogues, beyond their field of familiarity and comfort. . . . Instead, almost everyone stayed within their faith group." Fiona, who calls herself a "deeply spiritual person," admits that her naïveté about people coming together in diverse groups probably grew out of the fact that she does not practice any religion ("As a matter of fact, I'm allergic to institutionalized religion"), and that she had not understood the need for women to feel "safe and rooted" in their religious traditions. Nor had she fully appreciated the deep entanglements between religion and culture, between the expression of religious symbols and metaphors and their representation in artistic imagery.

Each session lasts for four hours, as women share their stories and spiritual journeys, talk about the limits of their faith, and exchange ideas for how their faith might be represented visually and aesthetically. These are hard and intense conversations, during which women learn to speak up, to listen, to compromise; as conflicts arise, differences are aired, temperaments clash, and efforts are made at reasoning and reconciliation. Learning to be together and produce something collaboratively is at least as hard as learning to design and cut and sew. "In this process, people come with deeply passionate views that often feel polarized. A big challenge is to navigate the conflicts and move toward collaboration," says Fiona a bit wearily. "My job is to try to keep it moving, to not let them become too discouraged, to keep them focused on the work rather than on some defense of their point of view."

Piles of beautiful fabrics of many colors and textures sit in big baskets around the room. Each person begins by producing a "self-portrait," an initial effort at self-reflection, a first attempt at working with the materials. There are few rules or constraints, but Fiona insists that everyone participate: "No one can just watch and observe." Fiona begins with self-portraits not because they are easy, but because she believes that they allow everyone to have a personal point of reference, and because she assumes that each person knows herself better than anyone else does. The exercise offers two major challenges. The first is technical: people find it hard to turn cloth into features. "How do you create a smile?" says Fiona. "It turns out to be very hard to make yourself look happy." The second challenge reflects people's reluctance to portray themselves, to choose and then reveal a core part of their identity to one another. Fiona believes—she has faith—that everyone is capable of mastering the exercise in her own idiosyncratic way, even though she knows that "many of them were told as children that they were not good at art, and that has produced in them a fear and a shyness."

Fiona offers words of encouragement as she works to demystify the process. She tries to inspire them with rich and colorful fabrics that "allow for a lot of imagery." Some people respond to the challenge in very adventurous and imaginative ways, but others get stuck on not being able to capture their images in a literal way. Quite soon Fiona is able to tell which among them have artistic ability—the women who might be technically able to tackle the more difficult pieces of the quilt design. After an hour or so, Fiona always asks the group to take a break and look at one another's work, to "see how other people are solving problems."

During the second session, the women begin to have a conversation about the ideas and conception for the quilt, about how they might want to portray the central tenets of their faith. It is often hard for them to give voice to the flood of feelings that come to them in the conversation. Inevitably, the dialogue brings up echoes from their childhoods—stories about the ways in which they resisted and embraced their faiths growing up; about whether they experienced their faiths as inhibiting or liberating, as safe or treacherous territories. Often, their voices struggle in drawing out the differences between faith and religion, between public and private expressions of spirituality. It usually takes two or three sessions for ideas and images to begin to converge, and the group finds a way to articulate a design for the "mandala." Fiona explains that the "mandala" is a "symbolic representation of the world." First drawn on a big piece of paper, this becomes the blueprint or design for the quilt; it also reflects the collective voice of the group and becomes the title of the quilting project.

From then on, the sessions focus on a refinement of the mandala as an expression of the spiritual themes of faith, and the development of the pieces that will be incorporated into the design. There is always a back-and-forth between the conceptual conversation and the art making, between the envisioning and the quilting. The quilts take months to make. Some groups proceed relatively smoothly; others get mired in technical difficulties that require patient problem solving; still others get mired in ideological haggles and personality conflicts. But all manage, in the end, to produce a quilt that is a "spiritual cry for peace"—"women's voices and art trying to make the world safer for their children." The fifty quilts are hung together in a large domed exhibition at the Boston Center for the Arts for all to see; the quiet and elegant end product gives no hint of the hard-won, heart-wrenching collaboration of the novice quilters.

In crossing the boundaries of place—from the private asylum

of her studio to the public project of quilt making—Fiona discovers "a whole new repertoire" of learning. She learns, for example, the mix of aggressiveness and restraint that it takes to reach out and recruit people from diverse backgrounds and neighborhoods all over the city. "I found myself behaving like a fearless ethnographer," she says about how she managed to stamp out some of the initial reticence she felt when she "made her pitch to people." As an artist who had always enjoyed working by herself, at her own pace, in "playful, fanciful imagination," Fiona also had to learn the art of collaboration. Over time, she learned to be patient with an inefficient, imperfect creative process; and she learned to be attentive to other people's ideas and feelings. She worked hard on learning to guide without dominating, teach without being patronizing, and listen more and talk less. Finally, she had to—and this was the hardest part of all—learn to "give up trying to control everything" and "have faith" that things would turn out okay.

Like Fiona—who claims to be a "lover of exotic opportunities" and uses the metaphor of ethnography to describe her Third Chapter learning—several of the women and men I interviewed speak of their explorations across new boundaries as "anthropological" expeditions. By that they mean that their new learning takes them to foreign places where they feel like awkward strangers, inept travelers, vulnerable observers. They must learn a new language, acclimate to a new set of norms and behaviors, and participate in strange new ceremonies, rituals, and routines. They must try as hard as they can to see things the way the "indigenous" people see them. After a while, they hope to learn enough about the place and its people to begin to see the strange as familiar, the exotic as ordinary.

Like anthropologists trying to understand another culture, new learners must sometimes act before they really understand what they are doing, throwing themselves into the action and being swept along in the momentum, hoping that through osmosis, intuition, and faith the learning will sink in. This was certainly the case for Roma Wolfe, who spent months traveling from her Hyde Park neighborhood to the West Side, standing up and mouthing the words she thought a teacher should say, but feeling as if she "wasn't making a dent, didn't understand anything, and didn't have a clue about how to communicate"—yet knowing all along that she had to jump in way before she was ready. "It was like play-acting," she says about the "hardest work" she has ever experienced.

In her book of essays, *Willing to Learn*, Mary Catherine Bateson talks about this act—of diving into the fray before you feel ready or knowledgeable enough—as one of the signatures of Third Chapter learning. "My own belief," she writes, "is that a commitment to lifelong learning is, for many people, a spiritual stance, requiring both humility and openness, for to learn, one must often participate before one understands."[2] Bateson gives the example of an Armenian grace she learned by listening to her husband's family recite it at the dinner table. She immediately began to participate in this ritual, saying the grace as she understood it. Years later, she realized she had been saying one of the words wrong, a slight change in pronunciation that changed the meaning. But by jumping in to participate, she was able to learn rapidly—even if not entirely correctly—and to be part of something important, to share a connection. Anyone who has traveled abroad, or tried to learn a new language as an adult, knows that learning happens best when we allow ourselves to be fully absorbed, to participate, to make mistakes. This kind of openness requires humility, the willingness to take risks, the capacity to look foolish, and, if we are lucky, a lightness of style and a well-developed sense of humor.

BOUNDARIES OF THOUGHT:
ABUNDANCE AND SCARCITY

A distinguished neurobiologist, sixty-eight-year-old Anna Nielson engages in new learning as she crosses disciplinary boundaries within the academy. Like Fiona, who moves from private to public work, from the quiet asylum of her studio to the messy reality of communal art, Anna travels from the "controlled environment" of a research laboratory to unwieldy forays into policy analysis and activism. And, like Fiona, several times during our interview she speaks of herself as an "activist anthropologist." Anna had spent most of her professional life in a university laboratory doing research on the tactile, nurturing relationships of primates, always working within the boundaries of rigorous empiricism. She had always loved the discipline and control of science: the data and the number crunching; the indisputable facts; and the authority and expertise that grow out of knowing what you know for sure. But all the time she worked in the lab, she had felt the urge to try to figure out ways of making her science relevant to the "real world." She had always asked herself, for example, if there might be anything she was learning in her observations of maternal attachment between female monkeys and their young infants that could inform our understanding of healthy bonding between human mothers and babies.

Ever since Nielson took a course her senior year in high school called "Problems in Democracy," she had wanted to "make a difference and participate in the struggle for equality and fairness in our society—in the world." The themes and perspective of this course—which she experienced as "so compelling and exciting" as a teenager—continue to be central in Anna's work today. As she remembers it, the curriculum was a blend of "critical thinking and interdisciplinary perspectives—

psychology, sociology, and economics—and the ways those frameworks shape our views of social problems and social remedies." Anna was so thrilled by this course, by its intellectual rigor and its grounding in real issues, that she decided she would apply for early admission to college. She planned to get a head start by enrolling in summer school, hoping eventually to major in psychology. Her choice was impetuous and naïve. Anna knew almost nothing about the academic discipline of psychology ("I didn't even know how to spell it! I didn't know whether it began with an 's' or a 'p' "), but she believed that studying psychology would prepare her to do "all these good things in the world." She thought psychology would be "a serious, legitimate way to make the world a better place."

Anna reminds me of the political context in which she was making these "urgent adolescent decisions." This was a time when the Cold War was waging, when people were talking about "the Russians brainwashing us," when Edward R. Murrow was courageously challenging the lies and paranoia of McCarthyism. But when she actually began taking psychology courses in college, she soon realized that they were not the best preparation for "changing the world." The courses were actually rarely about "doing" anything. "The real world," in fact, tended to be seen as a distraction from the rigors of the discipline, the reliability of the methods, or the validity of the findings. Anna quickly came to the conclusion that psychology was neither real enough nor scientific enough for her taste. Rather, it felt like some uncomfortable blend—an academic diet that didn't satisfy her taste for intellectual rigor *or* social activism.

"But all the while, I loved science," says Anna passionately. "There was this alluring reductionism to the empirical approach," she says, recalling her decision in her sophomore year to change her major from psychology to biology. "I loved finding out what actually happened." She relished the facts, the data, the certainty, the answers. She even enjoyed that the study was removed from the heavy political debates that were raging at the time, that it could be reduced to pure and objective truths. "You could experiment, manipulate things, and get an answer as opposed to use the work to support debates or conflicts, winning or losing." Anna also discovered—in retrospect—that biology kept her close to her Midwestern roots. "Being from the Midwest, I always felt that I was a barnyard socialist. I was fascinated with the idea of evolution, relationships, and likenesses among animal and plant life. In the country, you learn from the ways that animals exist and farms operate—in a holistic way. You learn that everything is interconnected, everything has a purpose."

But even after Anna had switched from "studying attitude change" as an undergraduate in psychology, and even after succumbing to the allure of the "reductionism" of experimental science, she wanted to find a way to "bring social-justice issues into the laboratory." She took a course with Harry Harlow, the famous primate researcher, and then joined him as a research assistant, observing how baby monkeys respond to a lack of maternal contact and stimulation. She saw these young primates develop into isolated, "autistic" creatures; she saw the wounds and scars resulting from the early physical and emotional deprivation. This was fascinating work—"rational, empirical, scientific"—that Anna hoped would one day be transferable to human issues beyond the laboratory.

Her rigorous undergraduate training in biology led to a doctorate in neurobiology, with Anna continuing to work in the laboratory on issues of attachment in primates. Early on, she was recognized as a rigorous and imaginative young scientist and as an excellent grant writer, able to raise research money successfully from governmental and nongovernmental sources. Her three-decades-long career in neurobiology included faculty and research positions at some of the most elite universities and labs around the country. Her work was well funded, her research published in the most distinguished scientific journals.

At her sixtieth-birthday party, Anna remembers blowing out the candles and feeling with a sudden urgency the finiteness of her life. She recalls, "It was like I felt this huge wave of anxiety come over me about the time I had left—like I had this big, newborn sense that I must do the things I had left undone for too long." Even though she did not act on her impulse immediately, Anna began to see everything through the "lens of time." A move to another university in a new city forced an immediate reappraisal. Anna remembers arriving at her new faculty position feeling a strong determination to "bridge theory and practice." She began to write grant proposals that explicitly focused on the integration of these realms, particularly on the ways in which good science might inform public policy. She was able to secure funding, for example, to study orphans in Romania, whose experience of deprivation and lack of stimulation made them behave much like Harlow's monkeys. The research included traveling to the orphanages in Romania and collecting stress hormones through saliva samples, to demonstrate the scientific connections between emotional deprivation and stress levels.

The Romanian research led her to ask, "Why can't brain studies be used to support public policies that further the development of children? How can these scientific studies be incorporated? How can the evidence be presented in such a way that it becomes part of the political discourse and decision making?" The questions consumed her, but the connections eluded her. She knew that in order to answer these questions, she needed to explore new intellectual frameworks, travel across new boundaries of thought. Just as she had begun to recognize the limits and constraints of her own discipline of neurobiology, she needed to understand more about public policy. She felt, for the first time since completing her Ph.D., the need for more "formalized training." Anna decided to return to school.

Later on, Anna tells me that her "new learning" is always a response to "wanting to get something done." It never feels like "a choice"; it feels more like an imperative. Whether it is her work in the Romanian orphanages, or the work that she is currently engaged in on HIV/AIDS in East Africa, Anna always feels compelled by the "need," and then tries to learn what she has to learn in order to be of some help. Her voice is as passionate as I have heard it when she describes her motivation for the new learning that helped to prepare her for her work in Africa. "It is not that I was good at survey research or really knew anything about virology, but we knew we had to do it, and in order to do it, we had to learn to do it. We had to experience it, and become students of the scene and of the methodologies that would help us understand what was going on and how to intervene effectively. This was obligatory. You think, 'I've got to be there!' We are global citizens, and we need to do it. This is not a guilt thing; it is an imperative for us."

A school of public policy seemed like the perfect place to seek the formal training that Anna needed in order to answer her burning questions and in order to bridge "science and policy" more effectively. She was admitted to a two-year master's program in which she studied with some of the leading figures whose work has joined research and policy, particularly the federal and state policies related to poverty, families, and children, and she found that this time around—now in her early sixties—she "loved" being a student. "I didn't want to sit in the front row, raise my hand, or take center stage," she recalls. "Instead, I liked sitting in the corner, reflecting, observing, curious, witnessing, listening." She felt both relaxed and fully engaged, reflective and turned on, playful and serious, and she loved witnessing herself as a learner, conscious of which things she could understand with great ease and facility, and which felt opaque and difficult.

Early on in her studies, she found her mentor: a world-renowned economist, a "gentle and generous man." When she enrolled in his class on "social economics," she felt immediately captivated by him, by "his brilliance and his kindness." She came to the class knowing nothing at all about the discipline of economics. (Laughing, at herself, she tells me later that when she took the admissions exam for the public-policy school, she had no idea what "S and D" meant, and had to be told that those letters referred to "supply and demand.") She soon learned not only that she had to learn a new language and terminology, but also that the discipline of economics was a "total paradigm shift" away from her work in neurobiology. Anna explains, "Economics is a zero-sum game. It is a science of scarce resources. By contrast, neurobiology is the science of abundant resources. We all have too many neurons, too many connections, too many synapses. The development of the brain is a sculpturing process, a carving out, removing, pruning of pathways that are no longer useful." Like most people who know their fields deeply and well, Anna offers this lesson about the development of the brain simply and clearly, hoping to communicate the major paradigm shift that her "new learning" required. As she began to draw the disciplinary contrasts, she began to realize that if "resources were to be more fairly distributed" then public policies needed to be driven not by the tenets of brain research but by the assumptions of economic theory.

It took deep and focused study to begin to learn the discipli-

nary boundaries and frameworks of economic theory, to begin to
master the language and the rhetoric, and to begin to recognize
the discipline's limitations and blind spots. This kind of book
learning required that Anna enter what she describes as an
"incubation period." "This was not a very social time. I was
curled up at home or stuck in the stacks of the library—this was
before we were all using the Internet—devouring everything I
could get my hands on, having a reclusive period. . . . I read
everything that my mentor had written." She also read Hume
and Kant, and eventually took on the opaque and difficult prose
of Jürgen Habermas. But this time Anna, in her maturity and
with a self-confidence that grows with experience, read not just
for understanding but also with a discerning and critical eye.
She wanted to learn not only how the various scholars saw
things but also whether their arguments made sense to her.
Interested in what was missing or left out, she probed the text
and the subtext of the scholars' analyses.

Fortunately, in her mentor Anna found a teacher who was
intellectually curious, who relished hard questions, who was always eager to learn something new. One day, after spending
weeks slugging through the "opaque, dreary, and thick prose of
Habermas"—first reading the translations from the German,
then the secondary sources that interpreted his theories—Anna
approached her mentor with a hard question, one that was a
direct challenge to his work. In reading Habermas, she had been
intrigued by how his theory emphasized the idea of "community," how he focused on the relational dynamics that bind people together and support collective action for social change. She
recognized that Habermas's perspective—which featured social
relationships and collective action—was quite different from the
views of her mentor, whose economic theory focused on the
actions and motivations of individuals.

Armed with a still-naïve understanding of Habermas, but

eager to share her emerging insights, Anna queried her mentor respectfully, pointing out what she thought might be missing from his approach. She asked, "Do you think your approach might be limited in not taking into account the social relations among people as a positive force for community change?" Her mentor could hear that Anna's question was motivated by genuine curiosity, and he knew that she was a very disciplined student, so he listened carefully before he responded. And his response was both openhearted and self-critical; he weighed her points very carefully. "It was almost like he received my question like a gift," recalls Anna. "There was reciprocity and respect there. At that moment, I felt like a student and a colleague. He was able to see the edge of his work. It is amazing when your mentor listens, takes you seriously, and says, go with it."

So, over the next several months, Anna bored into the Habermas texts even more deeply, and her readings helped her to see more clearly the connections between "thinking and doing"—the ways in which social science can inform social action and vice versa. As we talk together, Anna suddenly realizes that Habermas's work might also offer useful lessons to those of us in our Third Chapters who are trying to navigate the "borders of new learning." She explains to me that his theory outlines three stages of "boundary crossing." The first has to do with "perspective taking" or empathy—that is, with being able to take on the role of the other, and stand in his/her shoes. The second stage is "mutual understanding"—a place of resolve, where people decide to agree on certain key goals and approaches, even if differences and disagreements among them remain, because only then can the group work together to take collective action. Anna tells me that this is the hardest stage, requiring deep listening, patience, and mutual respect; requiring that people submerge their individual differences for the benefit of the group. The third and final stage is about taking action, actually doing something. "This is the transformative part," says Anna. "The whole thing is not just to sit around, ruminate, and talk. The talk must lead to action."

It is not that Anna believes Habermas has "the answer," but that his theory seems to be an important piece of the puzzle that she has been working on for decades now. Her senior high-school course "Problems in Democracy" was the first place where she tried to work through the relationship between thinking about ideas and doing things in the world; and ever since then—as a disciplined and rigorous laboratory scientist, as a student of public policy, as a social scientist working in the field, gathering data and designing interventions—she has been border crossing. In her Third Chapter, Anna has been engaged in "new learning" that has introduced her to the opportunities and limits of disciplinary thinking, the light and the shadows that are part of any single explanatory theory, and, like her mentor, she has begun to see "the edges of her work."

The stories of Roma, Jock, Katrina, Fiona, and Anna recall the intellectual, aesthetic, emotional, and relational dimensions of border crossing that lead to new learning in the Third Chapter for many of the women and men I interviewed. Whether they are crossing the borders from Hyde Park to the West Side, from face-to-face space to cyberspace, from the Midwest to the Northeast, from the commercial arts to fine art, from private to public arenas, from neurobiology to economics, from science to public policy, they follow many of the same steps, and these steps remind them of an ethnographer seeking to learn a new culture from the inside out.

The first step is curiosity. Women and men who decide to navigate the boundaries of learning begin with a deep curiosity about what they will find on the other side. They are interested in knowing something new, understanding the way something works, asking the probing questions, and seeking a new way of being in the world. Their curiosity makes them wonder what is happening behind closed doors; their questions are impertinent, persistent, compelling, nagging. In his book *Invitation to Sociology*, Peter Berger claims that good ethnographers have a temperamental inclination toward curiosity. They begin with the assumption that "things are not what they seem to be," which pushes them to examine the layers underneath the surface, the subtext underneath the text, the face underneath the mask. They discover that the uncovering of each layer transforms their understanding of the whole. Then they get ready for the surprise, the unexpected. As a matter of fact, Berger claims that the real challenge for curiosity seekers—especially those who are crossing boundaries of thought rather than traveling across geographical distances—"is to experience culture shock minus geographical displacement."[3] The curiosity almost inevitably opens the way for surprising experiences that transform what it is we expected to find, pushing the learning in unexpected directions.

The second step that border crossers must overcome focuses on letting go of the fear—the fear of the unknown and the fear of failure. All the people I spoke to talked about ridding themselves of fear as an essential step of the journey across borders. They spoke of first needing to recognize and name the fear, and then needing to conquer it—not by some rational listing of pros and cons, benefits and liabilities, but by deciding to take the courageous "leap of faith." Once they do take the leap and seize the opportunity, they face the possibility of failure, and the probability—at least in the short run—of making fools of themselves. Some people are fortunate enough to have temperaments that seem to blunt the fear, making the awkwardness and imbalance of new learning not seem so terrifying. Katrina Adams, for example, claims that her fearlessness is driven by a single-minded drive and a fierce determination to knock down the doors that were once closed to her. "I am like a pit bull," she says many times during our interview. "Once I get my teeth into something, I refuse to let go."

Anna Nielson also describes herself as "fearless." She almost never shies away from something "novel, or inappropriate, or unexpected." Her fearlessness is linked to a quality in her that just doesn't seem to respond to insults and other people's harsh judgments of her. It is not so much that she has a thick skin; rather, she does not even seem to notice the accusation. She remembers several times in her life—from childhood to recent adulthood—when she "just didn't take in what was going on." When she was in graduate school, for example, one of her fellow students said in front of a group of her peers that Anna was an "enigma." His tone was not kind; actually, it was a barely veiled insult. When Anna did not respond, another of the students translated for her. "So-and-so just insulted you, Anna." "Oh, really," said Anna, "what did he say?" She was "clueless." But the ability to withstand being "clueless" and the willingness to put up with "humiliation" are, Anna believes, a big part of a readiness to learn something new, especially, she says, if "you are making progress and if you are getting critical feedback." Finally, it helps if you can admit, out front, the things you know you can't do or don't want to learn to do better. "I'm a terrible hostess," Anna says without apology or remorse. "I can't dance, can't cook, I'm not musical—these things don't come naturally to me."

Even though most women and men I spoke to did not see

themselves as fearless or clueless, all of them spoke about "lightening up" and allowing themselves to look foolish in the face of learning something new. With maturity, they were willing to risk being the brunt of the joke; in fact, their best defense was to learn to laugh at themselves.

Losing the fear opened the way for step three of the border crossers' new learning—the willingness to be vulnerable, open, and exposed, to fail publicly, to experience embarrassment and humiliation. Several of the people I interviewed spoke about the value of failure as the most important diagnostic tool for learning, and the best way to learn how they learned. I visited the shop of a seventy-year-old furniture maker who had recently completed a two-year course at a craft-and-design school and was working on an elegant reproduction of a Victorian chest. A former FBI agent, he had always hated the paper pushing that chained him to his desk for too many hours, though he loved the exacting, probing, data-gathering detective work that he did in the field; most of all, he relished the problem solving. But his work at the FBI did not leave much room for mistakes, for lapses in judgment, for failure. Now, as he slowly, carefully, skillfully planes the wood for his chest—after spending months looking at furniture pieces from this period in museums and scrutinizing the details in the photographic plates found in books—he shows me evidence of things gone wrong: pieces out of balance, decorative elements cut too deeply, overly heavy, almost comic, claw-feet. These failures have taught him something new about the craft he is developing. He caresses one of the carefully saved, discarded examples, and claims, "This is the most efficient, most productive learning I have ever done." He sees the "public failures," which his fellow furniture makers in the shop are quick to point out, as an "invitation to learn something new," and he likes the new experience of not having to cover his mistakes the way he did in the FBI.

Developing empathy is the fourth step that boundary crossers must master in learning something new, or becoming someone new. They must be able to put themselves in the place of those who are their teachers, those whom they are seeking to understand, who have a different perspective or a strange way of doing things. Fiona discovered that she had to "inhabit the moccasins" of the women whom she was trying to recruit to join her quilting project; she had to figure out what might motivate them to participate, what might lure them into making art, especially since many of them had been told as children that they were neither creative nor artistic. Then she had to find a way to make them comfortable with the technical aspects of working with the fabrics, so she began by having them do self-portraits, not because it was technically easy, but because she figured that they knew themselves better than anyone else did. They could begin by working from a place of authority and strength. For Fiona, empathy became the bedrock of her new learning, the path toward mutual understanding.

The final step that boundary crossers recognize—they often see it in their rearview mirror—is that the new learning does not mean losing touch with life on the other side of the border. As a matter of fact, the work of the Third Chapter is integrative, like putting together the pieces of Fiona's quilts. Learners do not have to choose between this or that realm, this or that perspective. They find ways of embracing the contradictions and constructing something whole out of the disparate, divergent elements. Fiona Featherstone finds inspiration and fresh perspectives as she traverses the boundaries between her work as a solo artist, done all alone in her studio, working out her concerns—about the environment, globalism, justice, war, and peace—through quilt making; and her work as a public artist, seeking to build community among diverse groups and speak with a collective voice. Fiona claims that she needs to keep her public and private lives in "precarious balance." She needs the silence, structure, and reflective space of her studio in order to remain sane. But she needs the social contacts, the messiness, the discourse, and the energy from others to stay alive.

This pattern of movement that Fiona describes is why the women and men that I talked to rarely described the learning of discrete skills, or the mastering of a specific body of knowledge, as the result of their border crossings. Rather, they talked about more holistic changes in their character and "ways of being in the world." They recounted experiences of expanding their repertoire, broadening their range, "deepening their insights," "seeing the edges of their work," and learning patience and restraint. And they spoke about learning a way of listening, with attentiveness and empathy, that opened up a path to "new philosophical vistas." The border crossing allowed them to transgress and embrace the contradictions at the "natural site of creation," learning as they journeyed.

SIX

New Learning: Body, Voice, and Soul

The journey of learning in the Third Chapter crosses borders and covers landscapes that are rich with complexity and color. The geography is rocky and irregular, beautiful and tortured, full of hills and valleys, open vistas and blind alleys, and menaced by minefields. The path moves forward and circles back, progresses and regresses, is both constant and changing. The developmental terrain grows more layered; patience trumps speed; restraint trumps ambition; wisdom trumps IQ; "leaving a legacy" trumps "making our mark"; and a bit of humor saves us all. Earlier narratives framed the internal and external landscapes of our learning and the trajectories of our development; now we move to consider the actual processes involved in new learning—the interior, detailed picture of people actually engaged in learning. How do women and men in their Third Chapters find ways of changing, adapting, mastering, and channeling their energies, skills, and passions into new domains of learning? How do they experience vulnerability and uncertainty, learn from experimentation and failure, seek guidance and mentoring, join work and play, rigor and spontaneity, and develop new relationships of mentoring and support? As I listened to people's accounts of risk-taking and adventure in the Third Chapter, I was particularly intrigued by their processes of learning in three domains that I have named: body, voice, and soul.

There is a "different kind of knowing" that many people found almost impossible to describe in words—a knowing that resides in the body, in the hands, fingers, and posture of a jazz pianist, in the unconscious dream life of a painter, in the shifts "from left to right brain" in the craft of a furniture maker. This kind of knowing is confused and compromised by the mind's surveillance. Other interviewees talked about the empowering feeling of "discovering their voice"—a phrase they used both literally and metaphorically. Those who referred to it in the literal sense told stories about taking voice lessons, learning how to speak another language, and finding the courage to do public speaking. Those who used the phrase metaphorically, talked about discovering within themselves a newfound sense of authority and courage, of becoming truth tellers. Still others spoke about "becoming a different person" in their Third Chapters, a learning process that involved the depths of their souls, a reconstruction and a reorientation of their identity, their values, and their priorities. A businesswoman described the shift of focus in her life from "the external to the internal terrain"; an African American museum administrator and curator recalled the deepening of her racial identity and a "commitment" to her "ancestral legacies"; and an internationally renowned jazz musician claimed the full acceptance of his gay identity. "I used to say that I was a jazz musician who happened to be gay. Now I tell people I am a gay person who happens to be a jazz musician," he said without defensiveness.

I found these domains of new learning particularly intriguing for three reasons.

First, because, as men and women talked about their learning, their stories were threaded through with a palpable yearning, deeply felt emotions, and what one interviewee called an "unfamiliar inarticulateness." In telling their experiences of gaining mastery, people searched for words to express the "rush of inchoate feelings." They would have to "show" me, rather than "tell" me, what they were learning—a painstaking demonstration of "fumbling mastery." Words were rarely enough to convey their feelings about "the interior and exterior chaos" that they experienced before making a "small, barely noticeable breakthrough" in their learning.

Second, the learning in all three of these realms seemed to require that people challenge deeply imprinted cultural priorities and assumptions that had formerly dominated their lives and often defined their success. Said a woman film director, who was trying to change the "pace and rhythm" of her life, "My parents always pushed speed and competition—being fast, being first, being best—all very American ways of being. Now I'm trying to learn to slow down and go deeper. I want to live in the present, rather than spend all of my time anticipating—and fearing—the future." And many others told stories of seeking new ways of learning and living that cut against the grain of traditional definitions of achievement, success, and mastery that are typically reinforced in our society. Their new learning often felt like an "act of resistance."

Third, I was particularly fascinated by these domains of learning because of how they contrast with the relatively narrow cognitive learning that goes on inside classrooms, how they depart from the standards and measures of achievement that are the central preoccupations of educational practitioners and policy makers. As a matter of fact, people often spoke of having to unlearn styles of learning—ways of processing information, and expectations of reward and reinforcement—that had worked for them in school but now felt inhibiting and counterproductive.

Mario Delgado, a sixty-nine-year-old industrial chemist, had been a star student all the way through school, with honors and scholarships that propelled him through an Ivy League college and an elite graduate school where he earned his Ph.D. "I was always the lone Latino trying to dutifully fit in—making sure I didn't make waves," he says, his voice still full of regret. He speaks, for example, about how his "secretive, competitive" mode of learning all the way through his formal schooling— "where you dared not ask questions or fail publicly"—did not work for him when he began to train and work as a sculptor. In his studio, which he shares with three other artists, Mario has had to learn to "reveal" himself and his process, "expose" his failures, and submit to criticism from his peers. As a matter of fact, in order to make progress, he frequently has to turn to his fellow artists and ask for help in solving problems, in con-fronting aesthetic and technical difficulties, and in finding the energy to keep going when his "progress seems invisible." He has had to learn to trust that the knowledge he needs resides in his hands, not in his brain; and that his need to "control the process with my mind" often gets in the way of "feeling my way with my body." In all of these ways, Mario experiences what he calls the "interference of old school habits" of learning. He recognizes the ways in which the structures, hierarchies, priorities, and social relationships that served him so well in his climb to the top of the achievement pyramid in school, work against his comfort and mastery as a novice sculptor.

Likewise, several women and men who had been unsuccess-ful and underachieving students in school, and who had been socialized to think of themselves as "stupid" or deficient, spoke about their need to overturn the ancient negative identities laid on them by "insensitive and inept teachers" before they could begin to express the intelligence they brought to the new projects in their Third Chapters. Throughout our interview, for example, Fiona Featherstone, the quilt maker we met earlier, kept on referring to the "damage" done by the narrow categories, limited pedagogies, dull curriculum, and pejorative labels laid on by her teachers ("with whom my parents were often complicit") —damage that lodged itself in her psyche deep enough so that she still occasionally feels the lingering, leftover shame, even when she mounts a spectacular show to rave reviews. A self-proclaimed "right-brain" person, Fiona believes that if she were in school today she would certainly be diagnosed as having ADD. At the fancy private girls' school that she attended from kindergarten through high school, she always felt surrounded by "smart kids" who were "academic superachievers" and seemed to do it all with such ease and grace, "never seeming to break their stride or even sweat. . . . I always felt stupid by comparison," recalls Fiona. "I had the sense that everyone else was amazingly successful and able. Every time I got my report card, the message was the same: 'Fiona could do better if she put forth the effort.' " Her teachers interpreted her poor grades as a reflection of her laziness or perhaps her lack of interest. "They could not see me struggling all the time," she says, her voice still angry. They could not see her hurt, her alienation, or how marginalized she felt.

For both Fiona and Mario, then, Third Chapter learning requires a different approach to the acquisition of knowledge and the mastery of skills, one that is contrary to the ways they learned in school. Fiona has had to shed her old school identity, which made her feel inferior, stupid, and deficient. Casting off the ancient labels, she can fully discover her gifts and strengths, her unique and powerful kind of intelligence. Mario, an excellent student in school, rewarded for his discipline, commitment, and intellectual prowess, must discover a way to learn that by now feels "counterintuitive." He must replace competition with collaboration, secrecy with openness, speed with deliberateness, public rewards with a private vigilance. In each of the three realms of learning I will explore in this chapter, then, women and men resist former habits of mind, styles of approach, and sources of identity that may have worked for them in the past, and substitute for them others that open up new pathways of energy, expression, productivity, and pleasure.

NEW LEARNING: BODY

In soft blue light, the ballerina glides across the stage and takes to the air, her toes touching Earth imperceptibly. Sauté, batterie, sauté. Legs cross and flutter, arms unfold into an open arch. The ballerina knows that the easiest way to ruin a good performance is to think too much about what her body is doing. Better to trust in the years of daily exercises, the muscles' own understanding of force and balance.   —Alan Lightman[1]

Thinking with Your Body

As Josh Carter learns to play the jazz piano, he begins to think with his body, trusting his fingers' "own understanding of force and balance." A former journalist and newspaper executive, Josh decided to retire at sixty, when his managerial duties had come to overwhelm his relationship to the editorial side of the paper. The realization that it was time to leave his job—and a stellar career that had over the years brought him honors, acclaim, and status—did not come easily or all of a sudden. It was like a slow, corrosive awareness growing each day inside of him. He began to sense in his "bones" the emptiness that he felt walking into the office, the weariness at the other end of the day, the lack of passion that seemed to hover over him like an unwelcome stranger. "It became clear that I was wasting my time, and it became clear that my time was a very limited resource. The ability to control my own time had vanished in my executive job." One of his friends observed to Josh as he urged him to get out, "You have a day job that has metastasized." Josh had a huge salary, certainly nothing to be sneezed at, but it turned out not to be anywhere near enough to keep him at the company.

When he left, he was aware of trying to do so gracefully, without regrets or rancor. He realized, after all, that in many ways he had outgrown the job, that this was more about him than it was about his job, the paper, or the industry. And he also knew that he was heading toward a life that he had yearned for and anticipated for a very long time. "I was going toward something rather than running away from something," he says about the directionality of his motivations and his actions. He was, he hoped, heading toward a life that gave him more time to write a "great novel," and he already had one that was almost finished, ready for shaping and refinement.

For all of his professional life, Josh had enjoyed a stealth career as a fiction writer: rising very early in the morning, hiding out, and writing for an hour and a half in a tiny back office at the company, to emerge around 7:30 a.m., when the rest of the staff were arriving, and migrate back to his big executive office to begin his "other day." Even though journalism had been his profession, writing fiction was always his calling, and he took it very seriously. He sees writing as connected to his "core identity." "You have to understand," he says, "writing is not a discipline for me, it is an addiction—it is who I am." Also, it is through writing that he is "able to understand the world."

"Writing books is a very serious enterprise for me. It gives me purchase on a knowledge of the world. I write about things that elude me, that dog me."

When Josh left the company, he spent the first several months writing, "relishing every minute of rewriting the novel." When he would get tired of refining sentences and shaping paragraphs, he would sit down at his gorgeous Steinway grand piano and revisit the classical pieces he had played most of his life: Brahms, Mozart, Beethoven. Although he remembers enjoying the initial phase of the transition—so filled with unscheduled time and solitude—he also knows that it "wasn't all that wonderful." He laughs remembering his wife's comment, after he had been home for a few months and his time was being eaten up by "a punch list of things" around the house that had long been neglected while he was busy at work. "My wife noticed that it was not all that idyllic—not quite as easy or as pleasurable as I had made it out to be. I had these quotidian things I had to do that began assuming too much time—financial affairs, taxes, my will, heating units that were not functioning correctly—all these things needing my attention. I would get irritable when they consumed my days."

One afternoon, as he pondered the strange mix of pleasure and disappointment that had "dogged" him for several days—when the moment felt both exceedingly difficult and strangely promising—Josh decided to take a leap of faith. "I mustered my courage to take piano lessons from the best jazz pianist in the city." Music had been a big part of Josh's childhood. He remembers that there was always classical music on the record player at home. His mother, a church organist, could read and play anything in her "clunky, competent way"; and his father, who was completely untrained but very enthusiastic, could only read the treble clef. Josh smiles at the memory of his parents sitting on the piano stool together "playing two-hand duets": his father playing the treble line, and his mother the bass. When he was a young boy, Josh took tenor-sax lessons and played in the school band. By the time he was a teenager, he was playing in a pickup jazz band with kids from all over the city, most of whom were terrific musicians. He loved the jazz scene the most, and thought at first that he would one day become a professional musician. "I was really pretty good on the sax," Josh recalls. "But when I played with all of these kids who were really amazing musicians, I began to realize that practice would not make me great. I realized, in fact, that I am not wired for music the way great musicians are."

When he decided to return to playing jazz—this time the piano—at sixty years of age, Josh knew he was trying to learn something that did not come naturally, something that would turn out to be very hard, a huge challenge. So, when he decided to study with the best jazz pianist around—someone he knew to be a really serious taskmaster—he knew even before he started that it would be a "humbling and painstaking" experience.

Josh has warned me at least three times before we get started that I should not expect too much of his piano playing, that I should keep my expectations "very low." And he has told me that he is feeling "embarrassed and nervous" about playing for me. He sits down at the piano, back straight, hands and wrists in the proper position over the keys, and I sit in a chair right beside him. First he plays "Summertime" for me the way he used to play it before taking lessons—the way he once played it in New Orleans, jamming with "some of the greats." "Before, I used to play everything in root position," he explains, "very obvious, very funky." Back then, he could sight-read anything, but he was not able to improvise in the least.

The first thing his teacher told him to do was to change the position of his hands—"to line up the center of my wrists with the keys"—and then to spend three hours each day doing scales, always with the metronome. Josh demonstrates the exercises, which seem pretty straightforward but are, it turns out, excruciatingly hard to do. He sets the metronome, and tells me that his teacher actually does this same exercise sequence himself at the beginning of his practice sessions. Josh describes his learning as labored, slow, meticulous; he notices the smallest changes and minor improvements along the way. "I discovered that gravity holds the key down. You don't actually strike the notes, you fall into them . . . and after several months of practice, I no longer feel the tightness and rigidity in my wrists. . . . The mechanics are very hard."

Working up from the positioning of his hands, to the practicing of scales, to the feeling of greater control and fluidity in his playing of the notes, Josh's teacher then began to instruct him in musical composition. "He taught me how to write music—how to write it legibly," says Josh, taking out a piece that he has composed and playing it for me. "Once you write, you improvise the line and see what chords work underneath the melodic line. . . . Then, by making it, you discover within the original chord sequence that there is a whole rich world." As Josh demonstrates the steps—of improvisation and chord development—his playing is tentative and awkward, but there are definitely beautiful moments when things come together, when there seems to be a lovely balance between sound and silence. He wants me to see—actually to hear—the ways in which the conscientious and rigorous practice of the mechanics gets translated into the music. "All of these scales I was doing get incorporated into the creativity," he says. "I am just about a year into this, nowhere near where I want to be, but I am beginning to get the keyboard under my hands." Now he plays "Summertime" again, and it sounds completely different from the first version, both more spare and more lyrical. I smile at the extreme effort and uncommon devotion that have allowed Josh to produce this sound.

For the next hour, Josh continues showing me the drill—how his teacher has demanded that he play triplets, putting an accent on the first, then the second, then the third notes; that he always concentrate on the "physics and mechanics" of the playing; that he always be guided by the rhythmic precision of the metronome; that he not "get stuck in ruts." He would say to Josh, "When you find yourself doing the same thing over and over, fool with some other voices." Josh's teacher would also occasionally, and intentionally, ask his student to do something that felt impossible, that was way above his skill level. "He would jump way ahead of me, knowing it would be hard for me to keep up," says Josh about the frustration and overwhelming challenge that his teacher would insert into the lesson, in order to show him how far he had yet to go. "Sometimes I would think, I'll never ever get there!"

But Josh persisted through the most arduous times. He even found the difficulty fun, occasionally exhilarating. And he learned a lot about learning music, which turned out to be a very different enterprise from, say, learning philosophy or journalism or psychology.

First he began to understand the relationship between technique and creativity. "Swing doesn't come from looseness," he explains to me, "it comes from precision, from rigor and discipline, two hands working together precisely in the same groove." Just like the graceful ballerina in the quote that opened this section, Josh begins to understand that the years of rigorous daily exercises produce the "muscles' own understanding of force and balance."

The second thing he learned was that there is a pattern, a set of protocols and rituals, that every student of jazz follows. When Josh would feel discouraged by the slowness and the routine of his playing, and by the labor-intensive daily homework, his teacher would say, "Everyone has followed this path." The fact that he was not alone, that he was one among a multitude of musicians learning the discipline, felt comforting and helpful to Josh.

The third thing that Josh discovered was that jazz music is about "intervals and symmetries." In that way, it is very mathematical. "It is a whole different system of thought." He shows me the diminished chord, the minor chord, the dominant seventh, and their relationship to one another.

The fourth discovery he made was that the music is made up of patterns and interruptions in the patterns, about expectation and surprise, about "never doing the same thing over and over again," Josh explains. "The patterns relate to one another. The music needs to relate to itself in a coherent way." Searching for a sentence that will express the essence of it, Josh muses, "All art is creation in satisfying violation of expectation."

Finally, Josh tries to explain to me the part of his learning that has been the most difficult for him. It is actually hard to explain in words. Because he has been a journalist and a writer, words have always been his currency of discourse, his strong suit. His explanation to me about the music feels tentative, less articulate and clear than his expositions on language and rhetoric. Music is not about translating the notes from the page to the instrument, he explains, it is about thinking with your body. "It starts with the body, with feeling the intervals under your hands. In jazz, performance is everything. It is not just playing, it is composing something that will be a unique event." Josh contrasts learning to play jazz with studying higher-order finance and mathematical modeling (training he had mastered for his executive position at the paper); the first is in the body, the second in cognition. "Once I've learned the basic elements of the financial model, I can predict that there will be certain key questions that will need to be answered. I know what basic equations will produce the same results. . . . But music is aural modeling of the whole spectrum of hearing." Josh realizes that I am not fully understanding the distinctions he is making between the aural and verbal worlds, between learning that resides in the body and in the mind. Days after our interview, he sends me an e-mail that finally nails his explanation, and I begin to understand. His e-mail tells a story.

> At one point I mentioned that going deeply into music is different from every other learning experience I've had. You asked me in what way. I gave some answer.
> Here is a better one, a story.
> I was at a lesson with my teacher. We were discussing some of the nuances of tonality (roughly the question of what key a work is in, which is more complicated than it sounds). I mentioned a debate I had with a very good amateur jazz pianist over whether John Coltrane's *Giant Steps* had a tonal center. I asserted that it did not, with some good authority and arguments to back me up.
> "Can he play *Giant Steps*?" my teacher asked, meaning can he improvise on it.
> "Yes," I said.
> "Can you?" he asked.
> "No," I admitted.
> "Then he's right," my teacher said.
> It is a different kind of knowing.

Josh's ambition is still to write a great novel, not to become a world-class musician. Even though he spends three to four hours each day practicing and takes his playing very seriously, he does the work primarily for himself. "I want to be a competent, confident jazz musician," he defines his relatively modest goals, which turn out to be very hard to reach. "I want to sound good to myself and be able to play with other musicians . . . and I want to get to a point where improvisation makes emotional and musical sense to me." What he has discovered, as he has gotten into the habit of sitting down at the piano each day, is that in his Third Chapter, his learning is enhanced by his patience and by his ability to notice and appreciate the small and subtle signs of improvement in his playing. He reflects back on learning to play the tenor sax when he was a kid. "Back then, you couldn't get me to play scales for anything. Now I get great satisfaction out of the repetitive process—out of seeing myself get better and better." He explodes with laughter. "Now it is scary how much patience I have."

Josh has also discovered the deep connections between work and fun: the harder he tries and sweats, the more enjoyable it is. Again, he draws a contrast between his perspective on work when he was a young adult and how he approaches things now. "At thirty years old, I had my mind on accomplishing something, and I didn't have—or take—the time. My learning was all purpose-driven. Now I'm still getting used to the strange sensation that I have no purpose for this except to enjoy. I want to play for fun . . . and I am not used to working that hard for something that is for fun." Josh reflects on his motivation. "This is very unlike me," he says with wonder in his voice.

Thinking with his body, rather than leading with his mind, is an entirely new way of learning and expression for Josh, and it is painstakingly, breathtakingly hard. But the joy, the fun, is in the hard work, in the tiny baby steps of progress, in the exquisite pleasure of producing a phrase that sounds good, that is "emotionally and artistically satisfying." Sitting at the piano four hours a day, with the insistent, unforgiving pulse of the metronome, Josh repeats the same scale sequence over and over, following a strict protocol of practice that is strenuous and exacting, and that even the best jazz musicians have suffered through. The discipline and rigor of these hundreds of hours allow him, slowly and patiently, to begin to explore improvisation. He discovers reservoirs of patience that he never knew he had; he is "a stranger" to himself. The new learning in his body has "metastasized" to all parts of him, making him feel—in many ways—like a "new person."

Night Visitors: Using the Unconscious

Like Josh Carter, Katrina Adams, the portrait painter whom we met in the preceding chapter, sees discipline and technical proficiency as the bedrock of her creativity and artistry. She says forcefully, "You start with technique, with manipulation of the tools. You learn the craft deeply and well, and then you move from that to the creativity of art." And, like Josh, whose creativity grows out of a discipline and expressivity felt in his body rather than his mind, Katrina also discovers that when she is really in the "zone" her painting ceases to be a conscious activity: "The brush paints itself." For both Josh and Katrina, learning originates from a new place—"the body" and "the unconscious," respectively.

Katrina's second marriage, to William—in her early fifties—allowed her, for the first time, not to be the major breadwinner in the family. She did not have to worry about putting food on the table, or providing shelter for her children, who were now grown and out of the house. "It was the first time in my life that I didn't have to generate money," she says with huge relief. Finally, she could allow herself to revisit that moment thirty-five years earlier when she had wept at the feet of the old masters, and promised herself that one day she would learn to paint the way they did. "When I grab on to something, like wanting to paint like the old masters, I hold on for dear life. I'm dogged and determined," she says without bravado. In this new chapter of their lives, Katrina and her husband had decided to move to Santa Fe, a place where they knew no one, where both of them could start over. It was like having an empty canvas, a clean slate, a new beginning. But it was also lonely.

Katrina found her way, almost immediately, to a small art school not far from her home, where she began teaching a life-drawing course. While there, she noticed the work of one of her colleagues, a figurative painter whose portraits were as close to the old masters ("the paintings were luminous and layered") as any contemporary artists that she had seen. Katrina signed up for a weekend workshop that he was teaching. The following Saturday, she walked into the studio, saw the model, took out her brushes, and felt immediately at home. "I couldn't believe what came out of my brush. It was as if I had been working on this stuff in my unconscious for decades, getting ready for this moment. Even though I had never worked with oils, it all came so naturally."

Katrina studied with the artist for two years, learning the "technical stuff," and working through problems in class that she was not able to solve at home. She quickly learned which things he taught her would be useful, and which she knew she would later discard. After a while, she also realized that she was discovering her own methods for doing things, and not telling him. "You see, he was a very controlling man," she recalls. "Ultimately, I couldn't conform to his rigid rules, particularly the ones that didn't work for me." Her mentor had served an important purpose, but mostly she was self-motivated and self-taught—working sixty-hour weeks in her studio at home, feeling fully committed and very driven. Katrina believes that when people think of artists at work they often don't realize that every day—whether he or she feels inspired or not—an artist has to put in time. "People don't think in terms of time with artists. It's very hard work, and you have to work smart."

More than anything, Katrina loved learning how to paint; she loved the thrilling moments of uncertainty, frustration, and resolution. "I like not knowing what I'm doing. I like the struggle, the excitement, the period where I am questioning." When Katrina is faced with a problem—technical or aesthetic—the day and night seem to melt together. There is a thin line between the conscious and the unconscious that she uses to good effect. She takes the problem to bed, knowing that her dreams will help her find her way. "I've always gone to school in my dreams," she says. "I dream at night and have the resolution in the morning. When I started painting portraits, the old masters would actually visit me in my dreams. Titian would come to my bedroom and show me how to do something, show me a technique or offer me an insight, being very specific—and I'd wake up and go directly to my studio to paint."

Not only has Katrina welcomed the nightly visitors, but in this new learning she has also found the connections between "constraint and creativity." "The limitations are what force me to be creative," she explains. This is particularly true in painting a portrait, where the artist has one opportunity to convey the soul and spirit of the person. "It is a theatrical production, and you have to say it all in one flush with a weird set of objects that provide context and meaning." Before she begins to paint, Katrina takes literally hundreds of photographs of a subject, and then uses details of these—taking a smile from one, earrings from another, the forehead from another—to piece together the painting. She also asks them to bring in objects they cherish that convey the ways they define themselves. "People tell you who they are by the environments they create and the things they choose to display."

Most of the portraits take about a year to complete. It is the layering of paint—"thin glazes of oil"—that creates the luminosity; and each of those layers takes about two weeks to dry. Patience and restraint and great skill are required to build up the layers, and sometimes Katrina loses her way, what she calls "losing her eye." She never loses faith, however—she just knows that she has reached an impasse, and that no amount of perseverance will make it right. "When you look at something long enough, you can cease to see it. So I walk away from it for a couple of months, then go through all kinds of gyrations to trick my eye into seeing it differently, to make it fresh." Katrina estimates that she usually has more than twenty canvases going at once, so that she "will always have a dry surface to paint on."

Just as she knows when she has lost her eye and it is time to take a break and walk away, so, too, Katrina knows when the painting turns from being a technical challenge to taking on a life of its own. "I work like hell at the beginning of a painting. It is conscious, painstaking, manipulative work. But at some point—I never know exactly when, but it always happens—it ceases to be conscious; the brush paints itself. It is like watching a good movie. I'm holding the brush and watching it move." Katrina knows this sounds mysterious, but, as with her problem-solving dreams, she has learned to accept those moments and not question the role of the unconscious.

She also remembers something very much like this happening when her father, who was an inventor, would make a breakthrough in his work. "I remember his hard work, his struggle, his scribbling notes trying to make sense of what was happening, trying to solve an unexpected glitch. . . . Then, suddenly, it would all come together and fall into place." Katrina feels the same thing happens with her paintings. All the industry, energy, time, and commitment, all the tremendous struggle and problem solving, all the effort, seems to drop away, and everything comes together. This is the part of painting—the part she isn't consciously involved in—that Katrina loves the most. It has to do with letting go and "having faith."

The first time that Katrina painted a portrait professionally—of a six-year-old boy, commissioned by his mother—she worked on it for over a year, and felt enormous anxiety when the woman burst into tears upon seeing it. Katrina had known when she painted it that it was good work, that she was "in some zone" when her unconscious took over and everything fell into place. But the mother's tears were still upsetting. It turned out she was actually weeping tears of joy—deeply moved by a portrait of her son that had captured his essence, distilled in one image the way he was now and would always be. It also turned out that Katrina's first professional venture earned her one of the top international prizes in portraiture. Even though this first experience turned out beautifully, Katrina always feels some form of dread when, after months, and sometimes years, of working on a piece, she shows it to her subject. "It is hard to please people. It is, after all, not like looking in the mirror at yourself."

Katrina's clients are often surprised that she has not produced a mirror image, that she is not even trying to create a literal likeness. Instead, she is trying to capture their essence, their soul. "It is not the superficial that I'm after. It is not necessarily flattering," explains Katrina. "When I paint, I am painting a person; it is an archetype." I struggle to understand what she means, and finally, after many fits and starts, when Katrina swears that "words cannot explain" what she means, she says, "It is the best of who you are. It is you in ideal light. It is idealism, not real-ism." But she is quick to say that "idealism" does not mean per-fection. In fact, flaws are critical in capturing the person and humanizing him/her. "Flaws only enhance—they don't detract or diminish." She looks at me hard, squinting her eyes so that she can focus on the parts of me that are below the surface. "You would be the 'wise-woman' archetype, Sara, and I would be try-ing to visually capture compassion with shadows and lights."

Even though Katrina works so hard to distill an image of her subject's unique individuality, she hopes that the audiences who see the portrait will find themselves somewhere in it. "If I painted your portrait, Sara, I would hope that the twenty people who looked hard at it would see themselves in it. The similari-ties among us are always greater than the differences—we see the universals in the particular." She reminds me that painters always say, "God is in the details": the fold of her collar, the set of his jaw, the loose strand of hair. "I pay close attention to these tiny details," she says exuberantly. "In fact, I force them to hap-pen. They are the most delicious. . . . But behind them is some-thing much bigger." Katrina stops herself, worrying that all of this verbiage is beginning to cloud the picture. Finally, she sums it up in clear language. "I tend to think in terms of connected-ness. The portraits tell a story, a different story for each of us . . . that turns out to be the same."

Katrina's devotion and enthusiasm for her work are captivat-ing. At sixty-three, she claims to have more energy, more curios-ity, and more ambition than she has ever had. As she ages, she expects just to get "better and better," "bolder and stronger." Every day she continues to push herself to learn new things; she finds it most interesting to take the difficult path through her work. Recently, for example, she took up the challenge of land-scape painting, which turns out to be very hard, because it requires that the artist have a keen depth perception. "People are relatively easy for me," says Katrina. "I'm real good at the drawing, and two or three feet of depth is easy for me. But I have terrible binocular vision, so landscapes are very hard." A broad smile spreads over her face, because she has discovered a new set of problems to solve, a new setting for learning. "I'm in the place of messing around again—asking questions and seeking solutions." This unfinished, ambiguous, imperfect part of her work keeps her intrigued and motivated. She contrasts her appetite for learning in the Third Chapter with her growing-up experience of "loathing school." "I'm not good at endings and not good at questions that have one prescribed answer. That's why I hated school so much. It just brought out the rebellious spirit in me. . . . I'd be damned if I'd give them the answer I knew that they wanted."

Just as Josh Carter loves the serious, relentless work of learning the jazz piano, the small evidence of progress along the way, and the patience he never felt when he was younger, so Katrina Adams loves learning the things that are hardest to do: she seeks out the most difficult challenges. She does not want to take the straight route; she resists the path that will lead to a certain, successful conclusion; and she persists in asking the impertinent questions that were not allowed by her teachers in school. In portrait painting, she also discovers a compelling paradox: as she portrays individuals in all of their unique particularity, she discovers the universals—the "connectedness"—among us. What she first imagined as solitary work, an individual indulgence, both for the painter and the subject, she now sees as a communitarian process. If she is successful at capturing the "essence," the "soul" of her subjects—through the rigorous depiction of the details of their things, their clothes, their gestures, their facial expressions—then those who see the portraits will recognize themselves in the work; they will identify; it will speak to them in a deeply personal way. What began as a privileged, private enterprise becomes a collective experience. "This is one of the most significant things I learned in portrait painting," says Katrina as she reflects on the "ultimate purpose" of her life, which is to be "a part of a movement that connects and joins humankind."

NEW LEARNING: VOICE

> **there are sounds**
> **which shatter**
> **the staleness of lives**
> **transporting the shadows**
> **into the dreams**
>
> —Nikki Giovanni[2]

Stand and Deliver

Several of the women and men I spoke to referred to the "wonderful adventure" of discovering their voices in the Third Chapter. For many, this meant being in touch with the sounds that "shatter the staleness" of their lives. They used the term— "discovering my voice"—metaphorically, to signal a growing sense of their own authority, confidence, and newfound courage. Others used the term literally, to refer to making new sounds with their voices—learning to stand correctly and breathe deeply, using their diaphragms, and sending out a note that is confident and beautiful; or discovering their voice in public speaking, being able to move through the fear and nervousness of standing on the stage, finding ways of connecting with the strangers in the audience, and developing a way of talking that felt natural and authentic, "a sound that originates from within."

Lucinda Miller, the international relief worker whose story I told in chapter one, has become one of the most powerful spokespersons in this country engaged in fighting the genocide in the Sudan. She returns home from the front and speaks at large public rallies, at colleges and universities, at congressional hearings, and at fund-raising sessions in people's living rooms across the country. Lucinda describes the huge challenge of learning to "stand and deliver" her message—a challenge that she experienced as both "technical and emotional." She wanted her voice to sound more "authoritative" when she spoke, and she wanted it to carry the "passion and emotion" that she felt inside. Public speaking had always been an activity where Lucinda felt inadequate and awkward, exposed and very anxious.

In an effort to manage the anxiety, she would overprepare, spending endless hours composing and practicing her presentations. "I would labor over them, write them out, almost memorize them," she says of her highly scripted speeches. "It was excruciating for me. I wanted so much to deliver my thoughts in a compelling way. I wanted so much to have an impact." Part of her unease had to do with always comparing herself to her husband, whom she saw as having "the touch." From her point of view, he was so much more natural, intuitive, and charismatic. But she was also anxious because she felt "uncomfortable in front of a crowd . . . not liking being onstage being looked at." She recalls sadly, "I used to hide behind the screen of a well-crafted message, a screen of protection between me and my audience."

But in the last couple of years, as she has traveled around the country having to make so many speeches about her relief work in Kosovo and the Sudan, Lucinda has learned to "stand and deliver." It is more important to her that she get out the message than that she is risking exposure, embarrassment, or failure. On the road, she has had no time for meticulous preparation, for composing a perfectly controlled text. She has had to learn to speak from her heart, and to dare to connect with her audience. "I've grown much more comfortable through repetition and experience." Lucinda offers an example of her growing "naturalness" in front of crowds. Soon after returning from her second trip to Darfur, she was giving a major speech about her experiences to students and faculty at a local college. Rather than stay up all night fashioning a perfect script, Lucinda—as she lay in bed with her husband—briefly spoke to him about the three major points she hoped to raise the next day in her talk and then—"miraculously"—went right to sleep. The next morning, she woke up bright-eyed and rested and scribbled the points out on a three-by-five card. She walked out onstage, looked at her audience, took a deep breath, and "spoke with surprising fluency." "It felt so good to know that I can pull that off, but also to know that the message was the most important thing. This was not about *me*, it was about my being the vehicle for narrating the stories."

Not only has she learned to "stand and deliver" and feel a new confidence in her ability to capture the essence of her experiences and "put it out there," but Lucinda has also begun to recognize that different audiences and venues require different kinds of preparation and delivery. Recently, at a large business conference, with an audience full of her fellow CEOs, she was the opening keynote speaker. She was asked to speak about how business leaders can create and sustain productive and inclusive organizational cultures. For these "suits" in the audience, she prepared a PowerPoint presentation with colorful graphics and direct, pointed, "usable" information. "For this audience, the message was tangible and skill-oriented," says Lucinda without apology, "very different from the inspirational, challenging, passionate stories that I brought home from Darfur." A few weeks before our interviews, when Lucinda testified on Capitol Hill about her experience "being embedded" with the African Union in Darfur, she knew that her presentation would have to be supported by data, evidence, and rigorous analysis; that she would have to have a depth of knowledge sufficient enough to answer any question that came up in the hearing. So she studied, read, prepared, and listened to experts who knew the region well, and then she reminded herself that the thing that she brought, that was unique, was her "insider's perspective." Her job that day was to blend facts and vision, data, and personal insight, with an authoritative confidence.

Immersed in the Word "Spare"

Like Lucinda Miller, Pamela Stein wants to use her voice to speak to wider, more diverse audiences. With an artful, passionate voice, she hopes to inspire and inform her listeners. But mostly she wants to provoke them to take responsibility—with their bodies and their voices—for helping to "repair the world." For most of her adult life—as an activist, clinician, and scholar—Pamela has written nonfiction books about what she sees, knows, and understands, books designed to inform, set the record straight, re-evaluate the data, and provoke some action, some change in the status quo. In her mid-fifties, for the first time she felt "liberated" from academic assignments. Without a faculty appointment, and feeling disconnected from colleagues, friends, and community, Pamela found herself turning to—actually returning to—the theater. She wanted to—actually, she "desperately needed" to—do something new with her life, to find a "new community," a new purposefulness, a new arena of expression in her Third Chapter.

As she so often does, Pamela looked toward home: to her family of origin, to the things that animated their lives together when she was growing up. It was in the bosom of her family, Pamela recalls, that she got her self-esteem, her sense that she could accomplish whatever she set out to do, her "chutzpa." Her parents' devotion and support always made her feel safe and secure, smart and confident, even though their parenting strategies were very different. "My mother's and father's approaches to child rearing were a study in contrast," says Pamela, "but, taken together, they always made me feel secure in trying new things. . . . If you brought my mother a drawing that you had done, her praise was effusive. 'Oh, that's fantastic,' she would say, no matter what the drawing looked like. My father, on the other hand, thought that that kind of praise was unrealistic. Instead, he'd give tough criticism that always seemed to say, 'You can do better.' "

When Pamela thinks about how she got up the nerve to try to be a playwright, she quietly thanks her parents for their unconditional support, for the way they believed in her and challenged her, for their effusive praise and their discerning criticism. On looking back, she also recognizes that her family—for generations—always loved the theater. Her grandfather had done vaudeville, and her father had done serious acting in high school—serious enough to make him want to do it professionally. Pamela remembers a story that still makes her weep: of her father wanting to apply to the American Academy of Dramatic Arts in New York City.

He filled out the application, practiced for weeks for the initial audition, and walked over to the school. He stood at the bottom of the steps with his application in his hand and yearning in his heart. He was poised, ready.

Now the tears are flowing down his daughter's face. "He is a breathtaking actor. It is just so sad. . . . My father stood at the bottom of the steps and decided not to go in. He knew he wouldn't be able to afford it." But he passed on his love of theater to his daughter, and he continued acting in local and regional productions. When Pamela was approaching her senior year of high school, he even wrote to a distant cousin of his in Los Angeles who was involved in movies, to ask him whether he would take his daughter under his wing and help her get involved in acting. His cousin told him that Pamela should "first get an education"; then she could decide if she was still interested in pursuing acting but would have something to fall back on. So Pamela went off to an elite college, then a fancy graduate school, followed by a distinguished and productive academic career.

A few years ago, those "old passions returned" when Pamela saw a piece in the local paper advertising a free actors' workshop. All alone, sitting at her kitchen table sipping tea, Pamela could feel the panic and the excitement. "I was intrigued, but terrified," she recalls. She telephoned a friend—the friend she typically calls when she is divulging deep, dark secrets or admitting to unleashed passions. He told her, "Just do it for fun." So she did, and "fell in love with the theater all over again." One workshop led to another, until she took the next step, of applying to acting school in Los Angeles—doing the very thing that her father's distant cousin, now dead, had suggested she do once she had successfully completed her education. All the time, she kept telling herself that she was "doing it for fun." She was trying to adopt a perspective so different from the focused, serious endeavors that had shaped all of her other life choices. This was to be a playful adventure, not a disciplined piece of hard work. This was to be adventurous and improvisational, not linear and purposeful.

But when she got to Los Angeles, it was the opposite of what she yearned for. It was not fun; it was grueling and degrading. "I hated L.A.," recalls Pamela. "It is an extremely ageist place. I wasn't young, blond, and skinny. I was invisible. People condescended to me. They didn't want to be my scene partner; I was always the last one chosen. And the teacher was this brutal guy who kept on pushing students until they had a 'breakthrough,' but what he was really doing was abusive. He wanted them to have a 'breakdown.' He would try to make you weep and then leave you in a heap on the floor." Even though it was an awful experience, Pamela persevered and finished the semester. She did not leave unscathed; there were times when she felt all beaten up. But the experience did not leave deep scars, and it did not dissuade her from wanting to be involved in the theater. She had always loved acting, and she still loved it. From the vantage point of her maturity—a self-assured Jewish woman in her Third Chapter—she knew in her heart that she did not belong in Los Angeles, and that her negative experience had more to do with "them" (the superficial values and vacuousness of Hollywood) than it did with her.

When Pamela returned home, she immediately jumped back into taking acting roles in community theater, recapturing the magic of her early experiences in high school. "Theater is a spiritual experience," she says about the relationship between actors and audience, and how the play—well conceived and well done—can become a "transformative experience." The more she discovered the joys of acting, the more Pamela thought about the possibility of writing the words that actors speak. After all, she had always been a writer, a good writer, and words had been her medium. So, with her parents "watching her back," and her now grown children "by her side," she decided to write a play based on one of her previously published books. "I was a complete novice," she says, laughing, still surprised by her daring. "I said to myself, I bet I'll learn something. This will be a new adventure for me." Her daughter bought her a book about how to write a play, which she devoured in one evening. "I've always done the counter-phobic thing," she explains. "I do something before I know how to do it—so that I really won't have anything at stake."

Several weeks after our interview, Pamela wrote to me about "discovering my voice": a story about how she found out that she could actually sing, after believing for all of her life that she was tone-deaf. Her "chutzpa," her "counter-phobic" way of approaching new adventures before she had a "stake" in them, allowed her to "stand up and deliver" at the audition.

A woman a couple of years older than I, with whom I attended high school, told me that when she turned fifty she made a list of all the things she had never done and wanted to do, and then she set about doing them. When I turned fifty, in fact that very year, I had spent my life believing that I could not carry a tune. I knew every lyric from every Broadway show tune and many popular songs and sang all the time when I was alone, but I had the impression that I changed keys when I sang. Then I attended an audition for a play, with a friend. . . . She has a fabulous singing voice and has taken lessons for years. She auditioned with a monologue and then a Broadway song. They had a pianist and grand piano there. When it was my turn, I did the monologue and started to sit down. The director told me to sing something. I told him

I am not a singer. He said that there were no nonsinging roles in the production and I should sing. I said, "No, you don't understand: I don't even pretend to be a singer." He instructed me to go over to the piano, so I did. The pianist asked, "Do you sing scales?" and I said, "I don't know." He asked, "Can you hear pitch?" I said, "I doubt it, but I have absolutely no idea." He hit a note and said to sing it. I tried. He kept hitting notes and then a series of notes and told me to sing them. From somewhere I recalled that when you sing you are supposed to send a lot of breath through, so I took a deep breath before singing each note or sequence of notes. Afterward, my friend said, "Pamela, you hit every note." I said, "Hm, really?!" And then I started to change the subject, but she kept coming back to it and saying things like, "Most people cannot do that. I could not do that when I started taking singing lessons." Since I always loved to sing, I found a singing teacher by saying I needed someone who, one, had a sense of humor and, two, would be able to be very specific in telling me what to do, because if she just told me a note wasn't right, I would have absolutely no idea how to make it better. I took lessons for one and a half years and had a wonderful time. I even did a couple of auditions in which I sang—was not cast, but that was okay, because the very acts of doing two singing auditions were things I would have never in a million years have thought I would do, and it was fun. After I had taken a few lessons, my teacher said something I never expected to hear. I had warned her that I had once been told that I went off key when I sang, but after a while she told me, "You have this wonderful ear that has been in the closet all this time!" So that changed something about my sense of who I am. And I was taking those lessons during a very difficult, sad, particularly lonely time in my life. But every single time I started to sing, even just the repetitive exercises, I felt so happy. It was magical.

Pamela approached learning to be a playwright with the same exuberance, sense of adventure, and fun—and with the same requirement that her guides and mentors be very specific in telling her what to do and how to do it. After reading the how-to book her daughter had given her, Pamela got right to work, transforming the ideas from a nonfiction book she had written into the structure of a play, trying to learn how to write dialogue and how to develop the characters so that the audience would be able to identify with them. This was not easy for her. She had a hard time freeing herself from the flat, static language of academic prose, and she struggled with her natural verbosity—too many words, especially too many adjectives.

When Pamela had written a first draft, she showed it to the three people whose judgment she trusted the most, and who she knew would tell her the truth: a director friend, her father, and her daughter. From each she learned an important lesson. Her director friend told her to remove all of the stage directions from the script. "You're telling them how to act," she said. "You're trying to control the whole thing." When Pamela dutifully took out the stage directions, it surprisingly gave her "a great sense of freedom." She recalls, "I realized that there are lots of ways an actor might say that line. I found that I did not have to explain everything . . . or control everything." Pamela's father asked her only one question: "Shouldn't a play have some mystery?" "Yes," Pamela thought immediately, "of course it should . . . or else why would anyone be interested in reading it?" The third lesson came from her daughter, who was generous in her praise for her mother's first effort but told her, "You're telling the story. It's a play, Mom; you should be showing us."

With each draft, Pamela's work got better. The language became more spare, the characters more developed, the sense of mystery and wonder more intense. It was hard, fun work, in which she became deeply immersed. The more she wrote, the more Pamela began to feel as if she were entering a different world, one that was "emotionally enveloping." Now her voice is full of wonder as she talks about how her relationship to her writing changed. "Writing plays is like being immersed in the word 'spare'—creating an emotional space. I became completely consumed by it, caught up in the world of what I was writing about. After a while, I found that if I got very quiet I could actually hear the next line. I began to inhabit the characters."

Pamela's work in the theater expanded to directing plays, ones that she had written—and that began to win prizes in regional and national competitions. In a very short time, just a few years, Pamela went from being a novice, from following a how-to manual, to being a playwright whose work was being performed in off-Broadway theaters. It was exciting to find that the issues about which she cared most deeply—social justice and human rights—could become the messages that shaped her plays; that her art could be used to further the causes that she had worked on for most of her life; and that, most of the time, audiences could "actually hear" her voice more clearly when it was threaded into a play, when the lines were delivered by a character whom they had gotten to know and with whom they felt some sympathy. After working awhile in the parallel universes of art and social science, Pamela found a funny thing happening to her writing: those universes began to converge, influencing each other in unexpected ways. For example, she began to notice a change in the way she wrote nonfiction. As she composed her research-based articles and essays, she began to care about the aesthetics of her prose—the shape of her texts, and the voices of her protagonists. She listened for the sound of her sentences. Recently, as she finished a journal article on the physical and emotional wounds of vets returning home from Iraq, she stepped back from her text and noticed the change. "I could see that I was not writing this like a journal piece. . . . The language I was using was much more literary, more poetic. The voices of the vets gave the piece emotional weight. I felt as I wrote it, 'Where is this coming from? I don't write this way!' "

Coming Home to My Father

Luther Brown, social activist and educator, surprises me by using "voice" in both the literal and the metaphoric sense, for expression and liberation. He says simply, without an ounce of bravado, "Finding my voice was like finding my life." Music was a large part of Luther's upbringing. Both his father and his mother loved listening to music. His father loved classical music and would fill the house with the soaring sounds of Bach, Beethoven, and Mozart as he worked in his library or sipped his evening cocktails. He was also a generous supporter of the local symphony and other chamber-music groups around town. Luther's mother also loved music, remembering with pleasure the thrill of going to free concerts as a young girl growing up in Dublin. When Luther arrived at college, he immediately joined the chorus. He enjoyed singing, which felt like a good counterpoint to the strict academic diet that dominated his life. But by his sophomore year he had gotten swept up in civil rights and progressive politics, which soon displaced his engagement in singing.

As he reflects back on the shift in his passions, he remembers feeling that his political activism was more important, more worthy and serious, than his music; the singing began to feel pointless and trivial. When he graduated from college, and continued to devote most of his energies to activist causes, he still stayed away from community choirs, even though he missed making music. "I think I was a bit arrogant, thinking that the local groups were below me somehow. I was sort of a snob." And then, after marriage and children, Luther's life became increasingly "layered," busy, and complicated. He admits sadly, "Singing and poetry—my connection to my father—got completely squeezed out." Luther's return to singing after all these years feels in many ways like "coming home"—coming home to his father. It is also very much related to his other efforts to live more freely, more joyfully, and with greater expression.

A couple of years ago, he decided—"after a lot of soul searching"—to take voice lessons. During every lesson, his voice teacher would insist upon the same thing. "Let it go," she would bellow. "Don't be afraid; don't hold back!" she'd say, cheering him on. "Learning to sing and allow myself to be free is a big challenge for me! I'm a good singer, but there is so much more in there that wants to come out," says Luther. As he listens to his own voice and tries to push past the inhibitions and fears, he tries to get rid of the "inner judge" that makes "opening up" so hard. He has discovered, for example, that show tunes encourage a kind of "letting it all out," a kind of schmaltz and exaggeration that frees him up. He also finds that singing requires a welcome focus: you must concentrate fully on the present moment, and as you do, everything else falls away.

With some lessons under his belt and with the encouragement of his teacher, Luther began to participate in recitals along with other voice students, and this required another level of challenge and courage. Performance meant that he had to put himself out there publicly, and that he had to be "willing to screw up and fail." It meant that he could not take himself so seriously. He has been surprised by people's response to his efforts, however tentative and imperfect his singing might be. "For some folks, the sight of someone who has the guts to stand up inspires them," he says. "In some way, it is like a gift for others." Luther is quick to remind me that he will never have a serious singing career (even though he admits to sometimes being jealous of those with more training or better voices). That is not the point. Rather, singing is about "listening to the sound . . . focusing on the moment, letting it all out . . . not in a sloppy way, but in a controlled way." He has learned that his goal, of "letting go" and giving it all he's got, must be balanced against an equally important artistic and emotional objective: learning restraint.

Luther also talks about "discovering my voice" and listening to "the sound and resonances of other people's voices" as he works on "peace-building" missions around the world—in Kosovo, Macedonia, Rwanda, and Bosnia. As a faculty trainer working for an international pacifist organization, he leads workshops and seminars designed to bring people from polarized sides together for dialogue, conflict resolution, and peace building. This evolving, difficult process requires patience and courage, empathy and attentiveness. But first it requires that everyone recognize that "conflict is not bad": it can be "productive and creative." Luther describes the process when groups come together who have a history of distrust and violence (like the Jews and the Palestinians). First they begin by "mapping the conflict"—acknowledging it, naming it, establishing its scope and boundaries, and finding the points of greatest resistance and discord. Identifying the conflict is the first "way out of the growing circle of revenge." The conflict, Luther says, is like "the tip of the iceberg, but there is lots going on underneath." To begin to excavate the subterranean layers, the group members must engage in "deep dialogue." Each one must be courageous enough to tell his or her personal truths and "listen without denying." This is very hard. Emotions flare; people get defensive; they project their pain onto others. There are advances in understanding, moments of reconciliation, even epiphanies, followed by retreats and accusations as people slide back into their comfortable and familiar stances. The learning that goes on in the group is both individual and collective, personal and public.

Luther's work as a group leader and participant is to listen deeply and attentively, to guide and support, to help participants see where they have traveled and what they have learned, to keep the growing optimism alive even in moments of great despair. But there is a point beyond which he must not, and cannot, control the process, a moment when all hell breaks loose and he can no longer direct the dialogue. This is the moment when something amazing and terrifying happens; when, as Luther puts it, "we take a deep breath and we know that the universe will take care of this situation." He describes this moment as an expression of "collective learning," "where we learn to go where angels fear to tread." Luther's eyes are closed and his brow is furrowed as he takes himself to that dangerous place of great possibility. "That's when I feel the Holy Spirit," he says softly, mysteriously. Everyone feels "the opening up of possibilities, everyone recognizes it, and everyone feels somehow changed." Even though the group may have worked together for days and weeks with fierce purposefulness, this moment is "not planned, but it has been prepared for."

As hard as it is to come to this place of collective learning, however, it is not enough, says Luther, to let the understandings reside inside the circle of participants. The learning needs to lead out into the community, and it is only then—when the lessons are transmitted to others and learned more broadly—that there is transformation and change in the community. "Good feelings are great, but they are not sufficient." Though understanding and recognition are essential, it is the "doing" that creates the change. With experience and a growing self-confidence, Luther has learned to let go, to cease trying to control the situation. "Before these international experiences," he recalls, "I knew a lot about group process but I lacked the confidence. I didn't have the faith. I didn't trust myself to put it into the universe and believe that it will be taken care of." He didn't trust that the sounds of their voices—and the sound of the silence—would "transport the shadows" of their lives to a new place of understanding and reconciliation.

In these stories of Luther, Pamela, and Lucinda, we discover how the literal and metaphoric meanings of voice are joined. Creating the actual physical sound, projecting your voice across the footlights, letting it all out, and practicing restraint are all connected to feeling self-confident and authoritative, wanting to convey your message with dignity and passion, and building a broader audience for your work. In discovering their voices, all three of these storytellers ultimately find that less is more: small is beautiful. Pamela discovers that the secret of writing a good play is finding a language that is "spare": fewer words, especially fewer adjectives, and fewer stage directions to the actors. As she immerses herself in the characters, she lets go, and they begin to speak for themselves. Lucinda, who used to spend days carefully composing the scripts for her speeches—which put a screen between herself and her audience—discovers that she is more "real" and more fluid if she goes up on the stage with just three points written on a three-by-five card. She throws caution to the wind, and just "stands and delivers." And Luther discovers that his letting go with his voice must be balanced by restraint, a holding back. He also recognizes that when he works with international groups on peace building there comes a point, in the deep dialogue and in the excavation of conflict, when more talk is counterproductive. The sounds, the voices, must cease. Silence is the most powerful voice in the room.

NEW LEARNING: SOUL

My soul has grown deep like the rivers.

—Langston Hughes[3]

The External and Internal Terrain

When men and women talked about "becoming a different person" in their Third Chapters, they described a "reinvention of the self," a reorientation of their "core values," and a discovery of "soul." Rather than honing a new set of skills, learning to balance technique and improvisation, or discovering the sound, strength, and authority of their voices, people spoke about changes in their "core being." Meredith Travis, a successful businesswoman, describes her new learning as "a soulful pursuit." A few years ago, she sold her business, thinking that after her entrepreneurial success she would be a hot commodity, and her phone would be ringing off the hook, with people seeking her expertise, her wisdom, her networking. Instead, no one called, except the occasional young, up-and-coming businessman who wanted to seek her counsel and "pick my brains for free." Some of these contacts led to short-lived consultant jobs, but nothing interesting or major. Certainly the market's indifference had something to do with her age. On the eve of her sixtieth birthday, she was considered an elder in the business, no longer the talented young Turk or the ambitious young thing with bright and brash ideas.

Others' perceptions of her—as possibly over the hill—were complicated by the fact that a part of Meredith actually was ambivalent about rejoining the fray. She kept on thinking to herself, I want a life that affords me more leisure time, more opportunities for peaceful retreats, more moments for play and pleasure. She is smiling at what she now regards as a lie that she laid on herself. "I thought it would be great to take a shower during the day . . . to bake bread . . . to read wonderful novels . . . to linger in a bubble bath." Although she held on to that "fantasy" for some time (maybe it was a defense against the deafening silence of the telephone, which reminded her she was no longer at the center of the action), Meredith knew in her heart that a life of leisure was not what she wanted. She had to admit to herself that her days were dark when they were not filled with ambition and action, when she did not feel needed and visible. "It is so very hard when you've identified yourself as a professional, when you've put together a lot of currency, and suddenly the phone never rings—nothing! I realized how locked I was into who I was . . . how dependent I was on the external trappings." Letting go of the leisure fantasy and admitting her dependence on the external trappings threw Meredith into an even deeper abyss. She began to do a little bit of volunteer work to fill the void. She even briefly returned to her old company in a consultant role, but the blues continued unabated. "I had a lot of doubts and questions, deep ones, troubling ones, existential ones. . . . I was clinically depressed, even though I didn't admit it," she remembers sadly.

There was no great epiphany; her climb out of the dark hole

of depression didn't happen all at once. But slowly Meredith came to the realization that she wanted to do something in the world that was "important and meaningful," that she wanted to use her experience and skills to create something new; that she most certainly was not ready for a life of gardening and bubble baths. She wanted to live in, and create, what she calls an "ascending environment," and in order to do that, she needed to be "willing to be a different person." At sixty, she no longer could afford to see herself as "the in-charge diva." She needed to let someone else have the "hot new ideas"; she needed to learn to listen to others, and she needed to learn the "art of compromise."

After many fits and starts, Meredith decided to respond to a rare phone call from a young entrepreneur who was seeking her advice. He approached her with a half-developed idea, a huge ambition, and what she calls a "Peace Corps offer": wanting her to dispense her counsel for almost no money. Meredith, of course, refused the offer of a pittance, but she agreed to the compromise of a major consultant role, which in time, grew into a partnership (even though she knew going into it that "nine out of ten partnerships fail"). Although there was much about starting the new business that felt familiar, a lot was different, because she saw herself differently in it. Her professional role had changed, as had her view of herself as a person.

In order to explain to me the contrasts that she experienced with the new venture, Meredith draws a contrast between the "external and the internal terrain": the difference between what she perceived to be going on in the surrounding environment, and what she felt was going on inside of her. Both contributed to her sense of "being a different person." In the external world there was "bigger, new technology and a marketplace with a lot of opportunity. . . . I had seen and done a lot of stuff, but this time I found myself treating the whole process with more respect. I took it more seriously on this second go-round. I was more skeptical, more realistic, more self-critical. There was more restraint in my moves. On the interior side, I traded in my bravado for a new humility. I admitted I didn't know everything. I started from the bottom. I worked those new muscles. At sixty, I was learning to value and honor everything."

Without a doubt, Meredith says that the hardest thing that she has had to learn—especially in the partnership—is to "really listen." For her, listening does not come naturally; she "practices self-restraint every day." The second lesson she is working on is learning to "give up control," and tolerate the inefficiencies of collaborative decision making. Her partner, a man, is twenty-two years her junior, and appreciating the age and gender differences turns out to be very important. Meredith's voice reveals her frustration. "My partner is thirty-eight and I'm sixty. He's the young and the restless. He has the arrogance of youth, and I have to be careful not to let his aggressiveness get to me." It helps for Meredith to recognize how crucial they both are to the success of their enterprise, and how distinct their contributions are. "In this pack, there are two alphas. I am the alpha female— collaborative, inspiring, leading, mothering—and he is the alpha male—competitive, fighting for it with pointy edges." She shakes her head. "Through this experience, I hope I'm learning to be a better person, not just in relation to my partner, but in relation to all people." For Meredith, the "internal terrain" is the "soulful place" where she begins to discover new priorities, new values, and new behaviors. Her progress cannot be measured by the familiar quantitative indices that defined her earlier success in business. She is using different standards, working "different muscles," and hoping for different results. And Meredith not only wants to reinvent herself, but she also wants to create an "ascending environment," and carve a space for her work that will nourish the existential questions and the "ongoing search for meaning" in her life.

My Ancestors Came Right Down to Me

When I ask Olivia Cartwright to tell me what she means by "soul," and why she claims that "soul searching" has been the work of her Third Chapter, she sings me a little Etta James and I hear the answer in a blues line. "Race, ancestry, survival," says Olivia, as if these words are always joined in her mind. At seventy, Olivia, an elegant brown-skinned African American woman, has just retired from her position as an administrator and curator at a major art museum. Raised in a working-class black neighborhood, Olivia came from a close-knit family with several siblings, all of whom were bright and achieving students who went on to college and graduate school. Neither of her parents finished high school, but their home was a place that "nourished curiosity and inquiry." Olivia remembers her father sitting at the dinner table each evening, asking his children what they had learned from their teachers that day in school. Then he would drill them with questions. "My father never took anything for granted. At the table we would have to defend our statements with evidence, facts, and argumentation. He had an inquiring mind—always asking what is underneath this thing, what set of assumptions cause you to think this." There was never much discussion around the table about race, however. Maybe her father would talk about the need for black folks to get out and vote, but he never admitted to seeing the world "through a racialized lens." When Olivia or one of her siblings came home complaining about being teased or bullied by a white kid at school, her father would never say, "They don't want you around because you're black." Instead, he'd respond with pride in his voice, "They don't like smart kids."

Looking back on her childhood—in fact, reflecting on the first fifty years of her life—Olivia claims that "race was not an issue." "This was not how I located myself in the world," she says without apology or regret. Her family, she explains, "looked like the black bourgeoisie," but they actually "didn't fit into any cast or class structure." "We inhabited the in-between places," Olivia recalls, "a place that always gave me a sense of singularity about myself." Married at nineteen to a graduate student in philosophy—a white man—Olivia went on to have four daughters, and spent most of their growing-up years being an activist parent and community leader by day, and a poet by night. It wasn't until she joined the workforce—a real, paying job at a nonprofit community arts organization—that she became aware of the significance of race.

"Believe it or not," she says, smiling to see the disbelief on my face, "before that time I was so innocent, so obtuse. It was so off my screen." But from the very first day that she took over as director of City Arts, she began to see with great clarity the separations and hierarchies of race. City Arts was an interracial organization that served predominantly black neighborhoods. Its mission was explicitly inclusive and antiracist, but when Olivia took over as director, the reality was that the day-to-day decisions—both big and small—were being made by white people. "The white people had all of the power. They were the deciders, the commander men," she remembers wearily. At first, it all felt unnerving, shocking, even dangerous to Olivia, who had to learn quickly to watch her back. Over time, she learned ways of challenging the cultural and structural inertia of the organization; she found ways to "subvert the inequalities of power." "I ran into these tremendous clashes of white people's paradigms of who black people are."

For the next twenty years, Olivia's awareness of race "grew

hugely," moving from off her screen to the "bull's-eye center," from seeing the "singularity" of her life to recognizing that her racial identity was her "soulful place." Having reduced the asymmetries of power—but not eradicated racism—in her ten years at City Arts, Olivia moved on to a major administrative position at an art museum, where she ran into the most "profound racism" that she had ever experienced. Even though she arrived at the museum much more wary and sophisticated about the undercurrents of institutional racism than she had been at City Arts, she would still find herself, from time to time, caught off guard by arrogant claims of white superiority or subtle gestures of disrespect. As people tried to "chip away" at her dignity, Olivia honed her survival skills. She figured out what to pay attention to and what to ignore; she learned how to deflect the blows and move on. But all along she knew in her heart that surviving was nowhere near enough for her, that her defensive stance—her "jungle posture"—was taking too much of her energy and robbing her of her "creative spirit." "I fought very hard. It was often deeply discouraging and disappointing. I was always fighting the cynicism that was rising up inside of me."

Still, Olivia refused to be marginalized: "I wanted to be at the center." Over time, she began not only to see how she could work with the people whose insularity and prejudice did not allow them to see her clearly, but also to learn the ways in which she might begin to "broaden the interpretive structures" of the whole institution. "You see, the museum had been a very staid, anachronistic place, a place where people couldn't see lots that was accessible to change. . . . I was able to see those openings." Looking back on her ten years at the museum, Olivia claims that she would never have been able to learn to read the institution "like a complex cultural text" if she had been any younger. "This is the kind of learning that you can only do in your full maturity." She would not have had the patience, the restraint, the empathy, or the skills of analysis before her seventh decade. "When you are younger, you tend to think that the way you see the world is the way the world is," she explains. "When you are older, and have had years of experience working with people from so many perspectives, you learn the assumptive position of the people in power . . . and you learn the tools for breaking through that."

When I ask Olivia to name the "tools," she lists three "assumptive positions" that guided her activities. First, it was important for her to see the "educative necessity" of her work. She needed to find a way to help people see "how they got to be who they are." Olivia remembers talking to the curator of a show on French landscapes, trying to get him to think about how his exhibit might be designed to attract a more diverse audience. His response was immediately defensive. It came out in closed, choppy sentences. "I'm a curator. This is my art. That is not for me to worry about." Olivia persisted, gently and patiently asking him about his life, about his experiences as a child, about his passions, about the gardens and landscapes he loved. He answered her questions, first skeptically, and then more openly—pleased that someone was interested in him, the man behind the mask. And during their conversation, she began to see him newly, as a person who was "different but not wrong or bad." "I was able to face that place of saying, He is not like me, but that is okay. I am not threatened by him." In the end, the encounter was respectful, and Olivia was able to "move him slightly."

Which speaks to Olivia's second "assumptive position": "everything is incremental." Nothing changes quickly or fundamentally. We must recognize that people and structures have a long history—"many years of piled-on stuff"—and it is impossible to uncover and undo all of those layers of living. Change happens slowly, tiny step by tiny step, and if you accept that point of view, then you can maintain some measure of optimism and hope. If you don't, says Olivia, you're "dead in the water."

Given that change is minimal and slow—in individuals and institutions—and that people seeking change must see their role as empathic educators, the third piece of Olivia's learning at the museum was a growing understanding that she had to be "immensely creative" in launching and sustaining any project. She had to do her homework, use her networks, call in her chits, and gather her resources from a variety of places. She had to work underground, below the radar, until she knew that her success was assured; and then she had to make a big splash. Putting the pieces together, building the necessary relationships, deciding on the content and the venue, and scheming about the presentation were all part of her "creative process," methods of challenging the entrenched insularity and racism that stood in the way of progress.

But even with all of her hard-earned maturity and creative, purposeful learning, Olivia would occasionally be blindsided by an unexpected assault from an unlikely place. She recalls once being "knifed in the back" by one of her white women staff, someone who had worked for her for years, whom she had mentored and supported. When the lies that her staff person had disseminated came full-circle back to her ("not even by a circuitous route"), she was devastated. First by the racist insinuations of the lies, then by her own naïveté in allowing the woman to get close enough to cause her injury. Olivia's usual mellow voice is now raised in fury. "I was so rageful. I was nearly hysterical. . . . But there I was, just back from Paris, sitting in my brand-new Lexus, looking out at the lake, with my six-figure salary, my fancy leather boots, and my fur coat. . . . My ancestors came down to me." Suddenly she felt a quiet come over her, a quiet born of a strange blend of gratitude and grief. But "thankfulness prevailed" as Olivia said out loud to herself—all alone, sitting in her car—"Think of what my parents had to go through. If they could keep their autonomy and dignity, I can put up with this." At that moment, Olivia came face-to-face with "a sacred resource for survival and personal triumph." The ghosts of her ancestors, the legacy of her parents' strength and grace in the face of struggle and oppression, surrounded her and gave her courage to "keep on keepin' on." At that moment she felt "blacker" than she had ever felt, deeper in her "essential identity." "My soul has grown deep like the river," she says quietly about the person she has become and is becoming in her Third Chapter.

Throughout my interviews, men and women of color often mentioned that their new learning included a growing recognition of the dimensions of race and ethnicity as powerful forces in shaping their "essential identity." Like Olivia, they talked about a "deepening" of their racial identity, and a more complex and sophisticated awareness of the ways in which racism threatened to distort and obscure their contributions and achievements and those of their children. Mario Delgado, the former industrial chemist and novice sculptor, speaks about how working with his hands has given him a new sense of connection to his father and grandfather, who were both artisans and manual laborers. As he works the clay with his hands, he says, "I feel the imprint of my ancestors, my strong Mexican roots." Likewise, Carolyn Chin, a Chinese American woman who has spent her professional life "fixing and redesigning big organizations," says that turning seventy has made her turn east, toward home. After leaving Shanghai as a young child, and returning there in her early twenties as a Fulbright scholar, she wants to "reconnect to her roots."

Recently, she traveled with her middle-aged children and *their* children on their first visit to the homeland. And she is screwing up her courage to return to the manuscript she wrote almost a half-century ago—not because she holds out hope that it might be published, but because she wants to begin to examine her early experiences of self-discovery. There is something "soulful, spiritual really," she says, about coming closer to the end of her life, which makes her want to revisit the beginnings. When she rereads the manuscript, she hopes to be in touch with the young woman she once was—courageous, curious, spirited, and adventurous—and she might even draw inspiration for writing about the person she has become—a woman who is both "the same and different." "When I understand my Chinese self better," she says finally, "I will feel more complete."

Across the three domains of new learning I have explored in this chapter—body, voice, and soul—there are intriguing points of connection and resonance. First, all of these women and men speak about the importance of learning restraint. Luther Brown, for example, discovers that projecting his singing voice—making it bigger and stronger and more expressive—must be counterbalanced by restraint. In fact, true artistry, he learns, resides in holding on to the tension between letting it all out and holding back. The passion feels deeper when the sound is both open-throated and contained. As she moves from composing academic prose to writing plays, Pamela Stein learns the power of restraint. Her writing becomes more "spare," more modulated, and more controlled. She learns to listen for the voices of her characters, and not get in their way with her natural verbosity. And she pulls back on giving stage directions to the actors, letting them become collaborators with voice rather than mere vessels through which she speaks. The portrait painter Katrina Adams not only understands that "less is more," but she also believes that the constraints of her medium, in fact, incite her creativity. She gets only one chance—"it's like a theatrical production"—to project the context, meaning, and character of her subject onto the canvas. There is no room— aesthetic or emotional—for indulgence or melodrama. She says, "The limitations are what force me to be creative."

In what seems both ironic and paradoxical, most of the men and women I interviewed link the learning of restraint with their willingness "to lose control." In their Third Chapters, they are working on containing their work and their passions, at the same time as they are learning how to release them, allowing "faith to take over" and the "Holy Spirit" to enter. In his work with peace-building groups around the world, Luther Brown seeks to master the balancing act between facilitating focused, deep dialogue—where his efforts are controlled, attentive, and strategic—and knowing when to retreat, let go, and have faith that the "the universe will take care of itself." In shifting her priorities and values from the "external to the internal terrain," entrepreneur Meredith Travis claims that she practices restraint every day as she tries to become a better listener and a more productive collaborator. In her efforts to "become a different person," she also balances her restraint with a new willingness to release her control of the project, and let things take their own "organic shape."

Several of my interviewees, across all three domains, also spoke about the connections between discipline and spontaneity, between technical training and improvisation, between learning the "craft" and being in the "zone." In all cases, the former must proceed the latter. As he plays "Summertime" for me on the piano, Josh Carter reminds me that "swing doesn't come from looseness." It is quite the opposite: the physics and mechanics must come first. The scales have to be meticulously practiced every day before he can begin to feel—in his hands and in his body—the possibility and promise of improvisation. It is the same with Katrina's portrait painting. Her openness in receiving her night visitors and trusting her unconscious only came after she had spent decades honing her craft—developing her technique, and putting in thousands of hours at the easel, "working hard and long and smart."

As people master the craft that leads to improvisation, they also realize how Third Chapter learning combines work and play. For many, it is the first time that they have worked so hard, so strenuously, and so patiently on learning something for which they will not receive public acclaim or external rewards; on learning something that they know that they will never master fully. Josh has no hopes of being a great jazz musician. His daily practice is hard and exhausting, and he loves every minute of it. For Katrina, there is "fun" in taking the difficult route—in discovering the problems that need solving, in designing challenges that have no solution. Her greatest pleasure is "in the struggle," in walking the path where she is given no map and needs to find her own way. She has also learned that playful thinking—using her imagination, her ingenuity, her fantasy life—leads to new ideas, innovation, and creativity. For these folks, then, work and play become merged; serious work feels like fun, and there is deep pleasure in doing the hard labor.

Whether we arrive at a solution, a breakthrough, or new learning through work and play, discipline and spontaneity, in the Third Chapter people recognize that change—real change—is incremental. As Olivia Cartwright works to change the institutional priorities and access at the art museum, and meets with resistance from those who have a stake in the status quo, she does everything in her power to connect with people, empathize with them, and convince them to listen to her views and share her values. But she knows that, despite her best efforts, change—both individual and institutional—will be slow and incremental, barely visible to those looking for radical shifts in the landscape. In trying to move from being a competitive, striving, tough entrepreneur, "dependent on external trappings," to a more mellow, collaborative, listening leader, Meredith Travis learns that change comes hard and slowly. Her mission is clear—to change "my core being" and create "an ascending environment"—but her steps are tentative, often fumbling; and she finds forces within her that keep pulling her back to her old ways. Progress is also incremental, painfully slow, for Josh Carter as he practices four hours a day, trying to produce scales that are perfectly clean and rhythmic, trying to get his hands to submit to the gravity. Like Meredith and Olivia, he has to adjust his lens and modulate his expectations in order to stay on point and remain hopeful. He has to see achievement in the smallest evidence of progress.

All of these aspects of new learning—which balance work and play, restraint and freedom, technique and improvisation, and incrementalism and progress—become woven into the repertoire of people in their Third Chapters. Learning to control the tension and balance between these often contrary forces requires patience, a quality that seems in abundant supply for such women and men. Josh Carter laughs at his amazing ability to practice for hours on end, something he would have never tolerated when he was a teenager enamored with performing—but not practicing—his tenor sax. And Olivia claims that her steady, purposeful, empathic leadership at the museum would have been impossible if she were any younger. Maturity and patience give her a long view, an ability not to fear difference, and a gentle curiosity about where other people are coming from. "Patience," says the poet Nikki Giovanni, transports our "shadows into the dreams."

Conclusion: Cracks in the Mirror

> There is always something
> of the child
> in us that wants
> a strong hand to hold
> through the hungry season
> of growing up
>
> —Nikki Giovanni[1]

> in youth our ignorance gives us courage
> with age our courage gives us hope
> with hope we learn that man is more
> than the sum of what he does
> we also are what we wish we did
> and age teaches us
> that even that doesn't matter
>
> —Nikki Giovanni[2]

OPPOSITIONS

The juxtaposition of these two passages from Giovanni's poems
echoes with the oppositional images, metaphors, and perspec-

tives that thread their way through this book. In our Third Chapters we are completely changed adults who care little for the decorum and rules that have defined our public personas in the past, and within us there is still the young child reaching up for the "strong hand" of the adult protector who will hold us "through the hungry season of growing up." Our new learning makes us feel more evolved and complete, and strangely needy and infantilized. We are growing toward a maturity that is liberating and pregnant with promise and possibility, and we are deeply connected to the "ghosts" in our past. We are poised to navigate new boundaries and tackle risk-taking adventures, at the same time as we feel the need to circle back home and connect with the rituals and roots of our ancestors.

From the beginning of this text, contrasting and contrary perspectives have helped us explore the complex and layered learning that goes on in the Third Chapter. Erikson's theory of development, which underscores the dynamic of constancy and change—regression and progression—captures the soundings in Giovanni's poems, and offers a framework for examining the competing forces that challenge new learners across the life span. And each of the chapters in this book also highlights the oppositional forces and the potential for resolution. As we mourn the loss of the familiar, we are liberated to explore the exotic; as we seek ways of giving forward to the next generation, we travel home to revisit the anchoring values into which we were socialized; as we begin to chart our new learning and compose new life scenarios, we discover that we must confront ancient traumas and heal old wounds. As we cross boundaries of place and perspective that carry us a great distance, we discover that we have never left home.

As we try to master a different kind of knowing, we begin to understand that we need to undo many of the practices and presumptions that made us achievers in the past; we need to experience the knowledge deep in our bones, in our muscles, in our very sinews, not follow the familiar lead of our mind and intellect. We need to accept and appreciate the nightly visitors to the realms of our unconscious, animating our creativity and our passions, not rely exclusively on the conscious control that guides our skills. As we learn to use our voices—with new authority and courage, from the depths of our diaphragms—we need to unlearn the practiced silences and caution that kept us out of trouble and on the track to success in the past. And as we begin to focus on the dimensions and richness of our "internal terrain," we find we must relinquish some of the public acclaim and rewards that flowed from our status and accomplishments in the "external terrain." In our Third Chapters, as Giovanni writes, "we learn that man is more than the sum of what he does."

Erikson's model not only identifies these contrary forces that propel development, but it also helps us see these "crises" as generative and productive.[3] It is not, for example, that loss wins out over liberation as we move forward in our Third Chapters, but that we learn to anticipate and accept the pain and confusion of the transition (the "neutral zone") from one stage to the next— and that we find a way to balance the competing forces that move us forward and pull us back. We must also expect that the path will not be smooth or straightforward. It will be rocky and uneven. There will be faltering, falling, and failing from which we will need to draw lessons and the courage to move on. There will be moments of backsliding and regression. Forgiveness, humility, patience, and resilience are critical ingredients of our approach to the chaos and complexity of new learning; and these qualities seem to be central developmental markers in our Third Chapters.

As I listened to the voices of the women and men whose stories I have presented here, I was struck by how the creativity and trajectory of their learning in the Third Chapters drew energy from the ways in which they navigated and balanced these oppositional forces, managed the dialectics of progress and regression, dealt with the inevitable awkwardness, vulnerabilities, and failures, and found a way forward. It is fair to say that the people who joined this project were unusual in their capacity to embrace oppositional forces, tolerate the complexities, and live with the ambiguities. They were particularly adept at coping with the developmental crises, unusually curious about taking on new risks and adventures, and especially discerning and reflective in telling their stories. They all relished the opportunity to look "backward into the future"; they all saw themselves as both protagonists in, and narrators of, their own stories. They all saw their Third Chapters as both exciting and adventurous, and tender and treacherous. As a matter of fact, they often spoke about the exhilaration of being open to taking risks, submitting to vulnerabilities and confusions that they would have never allowed themselves earlier in their lives. Their failures offered opportunities for recovery; their awkwardness helped them learn a new humility; their slowness demanded that they practice patience; their intensity and impatience required that they go deeper, rather than farther and faster.

I would never claim, therefore, that the forty women and men I interviewed represent the majority of people who are in their Third Chapters, but I would argue that many of the lessons drawn from their stories are broadly transferable to a more diverse population of people between fifty and seventy-five, and that under certain conditions—economic, cultural, developmental, and temperamental—most people might be able to develop the capacities to embark on new learning in their Third Chapters.

Obviously, one important reason these women and men were able to seek out new learning opportunities was their privileged status. Although the majority of them would not be described as affluent, and many of them grew up in working-class or even impoverished backgrounds, none of them were currently worrying about paying their bills, feeding their families, and buying car insurance or health care. In other words, they all lived lives of real—or perceived—abundance that allowed them to make choices and take risks, and, more important, they all came from educational and work backgrounds that offered them access and networks to a broad range of relationships, resources, and institutions. I refer to the notion of "perceived" abundance because several of the people who had grown up in working-class families, for example, saw "plenty and choice" in the relative gains of their adult middle-class status.

CHERISHING

Katrina Adams, the portrait painter, whose ambition was to paint like the old masters, spent most of her adult life as a single mother taking on a variety of graphic-arts jobs that barely put food on the table for herself and her two sons. Much of the time, they lived a fragile existence, and when times got really tough, she "endured the humiliations of welfare." Her second marriage, a decade ago, when she was in her early fifties, allowed her, for the first time, not to be the sole breadwinner, and opened up an emotional space for her to recapture her life's dream of learning to paint like the masters. By any objective measures, she and her husband would certainly not be considered rich—her grown children both had to earn generous scholarships and take out big loans to pursue their college careers, and she and her husband lived frugally and simply in a "downsized existence"—but Katrina felt she had plenty: an abundance that allowed her the space for imagining, then seeking out, a new path of learning and creativity. Even though Katrina admits that the "lack of major money worries" opened up the space for new learning, she claims that her real emotional awakening and risk-taking came from being married to a man who believed in her, who was not threatened by her passions and her talent, who wanted her to "soar as high" as she dared. The emotional support he provided—not the extra income—was more important to her liberation.

In fact, several of the men and women I spoke to echoed Katrina in their focus on the significance of supportive and loving relationships that "opened up the emotional space" for risk-taking, adventure, and new learning. Some said their adult children had challenged them to take the leap of faith; others were spurred on and "well held" by a group of intimate friends; and several gave credit to partners and lovers. Josh Carter, the jazz pianist, claimed that his strong relationship with his wife, who resonated with his "artistic soul," helped him make the treacherous transition from the high-status, high-stakes entrepreneurial world he had inhabited as an executive of a big company, to work that was "much harder, more private, more demanding," and completely lacking in public rewards and applause; from a career in which he was skilled and expert to one in which he was a "trembling novice." "My wife's support, encouragement, and empathy not only gave me the license to immerse myself in this new learning, it liberated me," Josh says about the ways in which he felt her "standing by my side and watching my back." Like Josh and Katrina, Rachel Middleton points to the full and unconditional support of her husband, who was "secure in his own person," and was there "like a rock, like an anchor," when she made the difficult and excruciating decision to leave her leadership role in a nonprofit organization that she had founded and "mothered" and enroll, at fifty, in divinity school. "I am very lucky, actually blessed," says Rachel, "to have a partner who knows me in my adult self and loves me in my passions."

The opposite is also true. It is extremely hard for people to embark on new learning when their spouses—or children or friends and loved ones—feel wary, insecure, or threatened by their new learning and passions. Thelma Washington, a seventy-year-old lawyer, married for fifty years, decided to change course quite suddenly—although the urge had been building in her for almost a decade—and abandon her lucrative practice for a volunteer position working with the international criminal court. Money was not an issue; both she and her husband had amassed enough to cushion them, for any eventuality, for the rest of their lives. Nor was it the surprising suddenness of her decision to leave her legal practice, and an orbit that required much more international travel, that seemed to threaten her husband the most. It was the shift in the rhythms and routines of their lives, and a sense that she was leaving him behind as she entered a "strange and foreign arena that he didn't understand or appreciate."

Thelma describes her husband's actions as "subversive," "consciously and unconsciously" designed to make everything harder for her, to cause her guilt, to make her stop her passionate pursuits. When she moved her office to their home, her husband balked at the use of the space and exaggerated the intrusiveness of her presence there. "He said that my new study, which was actually one tiny room looking out over the back alley, was taking up our whole house . . . and yet he didn't want me to shut the door. He couldn't stand my presence or my privacy. He didn't want me there, and he couldn't stand to be separated from me," she recalls. Without her husband's support, Thelma drew courage from her own hard-fought determination, and from the "light and force of a higher spirit." "I actually believed," says Thelma with reverence in her voice, "that this opportunity was a gift from God, and that I had to be respectful of the gift. For the first time in my life, and in my marriage, there was no fuzziness, no negotiating room. I was immovable, and that gave me strength."

The emotional abundance that Katrina, Josh, and Rachel enjoy, and that Thelma yearns for, and ultimately sees as a "gift from God," is at least as important as the abundance of material resources, and turns out for many to be critical to nourishing new learning in the Third Chapter. In order to face the oppositional forces of loss and liberation, these men and women are helped by knowing someone will be there to catch them if they fall. They are helped by knowing that this person is willing to face the possible threats to their relationship and the changes in the routines and rhythms of their lives that follow new adventures. They are helped by—and this is another opposition— the realization that out of the intimacy and constancy of their relationships they are free to become more individuated and autonomous; the steady bedrock of support lets them take on the risks of change and reinvention. "There is always something of the child in us that wants a strong hand to hold through the hungry season of growing up," writes Giovanni.

In her book *Willing to Learn*, Mary Catherine Bateson enlarges the arena of care from the child who reaches up for a "strong hand to hold" to a society that offers a more compassionate and generous environment for lifelong learning. Like so many of the people that I spoke to, Bateson observes that new learning—particularly in the Third Chapter—requires a kind of openness, fearlessness, humility, and capacity to look foolish that most of us can only muster if we know that we will not be trammeled if we try. We will only dare to risk the casualties and discomforts of new learning, says Bateson, if we are surrounded by a caring society. When individuals are asked to "stand on their own two feet,"[4] with no one to look after them, then their capacity for learning decreases. In order to be open to learning, humans require a different situation:

> One of the things we know about the human capacity to keep on learning, to remain young at heart and willing to learn, is that it needs to be supported by cherishing. We needed to be cherished as infants, and as adults we need to cherish our children. But if we want a society of people willing and open and ready to learn, it has to be a kinder, gentler society, because we need a lot of mutual support to face change, to give up things we've always believed in.[5]

Though the need for cherishing and its links to learning is relevant across the life span, it seems particularly critical to adults in their Third Chapters, where the confluence of cultural ambivalence, social prescriptions, institutional norms, and stereotypes of aging conspire to undermine people's courage and spirit of adventure. In observing how people grow older, Bateson argues that "we will need to think further about providing care through an institutionalized and monetized system, but that will not be enough, there will still be a need to provide cherishing."[6] Without this cultural surround of compassion and empathy, learning will be inhibited and compromised, and our society will be deprived of the energy and productivity of Third Chapter learners. The prism of our societal views on retirement, for example—with its focus on leisure, isolation, and protective asylums—is contrary to Bateson's notion of a "cherishing society." An anachronistic view of retirement—where couples are "set loose, like passengers in a lifeboat,"[7] to move across the country to a golf course—means that people in their Third Chapters are forced to lose the networks of support that they have built up over time at a moment when they perhaps need those connections and relationships the most. In that situation, with less caring and support, they are less likely to be open to learning or to engaging themselves in society in new ways.

SCHOOLING AND LEARNING

As I listened to the learning narratives of men and women between fifty and seventy-five, I was continually struck by another apparent opposition: the clear contrasts between the processes and products of learning that were part of their formal education—from elementary school through college and graduate training—and the motivations, values, and goals that inspire their new learning in the Third Chapter. For many, the mastery and achievement that were dominant during childhood, adolescence, and young adulthood seemed, in retrospect, to be dissonant with how they hoped to evolve as learners in their Third Chapters. Several people spoke about having to undo the long-entrenched habits, values, and norms of school life in order to embrace the challenges of learning in the Third Chapter. The very aptitudes and attitudes that had made them stand out and excel in school seemed to be barriers to the risk-taking and adventurousness that allowed them to embark on new learning thirty and forty years later. Others talked not about the need to unlearn academic ways of approaching and mastering knowledge, but, rather, about having to shed the negative, pejorative labels bestowed upon them—wittingly or unwittingly—by teachers, which had left permanent scars. They could still feel the sting of being labeled slow or lazy or stupid or unmotivated in school—the hurt of being misunderstood, ignored, and rendered invisible by their teachers. New learning in the Third Chapter required that they confront those ancient pains, recover their dignity, and rise to the challenge of rediscovering their gifts and redefining their self-images.

These individual stories of people needing to unlearn the habits, norms, standards, practices, and labels of school in order to replenish their learning in the Third Chapter underscore a critical disjuncture between the patterns of socialization and learning that go on inside of school classrooms and the instigation of learning across the life span. Over the last thirty years, I have visited hundreds of schools across the country, carefully observing the teaching in classrooms, examining the pedagogies and curricula, documenting the culture and character of the school environment, and witnessing how children navigate the broader educational ecology. I have monitored the cycles of educational reform, the changes in the rhetoric and preoccupations of practitioners and policy makers, and been engaged in the discourse among theoreticians and researchers about the goals of education, the standards for measuring aptitude and achievement, and the habits of mind we hope to instill in our children.

What is fascinating—and disturbing—about most of the public discourse, policies, and educational practices is that there is seldom a reference to the longitudinal trajectory of learning across the life span. For the most part, school learning does not anticipate or help students prepare for lifelong learning. The

goals of schooling tend to be shortsighted and narrowly pragmatic. We work to prepare our young people for the next step up
the educational pyramid, or the first level of employment, and
we ignore the long view. Increasingly, our measures for whether
our students are ready for the next rung up the ladder are determined by their scores on narrowly constructed tests that capture
only a limited range of knowledge, and an even smaller spectrum of ways of knowing. And these are quantitative, evaluative
instruments that tend to focus on phenomena that are measurable—discrete, visible, and countable—not necessarily the
dimensions that are meaningful to the learning and growth of
students. Because the tests become the critical standard for gate-
keepers, teachers begin to teach to the test; curriculum becomes
increasingly focused and formulaic, questions are designed for
single right answers, and pedagogies become narrowly prescribed. Curiosity, risk-taking, questioning, experimentation are
largely written out of classroom conversations. Failure is feared
rather than learned from; aggressive competition becomes the
mode for rising above one's peers; rewards and incentives are
dispensed to the lucky few whose minds match the medium, and
whose biorhythms and priorities adapt smoothly to the school
culture.

The stories of Third Chapter learners recorded in this book
point to the ways in which these school values and practices
may distort organic learning across the life span, compromising
and masking the impulses that might make us productive and
creative learners when we are no longer living within the constraints of school or work environments. For decades, psycholo-
gists have pointed to the limited repertoire of learning that goes
on inside of schools, and the ways in which large percentages of
students are, therefore, excluded from opportunities for full participation and achievement. In his classic book *Frames of
Mind*, Howard Gardner identifies eight kinds of intelligence,

and claims that our schools tend to reinforce and systematically develop only two of them: the linguistic and logical modes of intelligence. That is, students are rewarded for the articulateness of their oral language, writing, and reading, and reinforced for developing minds that are rational and objective. They are not rewarded, for example, for developing their kinesthetic intelligence (the ways they move and feel in their bodies), their interpersonal intelligence (the ways they interact with and respond to others), or their intrapersonal intelligence (their capacity for self-reflection and self-interrogation), even though these seem to be important to their success in coping with the realities of their lives beyond school. Gardner, therefore, points to the narrowness of the curriculum and reward structures in classrooms, and the disjuncture between what is learned in school and what is needed for surviving and thriving in life later on.[8]

Offering another angle on the contrasting realms of school instruction and life learning, the psychologist Daniel Goleman identifies the individual characteristics of students that lead to success in school and life beyond. His book *Emotional Intelligence* does not deny the central importance of intellectual aptitude and acuity to the mastery of academic material, but he claims that these cognitive dimensions are nowhere near as meaningful or predictive of school success as the four temperamental qualities he identifies: commitment, discipline, restraint, and ambition. Further, he recognizes these qualities as better indicators of school achievement than a person's IQ or his/her scores on an SAT, and he reminds us that SAT scores are really only good for predicting a student's first-semester grades in college. They do not help us anticipate long-term productivity and success. Finally, Goleman argues that these four capacities in human beings cross the boundaries from achievement in school to sustained lifelong learning.[9]

Gardner's and Goleman's analyses are echoed in the voices

of Third Chapter learners whose reminiscences of school often include references to the ways in which their formal training did not help them adapt to the developmental and cultural changes they are now facing as new learners. In fact, many are able to point to the ways in which their school experiences were not only different from, but also oppositional to, productive lifelong learning. Orville Brim, a sociologist and one of the major contributors to life-span theory, uses an architectural metaphor as he offers a pointed assessment of the contrary expectations, practices, and rewards in school and those that support lifelong learning: "To study childhood without its life-long aftermath is to pour a foundation and neglect the edifice."[10]

I could not agree more. I believe that the designers of childhood education need to consider the developmental tasks of adulthood and old age as well as those of childhood when they construct curricula, develop effective pedagogies, and build school cultures. So much of childhood socialization in school is aimed at intellectual competence and achievement motivation, at helping children learn to compete successfully against their peers, gain public recognition for solo work, and demonstrate mastery by rapid response rates, quick articulation of ideas, and high scores on standardized tests. But these often turn out to be the very competencies that may interfere with successful aging and learning in the Third Chapter, where collaboration, relationship building, slowness and deliberateness, risk-taking, and irreverence are the coin of the realm; where work and play, restraint and expressivity, discipline and improvisation are joined.

I believe, then, that our contemporary preoccupation with testing, our quest for higher standards of achievement, and the tools we use for measuring and evaluating student skills and proficiency in schools lead to a narrowing and standardization of learning that neglects the building of the "edifice" of life. And I believe that the parts of the school curriculum—the arts and humanities, sports, and community service in particular—that are the first to be eliminated when school systems are facing budget cuts, may be the very arenas that support approaches to learning that will emerge as important to sustaining development across the life span. A shift to a more embracing, generous, complex curriculum, and a more "cherishing" school culture, will require changes in societal expectations, cultural priorities, and educational policies. In turn, it will require that teachers in our schools see themselves as lifelong learners, modeling for their students a curiosity about life and a fearless pursuit of new knowledge; this, in turn, will nourish the imagination, questioning, storytelling, intellectual discipline, and adventurousness of the students in their classrooms.

Again, Mary Catherine Bateson is helpful in observing how the institutional structures and boundaries of school can distort the processes of lifelong learning and compromise our ability to adapt to a rapidly transforming world. In the past, when people completed their matriculation through school (high school, college, or graduate training, depending on time and place), they were considered to be "educated." But education, says Bateson, can no longer be seen as finite and complete. The life cycle, she writes, "is no longer structured in terms of a separation between preparation and participation. Learning is no longer before, but whenever."[11] In order to make lifelong learning possible, then, institutions need to adapt. Historically, Bateson sees these institutional innovations as related to societal efforts to offer full participation to new social groups. "Each time we have newly understood that some social group had the right to full participation, innovations in education have been needed to make the transition possible."[12] Bateson points to the examples of the creation of schools for newly freed slaves after Emancipation, and the community-college movement that was a major expression of the push for equality in the Great Society. By extension and analogy, it would seem that now is a propitious time for considering institutional innovations that would help to spur the new learning of people in their Third Chapters, that would offer them more opportunities for generative work and creative civic engagement.

INTERGENERATIONAL RELATIONSHIPS

Not only do I think it is important that we begin to redesign school cultures, pedagogies, and curricula using life-span theory as a guiding framework, and honoring the central dynamic of continuity and change that moves across the life cycle, but I also believe that the boundaries of school need to be made more porous and permeable, that we need to reduce the generational segregation that defines life and learning in our society. The movement across school-community boundaries, however, needs to move in two directions. Children preparing to live as citizens in an increasingly complex, diverse global reality need to be offered opportunities for apprenticeships and service in the "real world" as part of their school and college experiences, and people in their Third Chapters must be seen as valued mentors who bring with them not only the accumulated knowledge of their work and careers, but also their wisdom, experience, and sense of perspective. The crossing of boundaries for both generations needs to express a respectful reciprocity—a dynamic pedagogy in which the old and the young are both teachers and learners.

Despite its importance, intergenerational learning is difficult to institutionalize in a society in which there is little if any spontaneous and frequent intergenerational contact. Social scientists have worried about how few opportunities our contemporary culture offers for intergenerational exchanges, and the extent to which this generational segregation deprives younger people of the opportunity to witness the generativity, engagement, and aging of older people. Absent these models, younger generations are given no road map for their journeys ahead; they are not able to witness the adaptations and learning of older people. In his essay "Generativity and Culture," John Kotre makes an argument for the ways in which the generative resources of people in their Third Chapters benefit both individuals and society. He claims that, for any culture to flourish, younger people need the stories and examples of real-life people growing older and acquiring wisdom.[13] By contrast, and no less important, the creation of these narratives that can be shared plays an important role in helping women and men in their Third Chapters realize and express their own generativity. This was certainly the case as I listened to Third Chapter learners who discovered, while they told their stories, new insights into their own motivations and capacities, and a new sense of control and agency over their actions—whose stories became their anchor and their compass.

In an essay included in the same book as Kotre's, McAdams and Logan write about the inspirational and educational power of life and learning narratives for the storytellers and their young audience of listeners.

The prospect of imagining how one's own life will end is not a welcome one for most individuals. The narrative beauty of generativity, however, is that it provides a way of thinking about the end of one's life that suggests that the end is not really the end. I may die, but my children will live on. My own story may end, but other stories will follow mine, due in part to my own generative efforts. Generativity helps to script how people see the end of their lives, helping to construct identities in which endings give birth to new beginnings.[14]

A half-century earlier, Erikson drew the connections between the storytelling of elders and the long view of youth. The narratives, he claimed, not only aid older people in their own self-definition, but they also help younger generations in understanding the life cycle, including the role of death in that cycle. Erikson asks, "How can we learn from our elders how to prepare for the end of life, which we must all face alone, if our models do not live among us?"[15] The voices of Third Chapter learners in this volume amplify another angle on aging. In hearing their stories, and witnessing their creativity and risk-taking up close, young people will not only witness the inevitable journey toward death, but they will also be offered lessons in living: lessons that teach the coexistence of urgency and patience, irreverence and grace, restraint and generosity, self-expression and altruism, each finding its balance in the midst of layers of complexity, human and cultural.

INNOVATION AND TRANSFORMATION

In fact, we are already beginning to see the seeds of institutional innovation that encourage cross-generational dialogues, offering opportunities for young and old to learn from one another. All across the country, increasing numbers of people in their Third Chapters are flocking to adult-education centers and university and college campuses to enroll in courses, and even to gain advanced degrees, in their sixties, seventies, and eighties. And many want more than classes. There is a burgeoning movement that *Newsweek* has called the "golden age on campus," where hundreds of thousands of people in their Third Chapters are moving to communities in order to be in close proximity to institutions of higher education.[16] Without a doubt, part of the lure is access to the cultural offerings associated with university life, and there is also a palpable yearning to belong to a community that many wistfully associate with their college days, and certainly a desire to catch the energy and vitality of the younger generation. But what seems to be the most attractive part of sharing—actually enrolling in—the same university courses as young students is the opportunity to cross the generational divide: to demystify "the other," to open up a dialogue, find a common language, and appreciate the contrasting cultural and historical perspectives.

The intergenerational dialogues that begin to challenge societal expectations and cultural presumptions are a first step toward a much larger, more embracing view of the potential and productivity—both individual and collective—of men and women in their Third Chapters. The narratives in this volume highlight the creativity, courage, and adventurousness of people who are often working against distorted popular and scholarly views of their developmental capacities; working against the harsh currents of a culture that does not fully value their wisdom or their experience; working against economic and public policy perspectives that cast young and old in adversarial roles competing for resources and services. Some speak about this work against these cultural currents as a subtle kind of "political resistance," reminding them of the noisier battles and street demonstrations they participated in as young adults.

But not everyone is like those whose narratives grace these

pages; not everyone has the resources, energy, grit, and determination to survive the difficult challenges. Growth and learning in the Third Chapter do not need to be solitary, lonely pursuits; they should not require that people gird their loins and spend their hard-earned energies resisting and confronting societal expectations, institutional inertia, and cultural ambivalence. We should not feel compelled to reveal the excitement of our new learning in hushed, confessional tones. Rather, societal views of lifelong human development need to be recast. We need to revise our perspectives on aging and retirement, redesign our institutional norms and structures, and look for different reflections in the mirror.

We must develop a compelling vision of later life, one that does not assume a trajectory of decline after fifty but recognizes this as a time of potential change, growth, and new learning, a time when our "courage gives us hope." Changes in life expectancy do not merely mean years added to the end, but an extension of the years of healthy and productive living. Bateson sees hope and potential in the channel of light ever expanding in the Third Chapter: "Life is not a building with an extra wing but one in which an atrium has been opened at the center, full of light and air, and passages toward new possibilities." In this way, the real changes "fall after fifty, in the years when it is now possible for the first time in history, to make new beginnings, new relationships, new careers."[17] Sighting a confluence of changes—in life expectancy, in developmental patterns, and in societal expectations—cultural historians Harry Moody and Thomas Cole call the Third Chapter "a season in search of a purpose."[18]

In order for individuals and society to take advantage of this "atrium . . . of light and air," institutions need to be flexible about the needs for time and space for explorations and new beginnings. We are missing the necessary institutions and infrastructures to harness the action and energy of people in their Third Chapters. "Most people can't just walk out their door and make a difference," claims Freedman about the unreceptive structures and systems that deny "ordinary" older folks access.[19] The gerontologist Matilda White Riley calls this a problem of "structural lag": a situation in which the organizational cultures, roles, and opportunities lag behind the capacities and interests of people between fifty and seventy-five.[20] Institutional innovations for people in their Third Chapters, for example, must allow for a malleability of time that enables people to find the space and a balance in their lives that may have eluded them when they were working full-time and full-steam-ahead. They must also be able to work in a way that offers them more autonomy and control, the "opportunity to switch the locus of control back to themselves; no longer . . . driven from the outside."[21] And they need to be able to establish relationships of mutual respect and collaborative learning with younger colleagues—relationships that honor their skills, maturity, and experience, and that are linked with purposefulness.

There may also be a need to rethink and revise the ways in which people move through—and in and out of—work much earlier in their careers. Perhaps the practice of crossing the boundaries of work and rest, the habit of navigating transitions, of trying on new roles and personas, should be established earlier, allowing people to become familiar with, and adept at, reinventing themselves. Bateson suggests a kind of prophylactic attention to both continuity and discontinuity in life, a need for experiences of reflection that anticipate and help prepare for the Third Chapter:

> One way to go for both effective planning and for intellectual vitality, is to look at the years of adulthood well before standard retirement age and invent ways to build

in a break, like a sabbatical leave, making it a norm rather than the exception. . . . For some, such a break might become a transition to a different sphere of endeavor, public service, perhaps, or the full-time exploration of an avocation. But for many such a break may be simply a refreshment of mind and spirit, energy and creativity, to be carried back to the existing career. . . . Without such a break, adulthood has simply become too long except in professions with a great deal of built-in learning and diversity. Far too many adults burn out and then plod through their later years, prevented by institutional and financial structures from making new beginnings. We need to punctuate a way to end and begin chapters, to break up the run-on-sentences of the same-old-same-old."[22]

Bateson speaks to the need for organizational innovations, and creative invention of other scenarios and arenas of learning, that support a more fluid and frequent movement across boundaries, allowing for shifts in our routines and rhythms across time, and offer us multiple opportunities to recalibrate the balance between work and love, between work, family, and community, and between work and play—all of which may help us revise and expand our definitions of a meaningful, purposeful life.

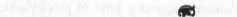

Giovanni's poems that open this chapter cast a light on the spiral of life that suggests both development and return: how moving toward the end of life allows us to be more in touch with our beginnings. A passage from Amy Tan's book *The Joy Luck Club*, a powerful saga about three generations of Chinese women, expresses this circular dynamic. In a voice alive with memories that are beginning to come into clear focus, the grandmother tells her daughter and granddaughter, "Now that I am old, moving closer to the end of my life, I also feel closer to the beginning."[23] The old woman has a yearning to tell her story—a story that echoes with the trauma and terror, and the resilience and courage, of a terrifying childhood journey; a story that is both reclamation and declaration; a story filled with inspiration and truth telling for future generations. Her voice is weary, but not cautious; whispered, but not tentative. She no longer needs to face the mirror with regrets for things lost or dreams deferred; she is no longer seeking a youthful image that has long since vanished. Her wisdom is recorded in her story and in her wish to tell it.

My final interview for this book was with a radiant and dignified African American woman, a seventy-year-old poet, who came to our session with "precious remnants" culled from her work—poems she had carefully chosen to chronicle the new learning in her Third Chapter, each one a courageous record of the changing, aging images of her face in the mirror, at fifty, at sixty, and now at seventy. The final poem, "Reflections," written just weeks before our meeting, honors all of life's imperfections, and recognizes "after long looking, that all of the mirrors are cracked." In the poem, she turns toward the darkness and discovers a path of her own unique invention. Her voice is full of pathos and hope, and her eyes search my face for understanding, as she looks across the table and reads me the final stanza:

> After a long seeking
> I gave up on all mirrors.
> Then feeling a way forward in the fog
> Without a lamp or even a candle

And absent any guide at all,
One starless night I stumbled
Upon this place of water where
Gleaming in its darkest deeps,
My own two astonished eyes.
Light.

NOTES

Introduction: Facing the Mirror

1. Julie Meyer, "Age: 2000," in *Census 2000 Brief* (Washington, D.C.: U.S. Census Bureau, 2001).
2. Eudora Welty, *One Writer's Beginnings* (Cambridge, Mass.: Harvard University Press, 2003 [1983]), 98.
3. Ibid., 14.
4. Ibid.

One: Loss and Liberation

1. Anatole France, in William Bridges, *Managing Transitions: Making the Most of Change* (Reading, Mass.: Addison-Wesley, 1991), 3–6.
2. Mary Catherine Bateson, *Willing to Learn: Passages of Personal Discovery* (Hanover, N.H.: Steerforth Press, 2004), 66.
3. Ibid., 70.
4. Ibid., 219.
5. Bridges, *Managing Transitions*, 3.
6. Ibid., 3–6.
7. Erik H. Erikson, *Childhood and Society* (New York: W. W. Norton, 1950); Erik H. Erikson, *Identity and the Life Cycle* (New York: W. W. Norton, 1959); Erik H. Erikson, *The Life Cycle Completed* (New York: W. W. Norton, 1982); Erik H. Erikson, Joan M. Erikson, and Helen Q. Kivnick, *Vital Involvement in Old Age* (New York: W. W. Norton, 1986).
8. Erikson, *Childhood and Society*, 266–67.
9. Ed de St. Aubin, Dan P. McAdams, and Tae-Chang Kim, "The Generative Society: An Introduction," in *The Generative Society: Caring for Future Generations*, ed. Ed de St. Aubin, Dan P. McAdams, and Tae-Chang Kim (Washington, D.C.: American Psychological Association, 2004), 6.

10. Erikson, *Identity and the Life Cycle*, 103.
11. For more on life-span theory, see Paul B. Baltes, Ulman Lindenberger, and Ursula M. Staudinger, "Life-Span Theory in Developmental Psychology," in *Handbook of Child Psychology*, ed. William Damon and Richard M. Lerner (New York: John Wiley, 1998), 1029–143; Orville G. Brim, Jr., and Jerome Kagan, "Constancy and Change: A View of the Issues," in *Constancy and Change in Human Development*, ed. Orville G. Brim, Jr., and Jerome Kagan (Cambridge, Mass.: Harvard University Press, 1980), 1–25; Rosemary S. Caffarella and Carolyn M. Clark, "Development and Learning: Themes and Conclusions," in *An Update on Adult Development Theory: New Ways of Thinking About the Life Course*, ed. Carolyn M. Clark and Rosemary S. Caffarella (San Francisco: Jossey-Bass, 1999), 97–100; Glen H. Elder, Jr., "The Life Course and Aging: Some Reflections," paper presented at the American Sociological Association, Chicago, Il., 1999; Glen H. Elder, Jr., "The Life Course as Developmental Theory," *Child Development* 69, no. 1 (1998), 1–12; Glen H. Elder, Jr., "The Life Course Paradigm: Social Change and Individual Development," in *Examining Lives in Context: Perspectives on the Ecology of Human Development*, ed. Phyllis Moen, Glen H. Elder, Jr., and Kurt Luscher (Washington, D.C.: American Psychological Association, 1995), 101–39; David L. Featherman, "Life-Span Perspectives in Social Science Research," in *Life-Span Development and Behavior*, ed. Paul B. Baltes and Orville G. Brim, Jr. (New York: Academic Press, 1983), 1–57; Tamara K. Hareven, "The Life Course and Ageing in Historical Perspective," in *Ageing and Life Course Transitions: An Interdisciplinary Perspective*, ed. Tamara K. Hareven and Kathleen J. Adams (New York: Tavistock Publications, 1982), 1–26; Bernice L. Neugarten and Gunhild O. Hagestad, "Age and the Life Course," in *Handbook of Aging and the Social Sciences*, ed. Robert H. Binstock et al. (New York: Van Nostrand Reinhold, 1976), 35–55.
12. Featherman, "Life-Span Perspectives in Social Science Research," 2–3.
13. Hareven, "Life Course and Ageing in Historical Perspective."
14. Elder, Jr., "Life Course Paradigm," 122.
15. Neugarten and Hagestad, "Age and the Life Course," 46.
16. Elder, Jr., "Life Course Paradigm," 121.

Two: Constancy and Change

1. Erikson, *Childhood and Society*, 141.
2. Thomas R. Cole, *The Journey of Life: A Cultural History of Aging in America*, quoted in Marc Freedman, *Prime Time: How Baby Boomers Will Revolutionize Retirement and Transform America* (New York: Public Affairs, 1999), 42.
3. Ibid., 43.
4. Quoted in bid.
5. Ibid., 41.
6. "A Place in the Sun," *Time*, Aug. 3, 1962.

7. Frances FitzGerald, "Sun City," in *Cities on a Hill: A Journey Through Contemporary American Cultures* (New York: Simon and Schuster, 1986), 205.

8. Ibid., 207.

9. "Place in the Sun."

10. Calvin Trillin, "Wake Up and Live," *New Yorker*, April 4, 1964, 120.

11. "Place in the Sun."

12. Paul O'Neil, "For the Retired: A World All Their Own," *Life*, May 14, 1970, 46.

13. Ibid., 45.

14. Freedman, *Prime Time*, 34.

15. "Place in the Sun."

16. Trillin, "Wake Up and Live," 145.

17. O'Neil, "For the Retired," 46.

18. Freedman, *Prime Time*, 59.

19. Ibid., 64.

20. "Place in the Sun."

21. Freedman, *Prime Time*, 62.

22. O'Neil, "For the Retired," 48.

23. FitzGerald, 1986, in Freedman, *Prime Time*, 71.

24. Ibid.

25. Ibid., 71–72.

26. Ibid., 73.

27. Meyer, "Age: 2000."

28. Kenneth D. Kochanek et al., "Deaths: Final Data for 2002," in *National Vital Statistics Reports* (Hyattsville, Md.: Centers for Disease Control and Prevention, 2004), 7–8.

29. WHO, National Institute on Aging, and U.S. Department of Commerce, "Aging in the Americas into the XXI Century" (Washington, D.C.: U.S. Bureau of the Census, 1998).

30. Experience Corps, *Fact Sheet on Aging in America* (Washington, D.C.: Experience Corps, 2000).

31. U.S. Census Bureau and Current Population Survey, "Percent of High School and College Graduates of the Population 15 Years and Over: 2004" (Washington, D.C.: U.S. Census Bureau, 2005).

32. AARP, *Staying Ahead of the Curve: The AARP Work and Career Study* (Washington, D.C.: AARP, 2002), 8.

33. Alfred Marshall, *The Principles of Economics* (New York: Macmillan, for the Royal Economic Society, 1961 [1890]).

Three: Healing Wounds: The Journey Home

1. Howard Thurman, *The Mood of Christmas* (Richmond, Ind.: Friends United Press, 1985), 10–11.

2. Jane Fonda, *My Life So Far* (New York: Random House, 2005), vi.

3. Selma Fraiberg, Edna Adelson, and Vivian Shapiro, "Ghosts in the Nursery: A Psychoanalytic Approach to the Problems of Impaired Infant-Mother Relationships," in *Selected Writings of Selma Fraiberg*, ed. Louis Fraiberg (Columbus: Ohio State University Press, 1987). Article originally published in the *Journal of the American Academy of Child Psychiatry* 14 (1975): 387–421.
4. Carol Gilligan, *In a Different Voice: Psychological Theory and Women's Development* (Cambridge, Mass.: Harvard University Press, 1993 [1982]), 42.

Four: Looking Back and Giving Forward

1. Frederick Buechner, in Parker Palmer, *Let Your Life Speak* (San Francisco: Jossey-Bass, 2000), 16.
2. Freedman, *Prime Time*, 178.
3. Bateson, *Willing to Learn*, 86.
4. Ibid.
5. Freedman, *Prime Time*, 165.
6. Ibid., vi.
7. Ibid., 111.
8. Ibid., 233.

Five: Crossing Boundaries and Embracing Contradictions

1. Toni Morrison, Unpublished speech, delivered at Radcliffe Institute for Advanced Studies, Cambridge, Mass., June 8, 2007.
2. Bateson, *Willing to Learn*, 348–49.
3. Peter L. Berger, *Invitation to Sociology: A Humanistic Perspective* (Garden City, N.Y.: Doubleday, 1963), 23.

Six: New Learning: Body, Voice, and Soul

1. Alan Lightman, "Pas de Deux," in *Dance for Two: Selected Essays* (New York: Pantheon, 1996), 3.
2. Nikki Giovanni, "Patience," in *The Collected Poetry of Nikki Giovanni* (New York: William Morrow, 2003), 223.
3. Langston Hughes, "The Negro Speaks of Rivers," in *The Collected Poems of Langston Hughes*, ed. Arnold Rampersad (New York: Vintage, 1995), 23.

Conclusion: Cracks in the Mirror

1. Nikki Giovanni, "Adulthood II," in *The Selected Poems of Nikki Giovanni* (New York: William Morrow, 1996), 205.
2. Nikki Giovanni, "Age," ibid., 202.

3. For more on Erikson's theories, see chap. one and the following references: Erikson, *Childhood and Society*; Erikson, *Identity and the Life Cycle*; Erikson, *Life Cycle Completed*; Erikson, Erikson, and Kivnick, *Vital Involvement in Old Age*.

4. Bateson, *Willing to Learn*, 126.

5. Ibid., 87.

6. Ibid., 85.

7. Ibid., 142.

8. Howard Gardner, *Frames of Mind: The Theory of Multiple Intelligences* (New York: Basic Books, 1983).

9. Daniel Goleman, *Emotional Intelligence* (New York: Bantam Books, 1995).

10. Orville G. Brim, Jr., quoted in Paul B. Baltes, "On the Potential and Limits of Child Development: Life-Span Developmental Perspectives," *Issues in Child Development* (Summer 1979): 2–3.

11. Bateson, *Willing to Learn*, 130.

12. Ibid., 134.

13. John Kotre, "Generativity and Culture: What Meaning Can Do," in *The Generative Society: Caring for Future Generations*, ed. Ed de St. Aubin, Dan P. McAdams, and Tae-Chang Kim (Washington, D.C.: American Psychological Association, 2004), 41.

14. Dan P. McAdams and Regina L. Logan, "What Is Generativity?," ibid., 25.

15. Erikson, *Life Cycle Completed*, 118.

16. Arlyn Tobias Gajilan, "A Golden Age on Campus," *Newsweek*, Nov. 9, 1998.

17. Bateson, *Willing to Learn*, 145.

18. Harry Moody and Thomas Cole, in Freedman, *Prime Time*, 21.

19. Ibid.

20. Matilda White Riley, ibid., 22.

21. Margaret Mark and Marvin Waldman, *Recasting Retirement: New Perspectives on Aging and Civic Engagement*, ed. Civic Ventures and Temple University Center for Intergenerational Learning (San Francisco: Civic Ventures, 2002), 4.

22. Bateson, *Willing to Learn*, 148.

23. Amy Tan, *The Joy Luck Club* (New York: Putnam's, 1989), 83.

BIBLIOGRAPHY

AARP. *Staying Ahead of the Curve: The AARP Work and Career Study.* Washington, D.C.: AARP, 2002.

Baltes, Paul B. "On the Potential and Limits of Child Development: Life-Span Developmental Perspectives." *Issues in Child Development* (Summer 1979).

Baltes, Paul B., Ulman Lindenberger, and Ursula M. Staudinger. "Life-Span Theory in Developmental Psychology." In *Handbook of Child Psychology*, edited by William Damon and Richard M. Lerner. New York: John Wiley, 1998. Pp. 1029–143.

Bateson, Mary Catherine. *Willing to Learn: Passages of Personal Discovery.* Hanover, N.H.: Steerforth Press, 2004.

Berger, Peter L. *Invitation to Sociology: A Humanistic Perspective.* Garden City, N.Y.: Doubleday, 1963.

Bridges, William. *Managing Transitions: Making the Most of Change.* Reading, Mass.: Addison-Wesley, 1991.

Brim, Jr., Orville G., and Jerome Kagan. "Constancy and Change: A View of the Issues." In *Constancy and Change in Human Development*, edited by Orville G. Brim, Jr., and Jerome Kagan. Cambridge, Mass.: Harvard University Press, 1980. Pp. 1–25.

Caffarella, Rosemary S., and Carolyn M. Clark. "Development and Learning: Themes and Conclusions." In *An Update on Adult Development Theory: New Ways of Thinking About the Life Course*, edited by Carolyn M. Clark and Rosemary S. Caffarella. San Francisco: Jossey-Bass, 1999. Pp. 97–100.

de St. Aubin, Ed, Dan P. McAdams, and Tae-Chang Kim. "The Generative Society: An Introduction." In *The Generative Society: Caring for Future Generations*, edited by Ed de St. Aubin, Dan P. McAdams, and Tae-Chang Kim. Washington, D.C.: American Psychological Association, 2004.

Elder, Jr., Glen H. "The Life Course and Aging: Some Reflections." Paper presented at the American Sociological Association, Chicago, Il., 1999.

———. "The Life Course as Developmental Theory." *Child Development* 69, no. 1 (1998): 1–12.

———. "The Life Course Paradigm: Social Change and Individual Development." In *Examining Lives in Context: Perspectives on the Ecology of Human Development*, edited by Phyllis Moen, Glen H. Elder, Jr., and Kurt Luscher. Washington, D.C.: American Psychological Association, 1995. Pp. 101–39.

Erikson, Erik H. *Childhood and Society*. New York: W. W. Norton, 1950.

———. *Identity and the Life Cycle*. New York: W. W. Norton, 1959.

———. *The Life Cycle Completed*. New York: W. W. Norton, 1982.

Erikson, Erik H., Joan M. Erikson, and Helen Q. Kivnick. *Vital Involvement in Old Age*. New York: W. W. Norton, 1986.

Experience Corps. *Fact Sheet on Aging in America*. Washington, D.C.: Experience Corps, 2000.

Featherman, David L. "Life-Span Perspectives in Social Science Research." In *Life-Span Development and Behavior*, edited by Paul B. Baltes and Orville G. Brim, Jr. New York: Academic Press, 1983. Pp. 1–57.

FitzGerald, Frances. "Sun City." In *Cities on a Hill: A Journey Through Contemporary American Cultures*. New York: Simon and Schuster, 1986. Pp. 203–46.

Fonda, Jane. *My Life So Far*. New York: Random House, 2005.

Fraiberg, Selma, Edna Adelson, and Vivian Shapiro. "Ghosts in the Nursery: A Psychoanalytic Approach to the Problems of Impaired Infant-Mother Relationships." In *Selected Writings of Selma Fraiberg*, edited by Louis Fraiberg. Columbus: Ohio State University Press, 1987.

Freedman, Marc. *Prime Time: How Baby Boomers Will Revolutionize Retirement and Transform America*. New York: Public Affairs, 1999.

Gajilan, Arlyn Tobias. "A Golden Age on Campus." *Newsweek*, November 9, 1998.

Gardner, Howard. *Frames of Mind: The Theory of Multiple Intelligences*. New York: Basic Books, 1983.

Gilligan, Carol. *In a Different Voice: Psychological Theory and Women's Development*. Cambridge, Mass.: Harvard University Press, 1993 [1982].

Giovanni, Nikki. "Adulthood II." In *The Selected Poems of Nikki Giovanni*. New York: William Morrow, 1996. P. 205.

———. "Age." In *The Selected Poems of Nikki Giovanni*. New York: William Morrow, 1996. P. 202.

———. "Patience." In *The Collected Poetry of Nikki Giovanni*. New York: William Morrow, 1996. P. 223.

Goleman, Daniel. *Emotional Intelligence*. New York: Bantam Books, 1995.

Hareven, Tamara K. "The Life Course and Aging in Historical Perspective." In

Aging and Life Course Transitions: An Interdisciplinary Perspective, edited by Tamara K. Hareven and Kathleen J. Adams. New York: Tavistock Publications, 1982. Pp. 1–26.

Hughes, Langston. "The Negro Speaks of Rivers." In *The Collected Poems of Langston Hughes*, edited by Arnold Rampersad. New York: Vintage, 1995. P. 23.

Kochanek, Kenneth D., Sherry L. Murphy, Robert N. Anderson, and Chester Scott. "Deaths: Final Data for 2002." In *National Vital Statistics Reports*. Hyattsville, Md.: Centers for Disease Control and Prevention, 2004.

Kotre, John. "Generativity and Culture: What Meaning Can Do." In *The Generative Society: Caring for Future Generations*, edited by Ed de St. Aubin, Dan P. McAdams, and Tae-Chang Kim. Washington, D.C.: American Psychological Association, 2004.

Lightman, Alan. "Pas de Deux." In *Dance for Two: Selected Essays*. New York: Pantheon, 1996. P. 3.

Mark, Margaret, and Marvin Waldman. *Recasting Retirement: New Perspectives on Aging and Civic Engagement*, edited by Civic Ventures and Temple University Center for Intergenerational Learning. San Francisco: Civic Ventures, 2002. Pp. 1–12.

Marshall, Alfred. *The Principles of Economics*. New York: Macmillan, for the Royal Economic Society, 1961 [1890].

McAdams, Dan P., and Regina L. Logan. "What Is Generativity?" In *The Generative Society: Caring for Future Generations*, edited by Ed de St. Aubin, Dan P. McAdams, and Tae-Chang Kim. Washington, D.C.: American Psychological Association, 2004.

Meyer, Julie. "Age: 2000." In *Census 2000 Brief*. Washington, D.C.: U.S. Census Bureau, 2001.

Morrison, Toni. Unpublished speech. Delivered at Radcliffe Institute for Advanced Studies, Cambridge, Mass., June 8, 2007.

Neugarten, Bernice L., and Gunhild O. Hagestad. "Age and the Life Course." In *Handbook of Aging and the Social Sciences*, edited by Robert H. Binstock, Ethel Shanas, Vern L. Bengston, George L. Maddox, and Dorothy Wedderburn. New York: Van Nostrand Reinhold, 1976. Pp. 35–55.

O'Neil, Paul. "For the Retired: A World All Their Own." *Life*, May 14, 1970. Pp. 45–50.

Palmer, Parker. *Let Your Life Speak*. San Francisco: Jossey-Bass, 2000.

"A Place in the Sun." *Time*, August 3, 1962.

Tan, Amy. *The Joy Luck Club*. New York: Putnam's, 1989.

Thurman, Howard. *The Mood of Christmas*. Richmond, Ind.: Friends United Press, 1985.

Trillin, Calvin. "Wake Up and Live." *New Yorker*, April 4, 1964. Pp. 120–72.

U.S. Census Bureau and Current Population Survey. "Percent of High School and College Graduates of the Population 15 Years and Over: 2004." Washington, D.C.: U.S. Census Bureau, 2005.

Welty, Eudora. *One Writer's Beginnings*. Cambridge, Mass.: Harvard University Press, 2003 [1983].

WHO, National Institute on Aging, and U.S. Department of Commerce. "Aging in the Americas into the XXI Century." Washington, D.C.: U.S. Bureau of the Census, 1998.

ACKNOWLEDGMENTS

New learning in the Third Chapter requires a willingness to take risks, experience vulnerability and uncertainty, learn from experimentation, improvisation, and failure, seek guidance and counsel from younger generations, and develop new relationships of support and intimacy. I am deeply indebted to the forty women and men whose voices fill this volume, for allowing me to witness their curiosity and courage, probe their wisdom and insights, and listen for the narratives they composed about their tender and treacherous adventures in learning. I am so admiring of their honesty and humility, their passion and generosity. Although their experiences, journeys, and stories have been faithfully documented and recorded, I have—by mutual agreement—altered names and places to protect their privacy and that of their families.

As always, my amazing assistant, Wendy E. Angus, was by my side and in my corner, bringing her wonderful insights, her balanced perspective, and her rigor to every phase of this project. My research assistant, Sarah Dryden-Peterson, combed through the literature with a discerning eye, wrote penetrating synopses, and cheerfully did the meticulous work of checking references and sources, bridging the big ideas and the tiny details. My wonderful, faithful friends—all in their Third Chapters—shared their stories, challenged my interpretations, and made my work feel like play. I am always thankful to Maya Carlson and Tony Earls, Andrea Fleck Clardy, Susan and Robert Berger,

Tom and Katie Cottle, Will and Jessica Davis, Ronne Hartfield, Judy Katz, Patricia and Loren Graham, Linda Mason, Mary Graham, Marita Rivero, Paul Solman, and Marti Wilson.

My family—now four generations, with the recent arrival of precious Paloma—calls me home and nourishes my soul. Mom Margaret—at ninety-three—continues to be deeply curious about life, radiant in her resilience, courageous in her questioning, and generous in her service. I am thankful for her lifelong example of adventurous living. My daughter, Tolani, loved this book idea from the very beginning, asking her impertinent youthful questions, offering her keen aesthetic and powerful metaphors. When things got too weighty and serious, my son, Martin, lit my way with his funky wit and playful encouragement. I am thankful to my brother Chuck and sister Paula, their spouses, and their progeny, for the conversations and laughter around the dining room table; for the soulful singing and colorful storytelling, moving back and forth through time. Paula found poetry and scripture that honored the spirit of the work; her husband, John, was the first in my family to read the manuscript, responding with recognition and tears. And my partner, Irving Hamer, brought his adventurous spirit, his huge appetites, his counter-narrative, and his penetrating questions to our lively exchanges, always pushing to find the universal in the particular, the rawness underneath the restraint.

Ike Williams, my agent extraordinaire, understood immediately the public and private dimensions of this work, and was strategic and smart in finding the right home for this book. I am always grateful for his ideas, insights, and advocacy. I'm also thankful to Hope Denekamp, his savvy assistant, who blends true grit and lovely grace; she's always there to help and guide me. Finally, I am indebted to my wonderful editor and publisher, Sarah Crichton, for her demanding pen, her clear-eyed incisiveness, her spirited cheerleading, and her truth-telling. She has been ably assisted by Cailey Hall, whose calm reassurance and good taste I always value.

THE THIRD CHAPTER

Passion, Risk, and Adventure

in the 25 Years After 50

SARA LAWRENCE-LIGHTFOOT

**A CONVERSATION BETWEEN BILL MOYERS
AND SARA LAWRENCE-LIGHTFOOT**

READER'S GUIDE

ABOUT THIS GUIDE

The following questions and discussion topics are designed to enhance your reading of Sara Lawrence-Lightfoot's *The Third Chapter*. We hope they'll enrich your experience as you explore this celebration of life's most transformative years.

INTRODUCTION

The Third Chapter of life, marked by the years between fifty and seventy-five, presents unprecedented potential for personal growth and fulfillment. Yet society often offers a murky view of this phase, unsure of how to view a population "neither young nor old." Challenging the notion that people over fifty enter a period of diminishing opportunities, the renowned sociologist Dr. Sara Lawrence-Lightfoot brings a rejuvenating new perspective to these debates. Brimming with profiles of men and women who approached these years with passion, innovation, and wisdom, *The Third Chapter* shares the insights of courageous souls from all walks of life who redefined "work," reinvented themselves, and tapped their emotional resources in creative new ways. The result is a revolutionary yet realistic challenge to all who are living in the Third Chapter, providing a gateway to liberation and greater meaning as each day unfolds.

QUESTIONS FOR DISCUSSION

1. Discuss the cultural challenges and myths surrounding life after fifty. How have these challenges and myths shifted over time? How do you, your friends, and your family regard the different stages of life? Do you exalt youth?

2. Chapter one, "Loss and Liberation," describes the fear that often comes with leaving behind a lifelong routine, or a career and an identity. How did the author's interviewees cope with this uncertainty and anxiety? What did it take to spur them to change?

3. How has *The Third Chapter* shaped your definition of learning? How do you think the reverence society holds for IQ-enhancing learning differs from its respect for learning wisdom and patience? What would it take to get society to change the way it prioritizes these different kinds of knowledge?

4. Chapter three describes those who courageously confronted the past. Were you surprised that emotional wounds from years ago can have a significant impact on the Third Chapter? What common threads do Luther Brown and Pamela Stein share in the way they managed memories of authority figures? What power lies in writing our own narratives, as Grace Clark did when she left her job in publishing?

5. How has the boom in retirement communities, and even Franklin Roosevelt's notion of social security for retirement,

changed our concept of the aging process? How would your life look if you never anticipated retiring? Has retirement had a negative impact on the way we perceive the Third Chapter?

6. Chapter five captures the sometimes daunting experience of venturing into new places, such as Roma Wolfe's sojourn from a physics lab to a low-income school. What are your "forbidden places"? What rejuvenation might you find there?

7. How do gender differences affect our approaches to the Third Chapter? Can age liberate us from gender stereotypes?

8. The conclusion of chapter five describes the stages of crossing boundaries: curiosity, letting go of fear, willingness to be vulnerable, developing empathy, and finally discovering that new learning doesn't mean losing touch with your known world. Have you reached any of these stages? What are the risks and rewards of the process?

9. Sara Lawrence-Lightfoot describes the unique history of the current Third Chapter generation members, many of whom were steeped in 1960s activism. What makes it especially hard for this generation to "recede"? What special potentials does it possess?

10. Discuss the impact of ancestors in shaping your sense of self. How do your expectations of the Third Chapter compare to those of your parents' generation?

11. Many of the people interviewed by Sara Lawrence-Lightfoot are artists. Does society encourage artistic expression? What are

the emotional costs of stifling artistic urges until after retirement?

12. The manuscript of *The Third Chapter* was finished shortly before the 2008 economic collapse. How do you think the recession would change the answers the people in this book gave? How does affluence affect the way someone experiences the Third Chapter? Can it be a time of significant personal growth regardless of economic status?

13. In that vein, if rejuvenation doesn't require a lot of money to spend, what does it require? How can you ensure a prosperous Third Chapter in times of limited opportunity?

14. What aspects of education, described in the book's conclusion, would most enhance a spirit of lifelong learning for future generations? How would reinventing the Third Chapter, beginning with the age groups that precede it, benefit society?

15. How did you respond to Erik Erikson's notion of the "penultimate" stage—a phase of production, not stagnation—and the impulse to guide the next generation? Which populations would you most want to "give forward" to? Describe your ideal legacy.

16. In uniting new learning with body, voice, and soul, what struggles do you face? What instincts do you possess to help you work through them? In what ways do your internal and external terrains reflect each other?

A CONVERSATION BETWEEN
BILL MOYERS AND
SARA LAWRENCE-LIGHTFOOT

The veteran journalist Bill Moyers sat down with Sara Lawrence-Lightfoot for an inspiring conversation about *The Third Chapter*, which aired on his PBS series, *Bill Moyers Journal*, on May 8, 2009. The following is adapted from that segment. The full transcript can be found at PBS.org/Moyers.

BILL MOYERS: I first interviewed Sara Lawrence-Lightfoot a generation ago, when she was a young professor at Harvard University. She has now been on the Harvard faculty for thirty-seven years. Sara Lawrence-Lightfoot, welcome to the *Journal*.

SARA LAWRENCE-LIGHTFOOT: Wonderful to be here.

BM: How time flies.

SLL: Yes. That's true.

BM: I can't believe it's been over twenty-one years since I last interviewed you. You were writing then about your mother—in *Balm in Gilead*, one of my favorites. Your mother is now how old?

SLL: Ninety-four years old.

BM: And here you are, writing about aging. What are you trying to tell me?

SLL: Well, what happened was that several years ago, at almost every cocktail party, dinner party, professional conference, and meeting, someone would lean in to me for what I began to call "confessional moments." They would tell me something about what they were truly excited about, passionate about, an adventure that they were on, that was new for them, and I would listen.

Their voices held both extraordinary passion and excitement, but at the same time, sort of a shyness or reticence—as if what they were talking about shouldn't be taken too seriously. But on the other hand, it was something that they felt deeply about. And I began to wonder: What were these moments about? People were talking about new learning in their lives, new adventures that they were taking, new risks. And they seemed so much more excited about these moments than when they would talk about their work, or even when they would talk about their family. So, I became curious: What is the text, and what is the subtext of these moments, these moments that I was calling "confessional moments"?

BM: Were you having any confessional moments of your own?

SLL: I probably was, but mostly I was experiencing this as listener, as receiver of these experiences. At the same time, there was always something that resonated with me about the idea that all of us, at this point in our lives, to some degree, are on a search for meaningfulness, for purposefulness. We want to find what this next twenty-five years, this penultimate chapter of our life, is going to be about. And we're ready for something new—for a new experience, for a new adventure.

I think all of us, to some degree, experience some burnout. Burnout is not about working too hard, or too diligently, or being overcommitted. Burnout is about boredom. And so, I think in some ways, this is about moving beyond the boredom—to compose, to invent, and to reinvent the path that we're on.

BM: And yet, you say that while they would talk excitedly and with passion about this vision or this confessional moment, there was also a note of fear in their voices.

SLL: I think two things are happening there. One is that we are still a youth-obsessed culture. And so, what we who have grown up in this culture all believe is that we should be in retreat at this moment. We should be, you know, kind of pulling back, feeling comfortable and staying still. But these stories that I was being told were about moving out, taking an adventure. They seemed to be going against the cultural norms that we have been embedded in for most of our lives.

It's hard to leave these roles that have given us responsibility and status; that may even have given us influence and power. Those roles become comfortable. And to go on this journey that takes us away from that feels terrifying at first.

BM: One of the most interesting revelations in the book to me is that you, in just a few pages, discuss the way the pendulum has swung back and forth in this country toward aging. I mean, there was a time, in the early days, when Americans powdered their wigs in order to look older—and then there was a time when aging was considered an incurable disease to be treated in old folks' homes, as we used to call them.

And now here you are, sitting before me, describing this aging, this growing old as a time of great excitement and adventure and passion.

SLL: Yes.

BM: What has happened to bring about the change in our perception of the elderly?

SLL: Well, we're living longer. That's one big piece. The arc of our lives has changed enormously. We're not dying at fifty. We are, if we're lucky, living to eighty, eighty-five, ninety. So that this period that I'm talking about, between fifty and seventy-five, is not our final stage, but our penultimate period.

BM: The next to last.

SLL: Right, the next to last. And I really believe this is perhaps the most transformative time of our lives—most exciting, in terms of new learning, and limitless in its opportunities.

Now, a lot of people may not have experienced this yet, because the cultural shifts and the institutional shifts haven't yet happened in order to support that in most of us. Most people still see this time as a time of retrenchment. They don't enjoy the beauty, the wisdom, the experience that comes with aging. And we continue to look at younger people as those people who have the energy and the drive and the new ideas.

BM: Well, there's something of a cultural and political factor there, because it was, what? in 1935, in the New Deal, that the

Social Security Act was passed, and people were told they have a "right to retire."

SLL: And a lot of people experienced stopping work as a kind of death.

BM: My father did. I mean, when he retired at sixty-five, something in him died. I know that's a cliché. But I could see it.

SLL: A lot of people continue to experience that. One of the things I found, in interviewing forty people across the country for this book, was that many of them had decided to retire—but also to continue to do work that's meaningful. They were figuring out ways to be productive. To be purposeful. To be creative. To be innovative.

BM: You acknowledge in here that these forty people do not represent the majority of people in this country. And it's also obvious that the book deals with people of an affluent class—people who have the means to make choices, and to go this way instead of that way. Whereas there are, you know, six, seven, eight million people in this country, over forty-five, who are living in poverty, and they don't have choices.

SLL: Well, we think they don't have choices. One of the things I talk about is "perceived abundance." How do we experience our life? Do we see whether we have a great deal of material resources or not; do we see choices in front of us?

A factory worker from Madison, Wisconsin, tells me that he was laid off, and that he and his wife went to the flea market every single Saturday with their stuff, trying to trade it or sell it, so that they could put food on their tables, and continue to feed their family. One Saturday, he saw these strange and interesting sculptures made by artists who were bringing their art to the flea market.

"You know what?" he thought. "I could do that. I'm a welder. I'm good with metal." So he went home, and began playing with the metal that he had around his house. He loves dinosaurs; has loved them since he saw *Jurassic Park*.

He begins to create these dinosaur sculptures. He takes them to the flea market. People become interested. He sells them for almost nothing. It catches on. And by the time he's talking to me, he's telling me that he's gotten his first gig with an art gallery. So, his innovation, his resourcefulness, and ultimately his pride in his own creativity have come through for him.

BM: One of the interesting insights in this book is that you say there's a difference between this new learning we have to do when we enter the Third Chapter, and the old narrow cognitive learning of the classroom. What's the difference?

SLL: Well, almost everyone that I talked to for this book—even if they were very successful students in school, and had very successful careers by all traditional standards—talked about the fact that the learning that goes on in the Third Chapter is often contrary, a contradiction, to the ways in which they were taught, and excelled in school. School teaches us to move quickly. To be singular in our ambitions. To be competitive. To not waste time. To not show failure or weakness. But in the Third Chapter, when people talk about learning, they talk about needing to be creative, needing to be collaborative. And that sometimes, in order to discover the best way that we can learn, we need to fail.

BM: To be willing to make a fool out of ourselves, you say in the book.

SLL: Absolutely. To be willing to fail and make a fool out of ourselves, at least in the short run. Of course, the ingredient that's so important here is humor: the ability to laugh at ourselves, lighten up, you know? Not worry about our facade and our persona, but instead really get into the process.

BM: One of the people in the book actually says to you that she's learned that patience is a major gift of life. That it's so important to do things slowly, which is something she had forgotten over the course of her life.

SLL: That's right. This is someone who had been a filmmaker, and she talked about the fact that it had always been rush, rush, rush with her. Her parents had actually talked about it, too: "Quickly, quickly, quickly." Be the best by shooting your hand up first, by making it to the front of the class.

BM: Tell me about it.

SLL: What she was realizing in this Third Chapter was how glorious it is to slow down—to be able to be reflective, to be meditative.

My favorite thing about this period, my own revelation, is restraint. How wonderful it is to know a little bit more about when *not* to talk. When *not* to move forward. When it's best to listen and sit back, to just witness and observe. And that slowness of pace offers us the opportunity to see things newly. To discover things that we hadn't seen before; to see the small, incremental steps, rather than expect the large leaps forward.

BM: You say in here that you looked into the eyes of these people, and saw your own reflection, with confessional moments of her own. Are you facing having to unlearn some things that have made you the success you are?

SLL: Well, I'm in one of those rare professions where I'm always able to engage in new learning. Each book I write is a new quest for me. And that's a huge luxury and privilege.

But I also see changes in the ways in which I behave within the context of my institution. For example, I used to reject the idea that I needed to mentor other people. It sort of made me feel old, to establish myself as a mentor and guide. But now, I embrace it. It is important that I let myself be a mentor to my younger colleagues. It is important that I work with and support them.

And, returning to "restraint," if I'm in a senior faculty meeting now, I listen more, and speak less. I've learned that timing is important. When I speak is important. I am comfortable waiting and waiting, and choosing my moment. And I'm likely to say what I think; I'm much less cautious. I want to be very honest, very clear. And even in a scholarly session, I will speak my mind and speak my heart, and say where my ideas come from, even if they don't come from cognition.

BM: Is it true, as I have heard, that you went canvassing, knocking on doors, door by door, last fall, in the presidential campaign with a twenty-four-year-old?

SLL: Yes, I did. One of the things I talk about in this book, that's so important, is that in our society we really need to engage much more in cross-generational encounters, discourse, conversation, and movements.

BM: But that's so hard to do, because we are separated into our different realities, right?

SLL: I think that's absolutely true. But I think that one example of young people working with old people in a common project was the last presidential campaign.

I went out campaigning in New Hampshire, three or four times, with a young kid, from Dartmouth. The campaign paired us together, and it was really interesting. I kept wishing I was a fly on the wall, or an ethnographer, watching us navigate our relationship and our encounters.

BM: How so?

SLL: Well, this was a kid who had voluminous knowledge about politics, and he was incredibly energetic. But he was also completely urgent, and impatient, and a terrible listener. He had stereotyped all of New Hampshire. He thought the people there were all backwoods, rural country people. Republicans. And he thought they hadn't really thought deeply about the issues, and that all he needed to do was feed them the information.

My approach, instead, was to start by listening to them. Not to assume that I knew who they were just because I knew where they lived. Not to begin with a stereotype, and to expect that they had the capacity to think deeply, as well.

And so the negotiation of our relationship was for me to help him wait, help him listen. And it was also for me to experience and catch his energy and drive—and his optimism.

BM: Clearly, he had more energy than you, right?

SLL: He had more energy. But his impatience often depleted his energy, you know, because he was so impatient to get the message across.

BM: Throughout your book, you quote someone who was on this show recently—Nikki Giovanni, the poet. She has a poem in which she says, "There are sounds which shatter the staleness of lives, transporting the shadows into the dreams." Most people I know, twenty-four years old or seventy-four years old, want to shatter the staleness. What have you learned about how to do that?

SLL: Well, one of the things that I found in talking to people was that, in order to move forward into new learning in the Third Chapter, they first had to overcome early negative experiences, often dating from childhood.

This was a very common theme among the forty I interviewed for the book. They needed to return to early hurts—to a time when they were feeling that they weren't being supported or nourished, maybe they were even being neglected and abused.

They need to return to that place of hurt, not to blame anyone—but to try to understand it. In some cases it's a metaphoric return, in others, it's more literal. It's literally going back to Ohio and walking up the steps of your father's house and knocking on the door, and talking to him, honestly, about what your experience was as a small child.

Sometimes people discovered those early hurts in the course of an interview. They would be telling some story that they had told many, many, many times before—which had been seen as a positive, affirmative, optimistic story—they would discover the underbelly of it as we were talking. And the discovery of that underbelly would illuminate their reasons for moving forward now.

BM: So, when they would identify these wounds, and begin to open them, what would happen? What do they tell you happened to enable them to go forward?

SLL: Well, let me give you an example. There's a public-health doctor, sixty-seven years old, from a middle-class African American family, and he is someone who's always worked very, very hard, most of the time in West Africa, working on eliminating malaria. And he has begun to take voice lessons, which he loves.

I ask him, "Why voice lessons?"

And he begins to tell the story of sitting in his mother's arms, at age six, every Sunday, listening to the Metropolitan Opera. And he loves this moment, because he is in his mother's arms, and because there's nothing more glorious than these resonant voices. And he says to his mother one day, "Mom, that's what I want to be. I want to be an opera singer."

She doesn't respond with any words, but what he remembers while talking to me is this dismissive look that she gave him. And he says, with tears in his eyes, now talking to me, "It's as if she thought that opera singers were sissies."

So he retreats, immediately. He never raises that up again. And he becomes a wonderful public-health doctor, giving to the world.

But then, at age sixty-five, he begins to take voice lessons, and he experiences, as he says, "a liberation I've never felt. A freedom I've never felt."

And the real kicker in this story is that, in conversation with me, he discovers that this new learning not only feels liberating in a physical and emotional sense, but also that discovering his new voice has helped him to become a better doctor.

BM: In contrast to that, there's a woman in your book named Pamela, a psychologist and an activist, who talks very poignantly about wanting, in this stage of her life, to do the "radical thing"—to make a difference. And she's disillusioned, or disappointed at least, to find that the solutions seem out of reach. That it's harder for her to rally people to a collective sense of responsibility than she had thought it would be. And she discovers that neither government nor private institutions are designed to prepare to help her make a difference.

SLL: Well, this is someone who is progressive, who has been an activist all of her life. And who sought to make a difference beyond the domain of psychology or clinical psychology. She is worried about death. Many of the people in her family have died early. She sees the finiteness of her life. And she wants to take on something big, right? She wants government, and hospitals, and the whole medical, psychological establishment to respond to the veterans coming back from Iraq and Afghanistan—to recognize that they're not crazy; that they've been through a trauma of huge, profound significance. And yet, she can't get this message across. She feels as if the institutions are not recognizing, or responding to, their trauma, and so she feels enormously frustrated.

BM: So is she going to spend the Third Chapter sullen and resigned?

SLL: No. She's keeping on pushing. But our conversations gave her an opportunity to really weep at the fact that she believes, "I'm at my most powerful now. I have the most to give. I'm the wisest. My voice is strong. My influence should be great—and yet I feel it diminished, at this point."

BM: Does it strike you that there are not enough people in our society who listen?

SLL: Oh, absolutely. Absolutely. I learned two important things in the writing of this book. One was the critical importance in new learning of curiosity. The other was the importance of listening, and in particular, the importance of cross-generational projects and dialogues. Young people listening to old people; old people listening to the young. Having a real discourse, with respect and with empathy.

BM: That twenty-four-year-old you politicked with last fall in New Hampshire. What does he want to do with his life and what did he learn from you about what he could do?

SLL: Well, one of the things that I think he learned from me was that he will have many chances to remake himself. Meaning, there will be many chapters and many challenges. I think the other thing that we talked a lot about in our walks from house to house was failure. That is, what I have learned, and what most people at our age have learned, as we look back on our lives, is the value of those moments when we have failed. We've learned that we need to pick ourselves up and move on. I talked to him about welcoming those moments.

But most of the time, he was talking. And he was talking about politics.

BM: The people in your book don't talk much about death.

SLL: No.

BM: Why is that? Was that deliberate on your part?

SLL: No, it wasn't. Pamela, who you just talked about, is one of the few people in the book who talks about death. The rest, well, they're too busy living.

BM: But, surely, they have to think in the back of their minds about it. They can see the grains of sand going down the hour-glass.

SLL: I think there is an expression of urgency in their new work, and in their new learning. This notion of limited time is very much there. So you do see an interesting paradox: the emerging patience of this period, coupled with a sense of urgency, of time moving on.

BM: So, I'll come back to you. Are you feeling that sense of urgency? You're only sixty-four. To me, that's just adolescence in the Third Chapter.

SLL: Well, I certainly am feeling the curiosity. I'm feeling the urgency. I'm feeling the patience. I'm feeling the courage to ask questions that may not have been asked before. To say what it is I need to say. It isn't that I think I'm invincible at all, but I have these qualities that have been, I think, deepened during this period of time—that I think will hold me and will help me move forward in this Third Chapter.

BM: People in the book talk openly about their own fears. What are you afraid of, at this stage?

SLL: Sometimes I'm afraid of loneliness. Even though I'm surrounded by glorious family and friends and have lots of love.

BM: What do you mean?

SLL: Well, when I look at people in their fourth chapters, I see the possibility of isolation. The probability—not just the probability, but the certainty—that as you grow older, your friends will disappear, they will die.

I look at my mother, who's ninety-four, who has deep curiosity, and who is very much engaged in the world. But most of her friends have died, and I think that I see that as a profound loneliness. So that's one of the things that I worry about.

BM: You finished this manuscript shortly before the great economic collapse.

SLL: Yes.

BM: How do you think the new reality would change the answers the people in this book gave you?

SLL: I don't know that it would change it very much. One of the things I've been hearing is that, in a time of reduced resources, when you need to sacrifice, when there is less stuff, there is a need to be innovative and creative. And the capacity to innovate is very much what these people are talking about.

I remember a time in my life when I was lowest and my mother saying, "Sweetheart, out of this suffering will come creativity." And she was right.

I don't mean to idealize what has happened, at all. But I think there are ways in which this reduction in our resources can force us to think more dynamically, more creatively, about how we can do more with less. In fact, how we can shape a new legacy in this time of sacrifice.

BM: You make me think particularly about the Baby Boomers. Not all of the people you write about here are Baby Boomers, but some are, and the Baby Boomers in particular grew up in a period of prosperity and relative abundance and they saw themselves as powerful actors who wanted to shape the culture and paradigm of their era. And they brought, as you know, considerable resources and wealth to the challenge. Now the rug has been pulled out from under them, and I wonder how they are reacting to the new reality.

SLL: Well, it's true. In our younger years, we Baby Boomers were, you know, bodacious, we were audacious. We were entitled, we felt we were empowered. And we felt that we stopped the Vietnam War. Right? We felt that we grew the women's movement. We were engaged in civil rights activities. We made a difference. We were the actors on the horizon. And even with the rug pulled out, as you say, it seems to me we still have this feeling about ourselves. We still believe that we can make a difference. We still believe that we can come up with good ideas that might help to solve what's happening now. But we must learn that we are not the owners of this intellectual capital or this cultural capital. That's why I stress the importance of bringing people together, across generations, to solve these problems.

BM: The book is The *Third Chapter: Passion, Risk, and Adventure in the 25 Years After 50.* Sara Lawrence-Lightfoot, thank you for being with me on the *Journal.*

SLL: You're welcome. It was a great joy.